FUTURE TIME STATUES: THEN AND NEXT

Robert F. Morgan

Copyright © 2023 Morgan Foundation Publishers

978-1-885679-32-1 (Paperback)
978-1-885679-31-4 (ebook)

All rights reserved. No part of this book may be copied or reproduced, stored in a retrieval system, or transmitted in any form, or by any means mechanical, electronic, photocopying, recording or otherwise, without prior written permission of the publisher:

Morgan Foundation Publishers. Email: **morganfoundation@earthlink.net**

Web page:
htpp://www.morganfoundationpublishers.com

FUTURE TIME STATUES: THEN AND NEXT

TABLE OF CONTENTS

Dedication ix
Acknowledgements xi

Introduction.. 1
THEN: Time Statues Prelude 10

1940s 12
Miss Kelly (1945)... 13
Barnyard Inspiration 17

1950s 19
And neither will they Small Business Owners 20
Madstop... 22
Hero of Fumes.. 40
Meals without Wheels (1959)....................... 42
Discovery... 48
Punctuation (1956)..................................... 54

1960s 56
Two Roberts (1967).................................... 57
The Prophecy 60
Anger: Three Cases (1997-1966) 65

Hong Kong 1967 81
Any Port in a Storm 89

1970s **93**
The Morgan House Ghost 95
Saying Nothing (1974) 106
Enter the Hippo 111
Trust (1944, 1972, 1996) 119
Secrets 124
Three Weddings (1972-1974) 128
Two Conventions 137
Andy Curry's Easter Story (1974) 141
Fun 145
The Flower 149

1980s-1990s **154**
Except For Your One Day 155
Sympathetic Enchantment 163

The Porcelain Protector **164**
The Raft 172

2000s **175**
Definition (2004) 176
Naming the Puppy 179
Bottomless Compliance (19th to 21st century) .. 182
Sharing (1930, 2000) 190

TABLE OF CONTENTS

2010s **193**
Cold Tale 195
Regifting 196
The Night Principal (2010) 199

2020s **204**
Random 205
Xi Misquoted (2023) 207
AI Support FOR the WGA 209
Falling Leaves (Timeless) 212

NEXT: Future Time Statues. **219**
Time Statues Encore 220
Previews 221
The Day of the Hobbit 224
The Curve's Frontier 231
Aye or Nay 236
ELIZA EARP 243
CHAT, Chaucer, & Aesop 251
Pooh and Pogo Find Romance 253
Banned. 260
Pollinating Terra. 262
Encore for Caterpillar 291
Celebrity Moon 295
The Monkey's Fist 301
Boga 304
Mausoleum with a Doorbell 305

Mother Duck Society 327
Ronin's Choice. 328
Honesty 347
OBEs in Plants and Trees 351
Is Gone Potato Soon 354
A Dreambridge Mother's Day 355

Archive: Dangerous Friends **360**
The Shark 360

Postscript: Life in the Last Lane **380**
His Last Word was Silent 384
Dodgeball... 388

Author... **395**
Other Books **396**

Dedication

Theme: *Amazing Grace* **Cherokee language version. Iveta Sunyata**

Becky Owl Morgan is easy to love. And loving the person you're married to after more than 30 years together would be expected. Time to work through baggage from past relationships, childhood, and those occasional scratchy differences in perspective. Now though, the few challenging days are overwhelmed by the mostly wonderful days Which in turn are swamped by the joyfully great days. First in the morning, last at night, us two together reminding us who we really are.

Eventually we get to a peace that allows a deeper level of love. For me, while I love her as she is, I have also come to love her as she was. Before I knew she was there. As that newborn baby needing protection, comfort. As that child full of joy, exploration, fun. Loving the woods, the river, being Cherokee. As that young woman, talented, brilliant, suffering, surviving, thriving, was finding her way. As the compassionate woman I first met in Billings, Montana. As the life companion she is now. As the woman she will be, as the years yet to come bring us the challenges and the benefits of age. To appreciate her through the whole lifespan is now to fully love my dearest Becky.

This book is for her.

*Black and white photo is of Becky Owl (Morgan) at age 13 as Cherokee NC's *Miss Fall Festival*.

Acknowledgements

Theme: *Honky Tonk Angels Medley* K.D. Lang, Kitty Wells, Brenda Lee, Loretta Lynn.

Thanks first to Asya Blue whose artistry and skills recently completed the 2023 five book revisited series, and now this *Future Time Statues*. Becky Owl Morgan's carefully thorough editing comment was essential for everything written here.

Otherwise, pretty much the same as in earlier *Time Statues* work: I thank my past editors from different printing opportunities who encouraged me to write whatever I chose, even if without statistics, graphs, tables, footnotes, or scientific jargon. I was told to just call it *"Commentary"*. Or just write it.

In this I think of Valerie Hearn, with the staff at the *Cambridge University Press*, and Valentine McKay-Riddell, with her staff at the *Four Winds Journal* and the *Winds of Change Press*. After decades of publishing about a hundred scientific journal articles and 14 earlier books, it felt good to write the seven time statues books freely and outside the confines of professional custom. I thank colleague Charles Tart who shared his own writing strategy: *'Just write what you really want to say. Then, as needed, you can add any citations, references, footnotes, and anything else an editor suggests.'*

ACKNOWLEDGEMENTS

Original material in this series is supplemented with my excerpts and illustrations from the *Four Winds Journal*, the Cambridge University Press *Journal of Tropical Psychology*, the *Bulletin of the International Association of Applied Psychology*: Supplement to *Applied Psychology: an International Review, Trauma Psychology in Context: International Vignettes and Applications from a Lifespan Clinical-Community Psychology Perspective, Opportunity's Shadow and the Bee Moth Effect: When Danger Transforms Community, Unfortunate Baby Names,* and the journal *International Psychology*.

As to the key mission of understanding the strange world we live in, and what we can do about it, I thank my Guides. Those include Robert Lee Green, Martin Luther King Jr., David Cheek, Michael Knowles, Rollo May, Nathan Hare, Fred Luskin, Sidney Farber, Robert Dattila, or mentors like Stanley Ratner, Bert Karon, Hans Toch, Lois Fisher, Helga Doblin, Cinnamon Morgan, Canadian-born Angel Morgan, plus the multitudes of my friends, teachers, parents and other relatives (my brother Nelson Morgan and forever sister Pat Norman come to mind, as do her children Elise, James, plus certainly Angela and her husband Conrad Laran). Also Michael Butz, Ben Tong, Ron Slosky, Len Elkind, Ann Yabusaki, and the other thousands of once students in six+ decades of teaching who have taught me much in return. I have special new appreciation for brilliant editor/inspiration Becky Owl Morgan, Mikael David Owl, guest contributor Angel Morgan, and the relentless motivating encouragement of Dr. Carl Word, Tom Hanrahan, Dorinda Fox, and Dr. Robert Lee Green. Dr. Roland Garcia impressively provided key focused feedback early on for a much improved reorganization.

FUTURE TIME STATUES: THEN AND NEXT

Respect is due the earliest *Time Statues* reviewers that mixed insight and comment with their own encouragement: Lois Bridges, Valentine McKay Riddell, Theodore Ransaw, Charles Tart, Hans Toch, Ann Yabusaki, with again Nelson Morgan and Robert Lee Green. Great thanks also to Ben Tong for his many contributing illustrations along with insightful historical context. And my cousin, the illustrious award-winning author, Tom Farber.

And a thankful appreciation for our friend Dr. Nathan Hare, founder of university Ethnic Studies in an era *then* while needed *next* more than ever now.

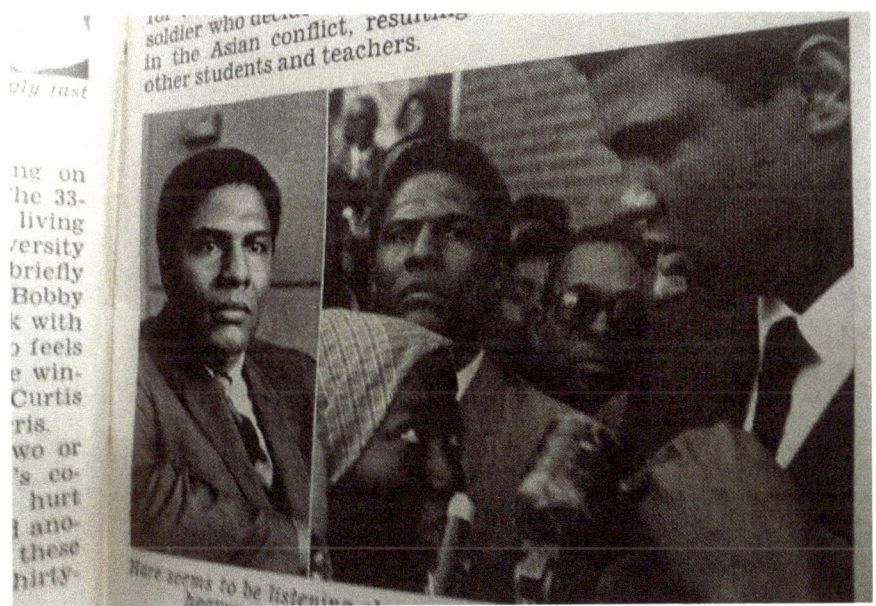

ACKNOWLEDGEMENTS

Finally, in memory of Ben Camo, my granddaughter Ava's father:

Some material from my earlier books has been updated, modified, or excerpted here where it necessarily fits to join the original material. Sure, with author permission.

Octogenarian memory can be tricky. You may be curious about anybody deserving to be acknowledged here that I inadvertently left out. Hope not. But an option we can always use is the answers source we learn about all day long on TV commercials.

Ask your doctor.

Introduction

Book's Theme: *Time Will Tell* Susan Anton

Time is a place. Each moment is a statue in time, always rooted in that time and that place.

> *When I was 5 years old, my mother always told me that happiness was the key to life. When I went to school, they asked me what I wanted to be when I grew up. I wrote down 'happy.' They told me I didn't understand the assignment, and I told them they didn't understand life."*
>
> –John Lennon

INTRODUCTION

"Because we are born for a brief span of life, and because this spell of time that has been given to us rushes so swiftly and rapidly that with very few exceptions life ceases for the rest of us just when we are getting ready for it. It is not that we have a short time to live, but that we waste a lot of it. Our lifetime extends amply if you manage it properly."
                                               -Seneca, 65BCE, 2004 AD

Mammaries to Memories Revisited

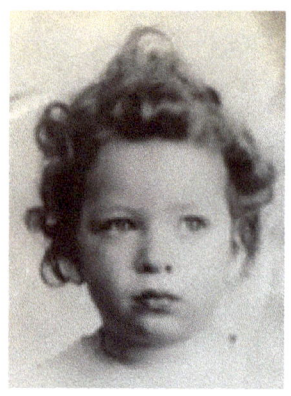

As a pre-school toddler, I already knew that I would grow up to be a writer. Everybody said I was a little Dickens.

Revisit: We were secure and warm, growing in safety. Growing so large that we began to be cramped. Here were the beginnings of desire for a larger apartment. Not to mention that the gentle rocking had become earthquakes.

In that moment or many moments later we first emerged into a new world. A mysterious world. Whirling shapes and colors, rumbling sounds. Made no sense.

We can explore though. Because we had the safety of the cord connecting us still to the warm safety we had left. Our air, our liquid energy. The lifeline is still there.

Hey! It got cut! Gone. Find a new way to breathe! We better figure out this weird place we are in. That's the primary mission. Fast as we can.

FUTURE TIME STATUES: THEN AND NEXT

It takes a lifetime. And then only a *little* bit understood. Too late to go back to the womb. (On Mother's Day she will emphatically agree.)

The newborn learns to breathe the alien place's air. For energy it can suck nourishment from a giant's huge breast. This perspective might lead to a lifelong craving that will never be fully satisfied. Males seeking ever larger breasts? Females seeking to *have* ever larger breasts? Here for some could be a primal critical period leading to wealthier plastic surgeons and silicon merchants. (What about bottle-fed babies? Maybe alcohol drinks would sell better in baby bottle shaped containers?)

Not us. We moved on. We need not climb the beanstalk to get to the giant. We grew up and *became* the giant.

Whatever else we learned to do, our survival still depends on the mission. To understand this strange world. Remember what we learn. The important stuff.

Time is a place. Each moment is a statue in time, always rooted in that time and that place. Memory allows us to visit them.

After eight decades of this, I have amassed a library of memories. Stacks after stacks of time statues archives.

So much that it can take minutes or more to access just one memory and only with patience. Elders do better at this when we imagine our search as an ordering at a restaurant. Then, usually, it will come. Arriving late? But it will come.

From the viewpoint of age, we can view these memories in their entirety as a grand tapestry. Not necessarily arranged in order, chronologically.

INTRODUCTION

What is a good guiding strategy for navigating these patterns, this treasure in an elder's experience? Maybe it's ones that were meaningful or fun. Sometimes both? Usually based on real past experience. Sometimes not. All of these can be shared.

Now: Well, at least some statues in time can be worth a visit. Or, on reflection, a revisit.

"Peter Rabbit" was a children's play I took my daughters to when they were very young. Peter began each day with great joy for the inevitable adventure. A day for him seemed like a whole season for us humans.

Remember in our own childhood how the beginning of the summer vacation seemed like the opening of endless days? For the shorter lifespan rabbit, each day was like that. It was a revelation for me. A fresh approach.

Jakob von Uexkull first made me more fully aware of the varying perceptual time world of animals:

"Karl Ernst von Baer has made it clear that time is the product of a subject. Time as a succession of moments varies from one Umwelt to another, according to the number of moments experienced by different subjects within the same span of time. A moment is the smallest indivisible time vessel, for it is the expressions of an indivisible elementary sensation, the so-called moment sign. As already stated, the duration of a human moment amounts to 1/18 of a second. Furthermore, the moment is identical for all sense modalities, since all sensations are accompanied by the same moment sign.

The human ear does not discriminate eighteen air vibrations in one second, but hears them as one sound. It has been found that eighteen taps applied to the skin within one second are felt as even pressure.

FUTURE TIME STATUES: THEN AND NEXT

Cinematography projects environmental motions onto a screen at their accustomed tempo. The single pictures then follow each other in tiny jerks of 1/18 second.

If we wish to observe motions too swift for the human eye, we resort to slow-motion photography. This is a technique by which more than eighteen pictures are taken per second, and then projected at a normal tempo. Motor processes are thus extended over a longer span of time, and processes too swift for our human time-tempo (of 18 per second), such as the wing beat of birds and insects, can be made visible. As slow motion-motion photography slows motor processes down, the time contractor speeds them up. If a process is photographed once an hour and then presented at the rate of 1/18 second, it is condensed into a short space of time. In this way, processes too slow for our human tempo, such as the blossoming of a flower, can be brought within the range of our perception.

The question arises whether there are animals whose perceptual time consists of shorter or longer moments than ours, and in whose Umwelt motor processes are consequently enacted more slowly or more quickly than in ours.

The first experiments of this kind were made by a young German scientist. Later, with the collaboration of another, he studied especially the reaction of the fighting fish to its own mirror image. The fighting fish does not recognize its own reflection if is shown him eighteen times per second. It must be presented to the fighting fish at least thirty times per second. A third student trained the fighting fish to snap toward their food if a gray disc was rotated behind it. On the other hand, if a disc with black and white sectors was turned slowly, it acted as a "warning sign," for in this case the fish received a light shock when they approached their food. After this training, if the rotation speed of the black and white disc was gradually increased, the avoiding reactions became more uncertain at a certain speed, and soon thereafter they shifted to the opposite. This did not happen until the black sectors followed each other within 1/50 second. At this speed the black and white signal had become gray. This proves conclusively that in the world of these fish, who feed on fast moving prey, all motor processes – as in the case of slow-motion photography – appear at reduced speed.

A vineyard snail is placed on a rubber ball which, carried by water, slides under it without friction. The snail's shell is held in place by a bracket. Thus the snail, unhampered by its crawling movements, remains in the same place. If a small stick is then moved up to its foot, the snail will climb up on it. If the snail is given one to three taps with the stick each second, it will turn away, but if four or more taps are administered per second, it will begin to climb onto the stick. In the snail's world a rod that oscillates four times per second has become stationary. We may infer from this that the snail's receptor time moves at a tempo of three to four moments per second. As a result, all motor processes in the snail's world occur much faster than in ours. Nor do its own motions seem slower to the snail than ours do to us." (von Uexkull 1957, Morgan 2005)

Learning to perceive the *Umwelt* (world view) of animals has the added benefit of enhancing empathy for own species.

For one, humans have great individual variations of time perception. Working with older people, I often saw anxiety about how few years of life it seemed that they had left. I had been working with the full spectrum of human aging and life extension experts, Jim Birren to Timothy Leary. They approached the subject with biology as cause and with psychology as consequence.

FUTURE TIME STATUES: THEN AND NEXT

What if we reversed the order? What if seniors with the life expectancy of less than a decade approached each day as a season in itself? Instead of ten birthdays and out, why not 3,650 individual seasons to savor, one at a time?

To do this, the senior would need to slow the rocketing passage of time engendered by similar days. Magnified by retirement or illness, one day is much like another. They go by in a flash. This may be comforting but life then goes by quickly. But if each day was differentiated as its own adventure, time will slow down. Life extension occurs experientially. For some, those who accomplished this, they said it helped very much.

We're not rabbits. We live much longer. Or so we can learn to do.

Can each of our days and the moments within them become simply statues of adventure in time?

Building on the first *"Time Statues"* book from 2021 and the five book series "Time Statues Revisited" two years later, once again we come to Einstein and Vonnegut: the temporal community is a place. Each day we finish is fixed for all time. Or is it? We can revisit, this time for new and more challenging ones.

This time we go to the even more interesting ones, although many are protected by metaphorical police tape. Worth the trip? (To help, each chapter begins with a link to a musical theme.)

As we get older, of what we usually regret, it is more often what we did not do than what we did. Either way, a revisit to worthwhile remote events seems worth the return trip. Despite some statues best forgotten.

INTRODUCTION

To navigate effectively in our own normal environment, it is entirely reasonable to consider time as linear and irreversible.

A nonlinear approach will naturally unearth exceptions. The passage through time carries us forward, evolving and adapting. In our nonlinear world, if we are open to it, we can find ways to detour against the current as part of our healthy development. It makes for a richer tapestry than had been expected.

Each moment we live includes our action as our art. Good art or bad art, all that we do sculpts a second-by-second statue to inhabit that time and that place.

The artist continues to live in the limited moments of this lifespan community.

Yet the consequences of this art can travel ever further, transcending dangers and obstacles, to shape a better future for our human community.

In this way, we can too.

Optional Music Themes   *Put another Nickel* in Teresa Brewer

Just below the chapter title is listed an optional theme, music or video. Some of readers may prefer to listen to this before, during, or after the reading of each chapter.

If before, you can play it soundlessly in your mind while reading. You enjoy reading as a kind of movie experience with music enhancing the experience. This feature is for you.

Other readers may find this a distraction. Or they may just want to avoid any online interference to their reading. These readers may have grown up in the early or even pre-television generations where radio stories dominated. That required imagination to supply the picture and any music. For them, we recommend skipping the optional themes entirely. This omission is for them.

THEN: Time Statues Prelude

Theme: *Unforgettable* Natalie Cole and Nat King Cole

Yesterday endures.

Visitors welcome.

How Poison Ivy Was Discovered

*"Two roads diverged in a wood and I—
I took the one less traveled by,
and that has made all the difference."*
                                                -Robert Frost

1940s

Theme: *Sweet Dreams* Annie Lennox

Miss Kelly (1945)

Themes: *"Honeycomb"* Jimmie Rodgers; *"A Woman's Love"* Willie Nelson; *Heartbreak Hotel* Elvis Presley

Kindergarten is the official year of public preschool in the American education system. Sure, outside earlier optional programs exist like Head Start in the United States and the historical Newstart in Canada. Not to mention the far out (in?) earliest effort: the actual controversial Prenatal University founded in 1979 for brain stimulation of the late term fetus (graduation options for Caesarian or Breach students?).

But in the USA public school system, passing Kindergarten is the gateway to First Grade. First Grade! Number one! Like First Prize, top of the line!

Then, after that, it's an annual descent into the less lofty numbers. Second Grade. Third. At the end of the next dozen years was Grade 12 (Grade 13 in Canada) and the high school diploma. But never as prestigious as that Grade #1.

Or so we told ourselves then. We needed to step up.

Children born in January or other winter months often had a problem starting kindergarten which began in September. They might begin early at age four or enter late at age six, a year older than the other children. School officials usually stuck to the latter option, thereby delaying the whole educational process up to high school graduation.

Since I was already taller than the other children, my public school let me in at age four.

Still, it was a whole new experience for me.

I was surrounded by humans almost my size that seemed pretty bizarre. One girl ran circles around me saying *"I'm a bumble bee!"* and then buzzing. A boy needed a teacher's help to *"Go Potty"* since he had no idea how a toilet worked.

I was way too young to know what a movie stereotype of a back ward in a mental facility would be like, but my young imagination felt like I was there anyhow.

Where had my mother dropped me?

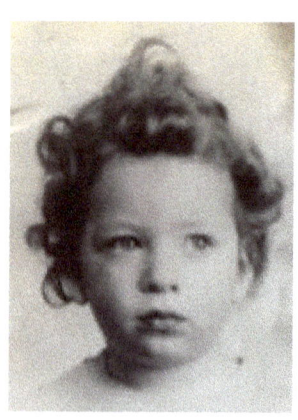

And then a giant came into my focus.

She said that she was my teacher, Miss Kelly.

And she welcomed me to the class.

I couldn't see her face though. She was standing and all I could see straight ahead were her legs.

That friendly but commanding woman's beautiful voice seemed to come through the clouds.

Too soon for a four year old but I was in love.

Miss Kelly seated me in a chair by a very small desk. She asked what I liked to do when I play. I said I liked to play chess or just walk around the city streets.

Neither of these choices seemed to engage her and she moved on.

President Roosevelt died that year. The ice man (no refrigerators then. just a wood ice box) asked me if I wanted to be the president someday. I said *"No! He died!"*

FUTURE TIME STATUES: THEN AND NEXT

I spent that school year thinking about radio stories I had heard or books I had read or stories I made up for myself. Often my imagination was interrupted by events which, if it came from Miss Kelly, my first love, had to be paid attention to.

My first report card, which I kept, had to be signed by a parent.

The written comment from Miss Kelly: *"Bobby is a very dreamy child and never feels the need to do a thing at once."*

World War Two had come to an end.

By my last report card, all the skills needed to begin first grade the following year were checked off.

I almost didn't make it because tying my own shoes was a problem to the last. I hadn't been paying attention when how to do it was explained.

At the final moment, just in time, I invented a simpler way to tie my shoes that I still do today, eight decades later.

I think Miss Kelly saw me do this my different way but as long as my laces were tied securely, she checked it off as done.

Love validated.

1940S

Afterthought:

My brother, Nelson Morgan, said:

"I sent your kindergarten story to ChatGPT with a request to rewrite it as a poem in iambic pentameter. Here it is (note that it doesn't get it all right, but still …)"

> *Born in winter's chill, a child so small Begins his journey, older than most all For school officials see him as too young To start his learning, with the throngs*
>
> *But fate has other plans, and off he goes To learn and play, with his new peers and foes A girl who buzzes, a boy who's lost His young mind wanders, at what cost*
>
> *But then a giant comes into his view A teacher kind, with a voice that's new She welcomes him, and takes him in His heart is captured, with a grin*
>
> *She asks him what he likes to do and play He tells her chess, or walking on the way But she's not interested, and moves along His mind wanders, to a different song*
>
> *The years go by, and he learns and grows His teacher's love, his heart bestows A report card signed, with a note so true "Bobby is dreamy, and never on cue"*
>
> *But as the war ends, and he moves ahead He ties his shoes, with a new thread A simpler way, that he still uses today His love for Miss Kelly, will never sway.*

FUTURE TIME STATUES: THEN AND NEXT

Barnyard Inspiration

Theme: *Surrey with the Fringe on Top* Gordon McRae

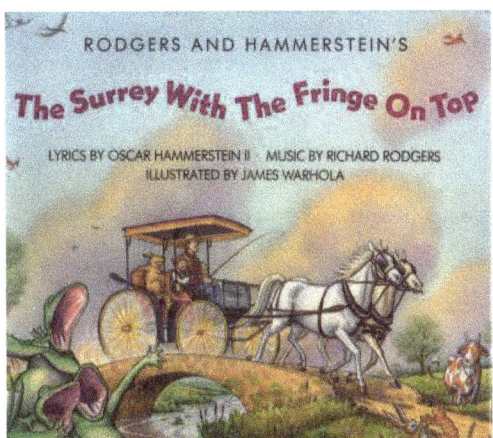

The brilliant Richard Rodgers was unsurpassed as easily the most prolific innovator of music in the history of musicals. Where did his inspiration for so much beautiful music come from?

One possibility, a reasonable one, is that Rodgers was a synesthete. These are people who re-experience sensory input in another sense as well. Words may have colors, varieties of sounds may immediately translate as music. When these overlaps are not suppressed in the child, they can become an artistic expression of the adult. When they are suppressed the adult may get Dyslexia instead*.

As a teenager, Rodgers spent his summers at Camp Wigwam in Waterford, Maine. Likely he had experienced a visit to chickens and their rooster along the way. Now: listen to *The Surrey with the Fringe on Top*, a song from the eternal Rodgers and Hammerstein 1943 musical *Oklahoma* as sung by Gordon Macrae. Do you hear the musical rhythm of the rooster, backed by his chorus of chickens? (Gordon Macrae was human though.)

*Stephan, Barbara Beard (2004) *Synesthesia and Dyslexia: Implications for Increased Understanding*. Ph.D. at Sofia University, Palo Alto, California.

1950s

Themes: *The Wall* Pink Floyd; *If I Didn't Care* Ink Spots

A rose by any other name

Won't know the difference

1950S

And neither will they Small Business Owners

Theme: *Short People* Randy Newman

Larry and Lenny Ciminelli were a year ahead of me in high school. They said they were identical twins. But one was normal height and the other was a foot taller. How could this be?

My own brother is normal height and I'm a lot taller. That difference I think I understand. My brother is a morning person, His school days began very early and he was up for that. As a child, he was high energy. Me, on the other hand, I was all afternoons and evenings. Those early school hours were (and are) bad for most growing adolescents. But, living in Buffalo, I missed a lot of school for snow days, sick days, and sleep-in days. My metabolism was relaxed, low body temperature. Then, once into my early teens, the longer I slept, the more I could feel my legs and the rest of my body stretch, grow. Today we know that is the high growth time option for teenagers.

Did that happen to the Ciminelli twins? Did the shorter one have an early morning paper route while the tall one slept in?

Height can also be an economic factor. Consider the happy organizations devoted to small business owners. Collectively the members help each other succeed. Government grants support them. Plus the gathering of small business owners in conferences and conventions shows all of us that short height can even be an advantage. *For you!*

FUTURE TIME STATUES: THEN AND NEXT

Yes, you!

And:

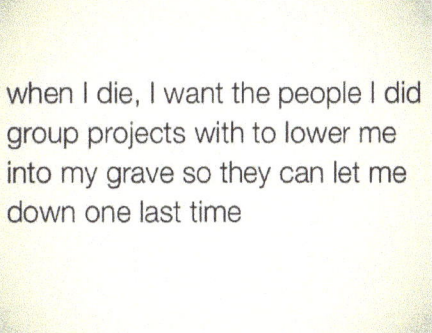

-The right side is from an internet meme DH Leonard grant writing services collection.

From Harper's Weekly Review: "The McDonald's corporation agreed to remove an advertisement for its McCrispy sandwich inside a bus shelter in Cornwall that is opposite a road sign for the area's crematorium."

From the book Gulp by Mary Roach: "Good luck to Deanna Pucciarelli, the woman who seeks to introduce mainstream America to the culinary joys of pig balls. 'I am indeed working on a project on pork testicles,' said Pucciarelli, Director of the Hospitality and Food Management Program at – fill my heart with joy! – Ball State University."

Madstop

Theme: *Great Grandfather* Bo Diddley

My first two years of college (1958-1960) were as a Physics major in an engineering college.

Clarkson College, now Clarkson University, was in North America's coldest spot at the top of upstate New York (yes, I lived in Alaska; Clarkson's town, Potsdam, was colder). The temperature was usually about 20 degrees below zero during the day, dropping to 40 degrees below zero at night.

"Madstop" was how we pronounced it (Potsdam backwards).

Clarkson College's motto was "The workman that needeth not to be ashamed". Though often our mentors could have used a little shame. My mechanical drawing prof was a fine example.

FUTURE TIME STATUES: THEN AND NEXT

Professor Myron Mochel taught using free hand diagrams designed to create products for those who chose to build them, often by his own demonstration. I'm not an artist and this was validated often as I did my best to recreate his personal masterpieces. Ones so complex most of us never really did them justice when we tried to reproduce them.

This probably didn't help. One day he dared us to bring any two dimensional drawing into class. He would then show us how effectively and rapidly he'll put it on the blackboard, exactly scaled and detailed such that anybody could build it.

When he said he was ready to pick a student's contribution, I deliberately yawned and looked out the window. So of course he took my drawing first, an object that was an illusion much like Escher's. After many heroic but futile attempts to schematically draw the illusion so that it could be built, he finally realized that it could not exist in real space. The class laughed loud and long.

Mochler though overlooked the comedic aspects completely. So I was not his favorite.

More telling as to his character was his grading scheme. His measurement of our work products, and ultimate grade, was on this scale: A, B, C, D, F, 2F, 3F, 4F, and 5F. This since, clearly, a single F could not accurately or fully express his overwhelming disdain for our work. The grade of 5F counted five times an F for a single work product grade and, by sure and certain design, devastatingly impacted each overall class grade.

In this measurement constellation, an average student's final grade would be "F". Maybe some pride in that as a grade from the middle of the range? By the end of the class I anticipated such an average grade at best. And yet, he passed me!

Pushing my luck, a common action, I asked him how I could have earned a passing (above the average F) grade in his class, given his measurement system. He scowled and said he just didn't want me to take his class again.

The Generational Secret of Clarkson College

It was the spring of 1959 in Potsdam. The snow was almost gone.

The school semester still had some months to go until the end of my first year in this remote engineering college.

Classes were held early, six mornings a week. Dodging man-size Damocles style icicles on the way to class was the usual gauntlet. Hard to breathe in this alien world of low temperature, ones found each day throughout the nine months of school. The slippery ice along the way for those morning trips was soon countered by shoes with massive treads at bottom, ones insensitively but literally called *"Guinea Ground Grabbers"*.

Why was I here?

I had been one of a few high school seniors that had won a New York State scholarship through high scores on a competitive written exam. There was a catch. It had to be a college in New York State.

Gone were my dreams of going to a university in the brand new state of Hawaii. Climate paradise for anybody growing up in Buffalo. My parents thought of the University of Hawaii as only teaching basket weaving and hula dancing. I had done research and knew better. My Hawaii plan had no backers though (later to be ruined by public awareness from the TV show *Hawaii Five-O*). Instead, the scholarship bound me to New York State. But where?

At 17 my career plans were more or less to actualize the best of science fiction. Learn the secrets of the cosmos. For this I chose to be a Physics Major.

By chance I met a graduate of Clarkson College. He said he had loved it there. And it was a great place to study the mysteries of Physics.

Never mind the cold climate and the all-male student population (shaving and bathing in the absence of females was sporadic). He thought that if I had survived 17 years in Buffalo weather, I could survive anywhere.

Finally, he shared the generational Clarkson secret: *"Don't tell them unless they can't figure it out for themselves"* he said. *"Give them some time"* he said. So I was sworn to temporary secrecy. And went to Clarkson. Well, the state was paying for it, most of it, so I gave it a try. Took me awhile to realize that no cosmology or actualized fiction would be taught there. Instead it seemed to be training us as electricians and plumbers. *"Workmen that needed not to be ashamed"*.

Also, not yet having mastered mathematics, or even having been casually introduced, I was in a strange country without knowing the required language. My only high grades were in "Liberal Studies" classes consisting of everything not Engineering or Physics. A message there.

I did enjoy doing a weekly satirical radio show on WNTC called **"Earaches"**. My opening theme was Bo Diddley's *"Great Grandfather"*, followed by *"My name is Morgan. Yours I don't need."* Between early rock & roll music breaks were my Stan Freberg style satire pieces and taped interviews, usually done in the spacious but busy dormitory restroom for the echo effect, barring flushes.

The satire pieces got me kicked off the air a few times. I had liked to have fun with our funding sponsor, Winston Cigarettes. Each time that happened I talked myself into being back on the air. So my listener base grew, eventually reaching near 100% of the students for that hour.

My favorite interview was with the Mayor of Potsdam who was being charged with gross embezzlement by a grand jury. He argued that as Mayor he was responsible for a million dollar operation, so that fact alone should mean he had better not be distracted by such charges. There was still a lot of money left. He refused to resign. As I recall, he finished his term still not in jail.

I was having fun in this little carrier current radio station, rooms sound insulated with empty egg cartons on the walls.

The show eventually lasted the two years I was at Clarkson. Although in year two I moved from all Rock & Roll breaks to playing Hawaiian Music while urging every listener to move to that warmer climate. Vic Dawley, in the class a year behind me, continued this good work after I left.

Future Roomies

Since we're exploring the tapestry of time statues in this book, we may just jump here and there to related events in other temporal geography. We'll come back to the originaal continuity though. Here's one of several such jumps.

I would leave after my second year at Clarkson, to transfer to Michigan State University (MSU) and a better choice of major then: in Psychology. Ironically, it was there that I finally learned math and how to use it. Too late for Clarkson. At MSU, even though I was a junior there, all students in their first year, transfer or not, were required to spend that year in a dormitory. I got the one for administration-defined misfits: foreign students, returning vets, transfers, discipline problems, writers. A truly creative mix. Here I will just include a nod to my own roommates in that dorm, Bryan Hall.

The first was Gilbert Moore, a poet from Montreal. He realized by the close of the first term there that his poetic future was somewhat ignored in Michigan. He needed to be back in Montreal.

Without a roommate, I began the second term gifted with a late entering freshman roommate, a local and very young Alan "Mike" Mikesell. Mike's father promised that if his grades for that beginning term were all "As" he would be gifted with a car. A gift for the rest of us on our dorm floor too we realized. We needed a sure thing. I had Mike enroll in the least challenging Football Players courses: Golf, Exercise, and "Ice Cream". The last class provided complete information on the history, manufacture, sales, and variety of the dessert. Mike got his As. But not the car. His father was not impressed with Mike's courses. Golf? Ice Cream? Mike got sent home, hopefully to try again eventually.

My third and last MSU roommate was Arthur David Otterbridge Hodgson. He was without a roommate too and we consolidated by moving into the same room before MSU could choose for us. Arthur had no roommate because he was black and his original roommate had been white. That roomie's mother would have none of that and yanked her son out of the dorm. Arthur was a soccer player and head of the Campus United Nations. From Bermuda, it was his ambition to go back there when he graduated and lead his country to independence from England. Looking like a young athletic Malcom X, I believed him. He had two strategies for this:

1. Sign up to give a speech at the real United Nations in New York. Any citizen of a member country can do this but the wait can take years. For Arthur, he had it timed for his graduation.

2. Apply for a Rhodes graduate award in his major of Economics. This would involve an apprenticeship with the head of state of a developing country followed by a more settled democracy in Europe.

As to the first, his timing was on target. As a member of his minority political party in Bermuda, their party leaders, faced with the reality of his speaking for them at the UN, appointed him forthwith as their representative on the (British) Governor's Council. Despite this prestigious and very visible role, he drove a cab during the day, dressing down in Tee shirt and jeans. He wore the same clothes to the governing Council, which delighted the younger generation. Moreso when he dressed up in suit and tie for his sister's wedding to make his values clear. Arthur was a fine orator and did a great speech advocating freedom from colonial status. As to the second, his Rhodes fellowship came through. He would wind it up studying economics in Scandinavia. First though he would be off to study with Fidel Castro, the new head of an independent Cuba. Castro was too busy it turned out, shunting Arthur off to Cuba's Finance Minister, Che Guevera. Arthur eventually went back to Bermuda and did his best to achieve independence. That hasn't happened yet, even in this current century, despite his best efforts. Bermuda remains the oldest British colony first with Queen Elizabeth and then King

Charles as the head of state. Arthur today is a retired judge in his home country. Bermuda has great beaches.

Before all of this though we both had one more year, outside the dorm at last, to graduate. Having become friends we rented a place together.

Back to Clarkson in late 1958. *(See?)*

Still, when 1959 was getting closer, I wondered: should I announce the secret?

First this: When I had left for Clarkson in the Fall of 1958, I was a tall skeletal teenager weighing 145 pounds. The food at the college was terrible but the cold weather and unrelenting pace made us ravenous for it. Sure we found pennies and hair in the food. The "mystery meat" remained a mystery. The cook's dog helped lick the used plates clean for her. Despite all this I arrived home for Thanksgiving heavier by forty pounds of muscle now weighing in at 185. My mother couldn't believe it. Or didn't want to. Let's explore this for a minute.

Food in the Fireplace *(another brief jump)*

My mother was one of fourteen children. Five of her nine brothers became medical doctors. One, Sidney, was, with the help of Ted Williams, a founder of Boston's Dana Farber Clinic. There his patients were children fighting Leukemia, a death sentence in those days. Every night he tucked each one of his child guests into bed, doing all he could think of to have them survive another day. He invented the first drug treatment for this, becoming the "Father of Chemotherapy". Another brother, Harold, became the President of his own insurance company. The eldest son, Marvin, became a philosophy professor, bringing the European phenomenologists to our country just in time to avoid being gassed to death by the Nazis. My favorite, Dan, was an adventurer, successful at enjoying life fully.

How did Simon Farber, the immigrant stevedore father of these 14 children get so many sons through school? He worked multiple jobs as long as he could and, as can happen in a large family, the older children helped the younger ones. This included my mother who always sent home as much of her salary as she could until she married at the advanced age for the day of 30. What career paths for her and her four sisters? Or any women living a century ago.

My mother, Evelyn, wanted very much to be a doctor too. But she had been born in 1908 and women in her day had but only a few career paths other than "housewife". These alternatives usually were Nursing or Teaching.

Evelyn got her teaching credential and continued through graduate work in Microbiology. Her family needed her help so she began decades of work as a teacher. At this she was successful, even teaching a high school Microbiology class. She was so loved by her students that, for several years in a row, their Yearbook was dedicated to her. Then she retired.

Microbiology was as close as she ever formally got to being a medical doctor. Still, retired, she now had time at home to increase her informal medical practice without a license. Her husband and two sons were the hostage patients.

Other than that, her new post-retirement career mission was to be a great cook. Food soon integrated into her realm of home medical practice, allowing what she considered to be healthy or restorative components to every meal.

Sadly, by her age she had been deprived of substantial taste bud competence. Her food then tasted awful. Who knew what she had added in any given meal? She was a great fan of laxatives for one thing.

My father worked hard and needed sustenance. He too came from a large family of nine children. He ate fast. He ate anything. He ate whatever we did not. This made him her star patient when it came to the culinary practice.

Not so for my brother, which may have helped him survive the streets during his Haight-Ashbury years.

As for me, I continued as a skeletal teenager, surviving on TV dinners and meals at the homes of friends. I also used every opportunity to make my own meals from whatever was available.

Complete feasts that way would be tomato soup and grilled cheese, a thinly sliced chip steak on a slice of toast, or the World War II specialty understood as "Shit on a Shingle" (ham and peas on a slice of toast). When we ran out of hot dogs, I learned that a hot dog roll filled with relish, onion, coleslaw, mustard, and ketchup tasted just fine without the dog.

Summer trips to Canada taught me that fries go fine with vinegar (try it) if you have no ketchup. The beverage of choice was tap water or Vernors Ginger Ale.

In later years I learned to make a few special dishes like leg of lamb slow cooked with green maraschino cherries or fried bananas with lemon sauce. Or omelets purple with grape juice.

When cooking for my two daughters though, they preferred to each do their own cooking. Maybe it was the green food coloring I added to scrambled eggs or most other things I served. I did green eggs and ham before Dr. Seuss made it known.

My mother was good at making deserts though. They were delicious and a staple. So our nutrition was impaired as well.

Years later I was invited to a home office party in San Francisco. My charge was to bring "green food". I brought green tea ice cream and green treats from the "Citizen Cake" store. Childhood strikes deep.

The grandchildren felt much the same as my brother and I about their grandmother's cooking. On holidays we would all gather at the home of my parents.

Grandchildren waited until Evelyn had stepped out of the room to dump their plates of food in the fireplace, covering it with ashes.

Eventually, at one holiday family gathering years into this clean plate technique, my father started a long overdue cleaning of the fireplace. As he worked through the years of holiday meals past, he was good natured about it all.

Finally finished, he stood and announced to us: "That was like an archeological dig!"

So Clarkson food was a step up. Not a great step. But up. Back to the tie statue story of Clarkson College, later renamed as Clarkson University.

Maybe photos might help. These are on the next page.

FUTURE TIME STATUES: THEN AND NEXT

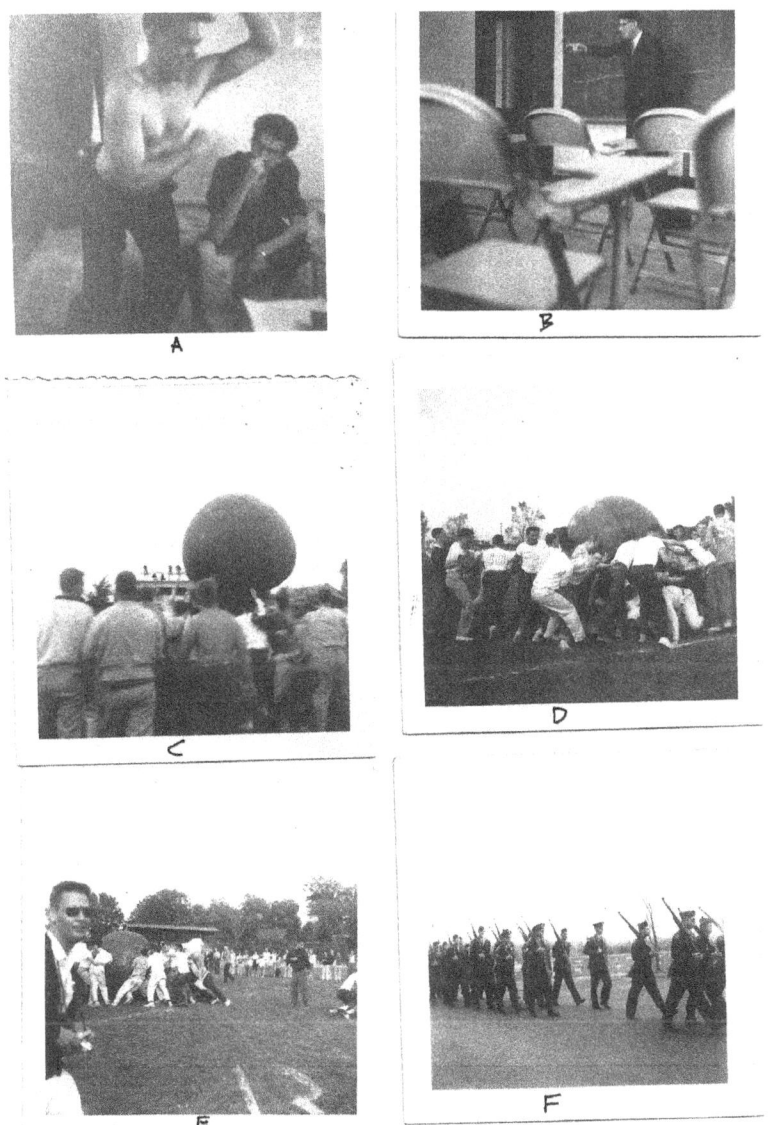

Photo A. A typical dormitory shot. Hygiene was sparse in all male dorms.

An earlier roommate of mine was from Japan. Hirofumi Matsusaki. His story is in the next chapter.

My substitute roommate that first year was George Zabriskie or "Zips". He was a great fan of Chet Atkins who I heard nonstop in our room for the rest of the year. Zips plastered the bulletin board over his dorm bed with Playboy Playmate pictures. We had a desk in the middle of the small dorm room, between the separate beds, so when we studied we faced each other from our respective sides. This gave me a scenic view of his Playmate photos.

To fill my own Bulletin Board, I posted a large very colorful chart my mother had sent me called "the infant stool cycle". Zips found this hard to view, despite the Chet Atkins perpetual soundtrack. Periodically he would lean back and throw himself at an angle so he could look at his own Bulletin Board.

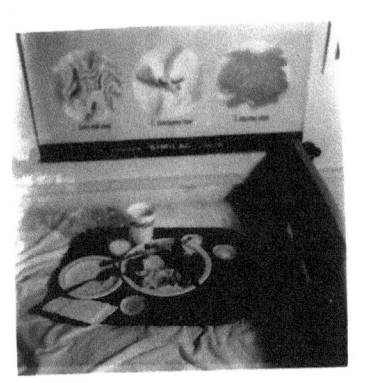 

Zips became a good friend. I missed him when he didn't return for the second Clarkson year. About 40% of the rest of our class weren't back that year either.

FUTURE TIME STATUES: THEN AND NEXT

That next year, I had the best Clarkson dorm roommate: Douglas Griffin, seen in Photo A sitting and holding his nose while our neighbor from the next room shared armpit fragrance in his typical gesture of sharing.

I'm still in touch with Doug, even though I was one of those not returning in year three. Doug went the full distance, got his degree, and had a career with IBM.

(I found a hole in the middle of my dorm mattress but, rebuffed for a better one, got used to it. I joked with Doug that the hole was for easing my sexual tensions though it was far too small. When his father came to visit, he asked to see my famous mattress hole. Left me impressed by the great relationship he had with his Dad.)

Most in the dorm were learning to be engineers. Different subspecialties could be competitive. For example, I announced on my radio show the rumor that the urinals were all about to be raised a few inches so as to keep the double EEs (electrical engineers) on their toes. Apparently they were deemed to be shorter.

The dorm had many characters, too many to expand on this here. The largest among us, for example, was Karl Trout who naturally was nicknamed "Guppy". Required to post our own shortened nickname on our room door, a neighbor, Spargo, posted "Sir".

The last I will recall here was Lynn Pagliarro (not sure of spelling). He had been dating a girl named Maureen whenever he went home for breaks. During one Visitors Day, Maureen's parents came by to have a look at (and judge) their daughter's new boyfriend. In this way I got to guide a very stern looking Ronald Reagan and wife to Lynn's room. Not sure how it all worked out.

1950S

Even Death Valley might have smelled better for Reagan than our own fragrant dormitory home.

Photo B. Clarkson College faculty were, if nothing else, undeterred by the bone chilling cold. A hardy lot, many had arrived from equally chilly or desolate places elsewhere on the globe.

This is a photo of our Economics Professor. From Switzerland, he spritzed substantially and with impressive range, when he lectured. The students were huddling in the last rows of the classroom, one with an umbrella as I recall, but the lecturer continued on oblivious.

Photos C, D, E. The death of hazing: Clarkson's generational secret emerges.

The hazing of freshmen by sophomores was continuing month after month with no end in sight. Freshmen could be ordered to streak without clothes from one dormitory building to another. This was a short run but at 40 degrees below zero risked pneumonia, certainly some respiratory damage. Freshman could have their head shaved for disobedience. In a good day, they would at least be stopped routinely and harassed. We got the freshman to walk in groups of five or six to or from class. It felt more like high school than College.

The few law enforcement individuals were nowhere to be found once summer ended. Rumor had it that they were "Snowbirds" migrating to warmer Florida to leave the snow behind. So a lawless place with little recourse.

Except for the one that needed to be realized. A secret passed on through the generations. I knew what it was. Should I announce it on my weekly one-hour radio show? Was the time right? Why not? This had gone on long enough.

On my next show: "*Have you ever noticed that the sophomores returning this year are a lot fewer than last year? They are down to less than 300 now. This means the freshmen class at more than 500 outnumbers them. So why is hazing continuing so long? Let it fill the whole year? Notice that no stop date has ever been given by the College? Here is the Clarkson secret passed on down through generations of hazing. It stops when the freshmen SAY it's over! That's all it takes. We just declare it done and it's done. Then the College gives us a little weekend ceremony to end it traditionally. How about it? Is it done*?"

Back at the dorm signs saying HAZING IS OVER were everywhere. So it ended then and there.

Except for that College ceremony promised for the next weekend to come. Fine for the freshmen to declare hazing over. For the sophomores a more vivid experience was called for to make their new situation clear and final. A ceremony was designed for exactly that.

The sophomore 300 lined up on one end of the football field and the freshman 500 on the other end. In the middle was a huge canvas ball. Officially the rules were to push the ball into the opposing goal posts. But with no referees to be seen that day (true to the Potsdam and College spirit of the times), 800 males met in the middle, more or less where the ball was, and conflict ensued. This blew off steam, followed by a more relaxed campus situation. Some bruises and bandages but no fatalities (a gentler time). They all moved on. This is what photographs C-E captured.

In my second year I tipped off the freshmen after just one week of hazing. They organized quickly. Hazing ended the second week, a Clarkson record.

Some of my classmates were not happy about this. They had looked forward to getting even with their oppressors from last year by taking it out on the new students this year. A way to pass on sadism over generations, prophetic of Eduardo Duran's intergenerational trauma insights so many decades later.

Well, I was against hazing then and I am against it now. Phil Zimbardo has shown how bad this inequity can get. On the other hand: *When* and *How* the hazing stopped was a rite of passage for Clarkson students. They gained the maturity of learning their own power to make change, to protect themselves by group action when no adult force was there to do it for them.

Sure enough, those passing through this ritual seemed to mature substantially. More self-sufficient, more independent critical thinkers. Less likely to succumb to dysfunctional authority. Very useful for citizens in our challenging world of today.

Photo F. Our Army ROTC marching stroll every Thursday.

We were scheduled for the Army ROTC training our first two years though an equal time of Physical Education (PE) could be substituted. Out of curiosity I stayed with ROTC. Turned out a very Clarkson/Potsdam approach to the Army. The commanding officer was Colonel Clarence Campbell. It was said that he was on leave from running the NHL, the pro hockey league, a big sport in snow country.

But for the ROTC back in the late 1950s, the Colonel was more of a front lines kind of leader. He made sure we knew how to shoot, how to do the manual of arms hefting the surplus M-15s we carried.

As to precision marching, he had disdain for that. Didn't think it would keep us alive in a shooting situation. So we marched as in coming back from the Front. When most are not in step, synchrony disappears. See photo F. Individuation very much in literal step with the Clarkson/Potsdam (CP: opposite of PC) spirit.

I marched, more or less, the first year. The second year I drew on my high school newspaper editor experience and offered to be the photographer and press liaison. The Colonel agreed. A very good man, that Campbell. The second year no more marching with M-15s every Thursday. I just hefted my camera.

A few years later, in the time of impending draft, I was in the USAF Officer Training or OTS. They assumed my Potsdam marching experience with ROTC was a plus. I did prove true to my Clarkson CP experience, marching at shifting cadences and directions when it intuitively suited my legs. Too boring for these legs to conform indefinitely to what everybody else was doing.

Did not go over well though.

I did eventually get to Hawaii where I did my postdoc internship.

After leaving Potsdam, it still took me six years to get there.

Hero of Fumes

Themes: *Magic Man* Heart; *Sweet Nothin's* Brenda Lee

Hirofumi Matsuzaki

For centuries Europeans avoided bathing, believing it led to disease or death. From this came various plagues resulting in a decimated population. The survivors developed immunity. Kept the lethal plague bacteria and its brethren with them.

Eventually, like the monitor lizard, their most powerful defense was these lethal bacterial inhabitants of their bodies. Offensive offense too. Witness the 80% of North America's original Native peoples who died from disease following European contact.

For me, growing up poor and of European descent (mostly), the once-a-week bath was on Saturday night; so-called sponge baths with a wet wash cloth were done other days.

That earlier college roommate of mine was from Japan. Hirofumi Matsuzaki.

Japanese are tightly packed on an island country. They tolerate this by daily bathing and devoted cleanliness.

Not so in our dormitory. In our all-male dorm of teenagers fresh from high school, I was one of the cleaner ones. I know, a low bar. In the day-to-day absence of females, the norm was unshaved faces, untrimmed nails and hair, and unchecked body odor. Not to mention the gaseous fumes provided regularly to applause and laughter. (See Photo A again below.)

FUTURE TIME STATUES: THEN AND NEXT

Our profs were better dressed and groomed but not by much. Our Swiss economics prof spritzed so fully when he spoke that the seats in the front half of his classroom were always empty. Though well moisturized. Phased him not a bit. (See photo B again below.)

Hirofumi and I definitely influenced each other. He maintained his composure admirably. Bathed regularly. Thereby lacking any noticeable or original body odor. Not me. My poor roommate. For me, it didn't take until a year or two later. I eventually arrived at a devoted daily bathing regime. Dating maybe had something to do with this.

But back then in the dorm there were no women to impress, or to not repulse.

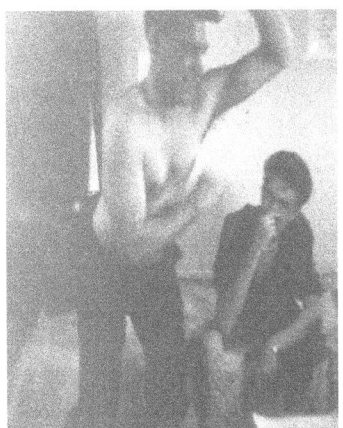 

Photo A   Photo B

Hirofumi, for his part, did not return after the first Thanksgiving break.

Looking him up on the internet in this more current century, I found him to be celebrated in Japan as an inventive chemical engineer, one successful with fragrance products.

Those fully appreciating his products called him the *"Magic Man of Fragrance"*.

Or, playing on his name, tourist customers called him the *"Hero of Fumes"*.

Maybe I had a little something to do with his successful career choice.

Meals without Wheels (1959)

Theme: *The World is waiting for the Sunrise* Les Paul & Mary Ford

The Trip

Doug Griffin, a past college roommate, forwarded this memory to me from a friend from that long ago era. All I recall now from this holiday trip from Potsdam to Buffalo was that the hole in the floor of the car gave a fresh view of the road we were traveling on as we progressed.

> *"Dear Doug,*
>
> *Doug were you part of the group going back to Clarkson after Christmas break in Jim Lepsch's old Plymouth? The old car that did not have a heater nor a defroster; so that in a snow storm one had to drive with some window open. Well Bob Morgan was part of the crew of four or five. After Syracuse the snow storm got quite strong. It was getting dark and some of us were afraid of ending up in a ditch. It was decided that the next time we saw a hotel or motel we would stop for the night. So we stopped at an old hotel in some tiny town in Northern New York in a snow storm.*

FUTURE TIME STATUES: THEN AND NEXT

The quoted price was maybe $65 each or maybe $85. So Bob says, "Let's see what happens when we appeal to the compassion of the folks who live here. We will knock on doors and say we are poor college students caught in a storm with no money for the hotel (all true). So can you put us up for one night?" Well it seemed like a good plan to 19 year old students. There was a small green in that town and we went to about 8 houses around that green. There were no offers of hospitality. We than came upon a house that looked like a share croppers. It has a low porch between it and the sidewalk. It lacked paint. Light streaming out its big front window, which was not the well-insulated type seen in New York State. It was clearly a home for a low income family. I am pretty sure there was a fireplace and a roaring fire inside and the place was crowded with happy people. So we knocked. They swallowed us up with kindness. They helped us warm up and then gave us bacon and eggs to eat. They did not have room for us due to the number of their guests. But they told us where their pastor lived. We tried the pastor's door. The pastor had a grand house. We may have said the generous people down the street sent us here. The pastor and his family looked as us askance. But did us up for the night. And served us a nice breakfast the next day. As I recall, an icy air hung over the table. I was embarrassed then and am still embarrassed. But Bob Morgan loved it."

Arthur and Larry (1960-1962)

Maybe that earlier trip was the beginning of this pattern. Meals without wheels.

In 1960 I transferred into Michigan State University (MSU) for my last two undergraduate years, this time as a new psychology major.

The first year there we were obligated to stay in a dormitory. Mine was reserved for keeping bad influences away from the younger first year students fresh from high school. Those bad influences were university defined as a year or two older transfers like me, returning military, discipline problems, and international students. So there was the great luck, being in the most creative multi-cultural multi-racial nonconforming MSU dorm location there was that year.

Top novelist Tom McGuane was there, also a paratrooper who loved to jump from his fourth floor window, past my second floor one, on to the rolling hills below, a few highly amusing alcoholics, some super athletes (eg. Hockey), and students from all over the world.

Arthur, who you have met now in an earlier chapter, was my roommate for most of this time. He was the one from Bermuda who looked much like a younger beefier Malcolm X. You may recall that he played Soccer, headed the campus model United Nations, and played Bid Whist cards with me and our Detroit dormitory friends in our room every Sunday.

I soon learned that Bermudians had some unique words and accents, still in the King's English, but far from the Midwest pronunciations found in Michigan. Gave me an idea.

Our second year at MSU, my last as an undergraduate, we were free from the dorms, and their excellent cafeteria food. So, along with our friends, we moved into cheap town rentals. Food though was now a problem. Few of us had much money.

A day's meal at times might have been the 25 cent hamburger at that brand new fast food chain, *McDonalds*.

This would not do.

Time for my plan.

We put up notices all over town like this:

Share Your Dinner with a Foreign Student Guest

(Interpreter will accompany)

And a local number from a favorite hangout.

A few takers were all we needed and their invitations did come in.

Arthur borrowed an African Dashiki from Larry, another of our past dorm pals. Larry was from Ghana.

Arthur showed up at a welcome dinner in his African garb and I translated. This involved a few Bermudian words like "*di*ckty*"*, meaning "*goofy*" or in Michigan parlance "*Not really pleasant*". I added a few cooking specialties involving sugar and salt on chicken. But mostly, Arthur just spoke plain English and then I would translate with cultural anecdotes, traditions, mating patterns, and, maybe, a few stretched possibilities that came to mind. Arthur struggled to keep a straight face during all this but managed in the end to smile rather than laugh. After dinner, we collected our borrowed Bermudian flag and left to applause, satiated by a great meal.

Larry soon joined our effort as the foreign student from Ghana. He was in fact from the capital, Accra, and was very sophisticated. Still, once in his Dashiki, and a bone over his nose, he was the very expectation of local dinner hosts who assumed he was fresh from an African jungle. Larry loved this and in fact gave me many cultural phrases to translate. Though Larry, as did Arthur, spoke perfect English the entire dinner.

Of many delicious courses.

After

Once we graduated, Arthur had a Rhodes scholarship to study economics in Europe but with a stop on the way in Cuba. There he spent a few weeks with Cuba's Economics Minister, Che Guevera.

Back in our dorm, Arthur had mailed a request to the actual United Nations in New York to, as a citizen of Bermuda, address the General Assembly. Turned out that any citizen of a member country could make such request, at least then, but they made you wait years to do so. Now, Arthurs years of waiting had ended and he had his invitation. The timing came just after the end of his Rhodes experience and was perfect for him. Arthur's minority party in Bermuda had to choose between ignoring this opportunity or letting the young recent graduate represent his country. They chose the second option.

Arthur spoke eloquently at the UN for his country's independence from Great Britain. In the dorm he had drawn me out often about why my country wanted no monarchy. He enjoyed this debate, asking, for example, why we wouldn't want this living reminder of our past. For that, I asked him if he would want to keep his burst appendix on his mantle to honor its memory. Arthur found a way to use some of these remarks in his address.

Still, even after all these many years of his best efforts, Bermuda is remains part of the British Empire, though with reduced compliance. And Arthur is now a retired Bermudian judge, also still of little compliance.

We lost touch with Larry, who returned to Accra after his graduation.

It is reasonable to assume he left his over-the-nose bone behind him in Michigan.

Back in his home country his dinner invitations would have no need for an interpreter any more.

1950S

Discovery

Themes: *Hello I Love you, won't you tell me your name?* Doors; *Every Breath You Take* Police

In the late 1950s Potsdam, New York, had very little law enforcement. The local version of this went to Florida for the ten snow months of the year.

The exception was at the Clarkson College campus. There law and order came only from the very formidable Dean of Students. He was more than enough.

The Dean seemed bigger than life and hard muscled enough to intimidate Arnold Schwarzeneger. He had survived World War Two as a young man. Stern as he was, he liked to tell us about his exploits then.

A favorite was when he faced down a Nazi tank, realizing that his drawn pistol was not going to help him. He fired anyway. The tank didn't fire back. Turned away, left him standing there. He said he liked to think they had been impressed by his courage. But on reflection, decided that they were just laughing.

These stories I just heard from a group of first year students. Never talked to him on my own. Until I had to.

Our all-male college did have periodic mixers with the women at the state university a few miles away. My first there was in that earliest 1958 fall semester.

Our dorm then saw our normally homeless-looking crew shave, shower, and put on unusually clean clothes for the event. Me too.

FUTURE TIME STATUES: THEN AND NEXT

Once at the mixer, I stood at the edge of the dancing, looking around. Even though I was still only 17, the female students looked way too young for me. Felt like high school.

But then a beautiful young woman came up to me and introduced herself. She wanted to sit down with me and have a conversation. Sure!

She had long black hair, violet eyes, and, though she said she was my age, she seemed mature, confident, even worldly. We clicked.

I was very interested in seeing her again. She gave me her campus mailing address and invited me to stay in touch. (Days before internet or even reliable phones.) I agreed. Definitely.

Now in those days, if I liked a girl, I'd write her a story. Something brief and just for her. My version of flowers and candy.

Still do I guess. Though for the last 30 years my target recipient has been my wife. Like this book.

So, back then I wrote a short three page story about a brave heroine described much like her. The narrative was pure imagination. I just thought about her and the words poured out. Only, pure fiction.

In the story, this heroine had been homeless since childhood. Survived on the streets of a city, barely. She was smart, spent much time in libraries and was ready for more education. Even a university one. In her later teens, she still went to school and had girlfriends there. They had homes and families, resources. Heading to college.

By their high school graduation, most not already married had become sexually active, shared stories. But for her, she decided that sex was a way out. Out of the street and into college.

She was very careful and absolutely selective. But once into somebody, it became transactional. Money changed hands. And then she'd move on.

It took her a long time but eventually she had enough money to go to a university. She chose a place far from her home in the state's cold north. Where nobody knew her. Her past was really past.

Ending this story, I was clear that she was my hero. Deserved the great future she was sure to find now.

Mailed the story to her with a note that this was my way as a writer to say that I'd like to meet her again.

Waited patiently for an answer.

Back then, the post office was pretty fast, reliable. Only a few days had gone by when I got her response.

The Dean of Students summoned me to his office.

I got that I was in trouble. Thought maybe from one of my weekly radio shows?

Once I was seated across from him, he stared at me for a minute. Then said he had not yet decided whether to expel me or send me to jail.

Worse than I thought.

He picked up an envelope and pulled out the story I had sent to the state university student. Said her Dean had complained to him that I was blackmailing one of her girls. Wanted justice.

I was stunned. The story was true?

My Dean said he wanted to hear my side before he acted.

I asked him if he had read the story. He had.

FUTURE TIME STATUES: THEN AND NEXT

I asked him if he liked it.

Said that was not the point. Was this meant to blackmail her?

Nope. No request for money. Never met her before the mixer. Knew nothing about her past life. Pure imagination, just meant to impress her. Sorry that it hurt her instead, Probably this relationship wasn't going anywhere good. Future doubtful, Right?

He gave me a grudging smile at that. Said he believed me.

I reiterated my question. Did he like the story?

Sure he responded. You write well. Too bad for this story though.

He asked if that was my only copy.

No, I had a carbon copy version. Took a while on an old typewriter with my hunt and peck skills.

He told me to go get the copy. I complied. Gave it to him. He tore up both copies. Filed the pieces in his waste basket (aka circular file. Said he'd tell the other Dean it was all a mistake and the matter was closed.

With him, I knew that would be it.

Before I left it almost looked like he was reconsidering.

He said, with some puzzlement, *"But you had all the details right!"*

I agreed. A mystery for sure. And exited fast.

Not a mystery to me though. A discovery!

I had been in an altered meditative state when I thought about her and wrote. My science fiction readings from age eight came back to me.

I could use this somehow. To be helpful some way.

In my later life as a clinical psychologist it would come in handy often.

-

Years later my wife and I were working at the Native American Health Center (NAHC) in Oakland, California.

Oakland. Just across the Bay Bridge from San Francisco, it was a different world.

Living in San Francisco was being part of a strangely small community. No matter where else in the world I would go, I usually met a neighbor from there.

Oakland was different. We never met anybody from the city across the bridge in all the time we were working there, or traveling anywhere else on the planet. A world unto itself.

After our work was done, we still kept flying from or to the Oakland airport rather than the San Francisco one. Less crowded, friendlier, more reliable.

Near that airport was a great restaurant, *Francesco's*, gone now. We stayed at the Airport Hilton or smaller hotels nearby.

One sunny day, walking around outside one of these hotels, I noticed a ladder on an alleyway leaning against a building with an indoor pool. Went over to it. Climbed up. At the top was a small hole through which you could see inside the pool and the hot tub next to it. Hmmm.

William Braud, friend and parapsychologist, wrote about his research that found that people could learn to know when they were being watched from a distance. William was a pretty thorough scientist. Seemed valid*.

So I went into that same altered state I had discovered writing in my teens back then at Potsdam until I had identified the feeling of being watched. Not easy and I had to invite it in. But it worked.

Later that day, we were relaxing in that hotel's inside hot tub by the pool. I got the anticipated tingling feeling about being watched. Looked up where the spy hole was, some twenty feet up by the ceiling in a dark corner, and waved. Got everybody in the hot tub to do the same.

Before we checked out later in the day, the head of hotel security came by.

Said I had freaked out his whole crew. The spy hole was just to maintain the safety of visitors, he insisted. But now all the staff knew I was some kind of magician with nobody's secrets safe.

I offered to show him how to learn the technique. But he declined.

He stayed friendly though.

And a little fear in the right place and time can keep things honest.

Source
*Braud, W. (2003) *Distant Mental Influence: Its Contributions to Science, Healing, and Human Interactions (Studies in Consciousness)* Newbury Port, Massachusetts: Hampton Roads.

Punctuation (1956)

Theme: *Young Love* Sonny James; *Great Balls of Fire* Jerry Lee Lewis

My mother was one of 14 children. As an adult, she asked her mother why she never used birth control. The answer: *"Is it legal?"*

At first we thought that response was cute. But Grandma was right. In her era. birth control wasn't legal. No birth control pills yet. All back when America was just *"great"*. Making it that kind of great again has surfaced in our era. Struggle ensues.

In the 1950s, my high school era, birth control pills weren't available yet. Abstinence by choice rare.

There was the very Catholic *"rhythm method"* which tried to avoid the female fertile ovulation time. And produced many more Catholic babies which I suppose was the point all along. Other religions were known to try this though those children were more likely to be expected to wait until marriage. Sure.

We also had condoms. It was common for teenage boys to carry one in their wallet, *"just in case"*. But for most that opportunity was years away.

Some of my male classmates one day came to school bragging that they had *"created life"*. By visiting the condom section in the shelves of a pharmacy and used a long needle to poke tiny holes in packaged condoms yet to be sold. Okay, sadistic morons.

But if that bragging was true, it could have led to tragic consequences for the girls their age. Pregnancy for them usually meant being dropped out of school, compelled to be a mother years too soon. Forced marriages. Unwelcome children. Unhappy spouses.

FUTURE TIME STATUES: THEN AND NEXT

Is 21st century America in danger of going that way again?

In my 1950s high school, one female teacher with a very strange sense of humor wrote this on the blackboard: **FUN FUN FUN WORRY WORRY WORRY**.

She dared us to punctuate it. No takers. So she did:

"Fun period, Fun period, Fun no period, Worry! Worry! Worry!"

1960s

Theme: *Age of Aquarius* 5th Dimension; *Love Tastes like Strawberries* (or bouillabaisse and, maybe somedays, egg drop soup) Miriam Makeba

I entered a San Francisco organic grocery store reputed to have great fresh produce, fresh from the farm. This turned out to be true. Once my grocery cart was nearly full, I checked my list. Oh. Asked a clerk where their meat section was.

She stood up ramrod straight, growled *"WE DON'T SELL FLESH!"*

I assured her that I was not a cannibal, but to no avail.

I moved on from this vegetarian oasis.

At the door I left her with: *"Vegetables and fruits have feelings too! Unhand their young!"*

In fairness, I considered whether an omelet was made from poultry abortions.

Well, rather than die from hunger, mayhap the best solution is the indigenous practice of, before eating, thanking the animal or plant sacrificed for your survival.

Forget any *"You're welcome"* back though.

Two Roberts (1967)

Theme: *A Change is Gonna Come* Sam Cooke

Psychologist Robert Lee Green was a visitor to the United State Senate cafeteria, a guest of Senator Robert Kennedy. Doctor Green was at the time working as a top associate of Dr. Martin Luther King at the Southern Christian Leadership Council (SCLC). He was the Director of Citizenship Education there. And my stalwart mentor and friend. Only later in life would he become a university president, published giant in education, and, to the day of this writing, a distinguished public speaker.

Bob grew up in Detroit, so on arrival at SCLC he found that, while respectful, he may have been a tad more direct, somewhat less constrained, than others raised in that era of Southern gentility. *Jet* magazine and other media began immediately printing his ventures. There was his leading a protest against a Black-owned Black-staffed Atlanta barber shop that refused to serve Black customers. There was his planting the American flag at the Jefferson Davis Tomb in Richmond, Virginia. Bob was clearly intolerant of injustice, hypocrisy, or the historic flag of slave-owner treason.

Now back to the meeting in the Senate Cafeteria.

Senator Kennedy wanted to arrange a cooperative alliance with Dr. King. It was the late 1960s, not long before the year both Kennedy and King would be murdered by their enemies.

While sharing a meal, Green noticed the lead segregationist from the racist wing of Kennedy's own party sat at the very next table. That senator was a strong force against any legislation that might provide justice to Americans of color. The segregationist senator waved and smirked.

Dr. Green grew as angry as he had ever been. Rage welled up but was controlled.

He was a master at this. Many times we were in situations so full of stress that anybody else would have exploded in anger. But in a split second he always became calm and focused. This was no exception.

He turned to Kennedy and quietly said *"How would that senator like it if I punched him in the nose?"*

Senator Kennedy took a few seconds to consider this question.

I imagine he visualized headlines about his guest, this young strong African-American colleague of the non-violent ML King, assaulting the racist senator in his own cafeteria.

Kennedy finally smiled and said *"He would love it."*

The Prophecy

Theme: *Summertime* Billie Holiday/Janis Joplin/Audra McDonald

A Lost Generation finding their way

Early 1960s. To push back against school desegregation in Virginia's Prince Edward County, an entire school system was closed for its Black children.

For years.

When federal intervention finally reopened those schools, the children were placed in grades by their age. This meant that the first cohort of high school graduates that was going to college would be missing years of their education.

They were termed the *"lost generation"* in the press.

The missing school years had depressed their tested IQ scores, as compared to similar children in a neighboring county.

That's how it was proved that the Tested IQ used in schools in that day actually depended on prior education. It was not particularly genetic as usually measured.

Analyzing learning deficits based on the age children had suffered from closed schools, we identified critical ages for skill in reading and math. Potentially lifelong without help.

A federal grant through the United States Office of Education was launched with the goal to bring this *"lost generation"* up to speed before these children began their higher education.

A large cohort of dedicated teachers signed on to attempt this jump of years in a single summer.

Dr. Robert Lee Green was in charge of this program, including the before and after evaluation of both these students and their summer teachers.

As Bob's graduate student associate, I took on the assessment of the teacher cohort.

The large group of teachers began their own pre-training that summer by assembling for the first time in a testing room with a demographic form to fill out.

They began.

Most were of the same race as their intended students though here and there were a few different faces. One of those with a white face raced his hand.

He looked to be in his early twenties, much like me.

I acknowledged him.

He said *"I see you want us to list our race here. Why do you want us to do that?*

I answered *"Sure. Understanding why anybody would ask a question like that is important. In our case, we need to prove to the grant provider that we have a racially diverse group here. This is a desegregation effort."*

He frowned and said *"I object! I don't see race. We are all just human here."*

By now the whole room's occupants had put down their pens and were paying attention. A few looked at this young man with concern.

I had to get things back on track. Not for the teachers then. Then and always for the students.

"Yes, far as I can tell, we are all of the same human family. Now look around the room and also see the beauty of this rainbow of skin tones. We are here because the School Board has damaged your soon-to-be students because of discrimination against their non-white shades. Children held back from their better future by the School Board's ignorance. We are here now to do something helpful for those children, now young adults going to college. Something valuable."

But the indignant volunteer teacher wasn't about to quit.

"Well, I'm telling you right now. I'm not going to write my race down here on your damn paper! For me it will stay blank."

I thought sure, his tell-tale blank would be as white as he was. But he meant well.

I just responded with: *"That's your right. Go ahead and leave it blank then. As to race, when I collect your completed form, I'll just make a wild guess."*

The teachers went back to completing their evaluation forms.

After drowning me in a sea of smiles.

After

The best question I asked on the evaluation form was to ask what percentage of their students would, by the end of the summer program, test at the educational level of children ready to begin college.

The results were significant, statistically and psychologically. Each teacher's class progress matched closely with their own teacher's predicted percentages. A Robert Rosenthal and Lenore Jacobson self-fulfilling prophecy effect: A teacher's positive belief in their ability can enhance their student's progress. Their learning. Their better future.

In the summer project results, the same happened. When a teacher expected good results, their students mostly succeeded at that level. Or: low teacher expectations of their students were matched by low student outcomes.

How else did the children do?

By the end of the summer program, as a whole cohort, they had advanced substantially in their readiness.

Most though had not caught up fully for all the lost school years. The college challenge to come would test them sorely.

Once the cohort had finished their time in college, those who made it to graduation were best predicted by one factor. A psychological measure.

Their motivation to succeed.

Those who cared the most, those who believed they would prevail, they stayed the course. They got to the finish line.

And the better life beyond.

Did these graduates get some success experiences from a teacher that believed in them back then in that early pre-college summer?

Looked to us that the children got to follow what had become their own self-fulfilling prophecy.

Sources

Green, R.L., Morgan, R.F., and Hoffman, L.J. (1970) 'Effects of deprivation on intelligence, achievement, & cognitive growth."
In Robert Wilcox (Ed), Chapter One, *The Psychological Consequences of Being a Black American: Research by Black Psychologists*. New York: Wiley.

Green R.L. & Morgan, R,F. (1970) "The effects of resumed schooling on the measured intelligence of Prince Edward County's Black children."
In Roger Wilcox (Ed.), *The Psychological Consequences of Being a Black American: Research by Black Psychologists*.. New York: Wiley.

Green, R. L. & Morgan, R.F. (1969) "Compensatory education and educational growth."
In Robert L. Green (Ed.), *Racial Crisis in American Education*. Chicago: Follett, 1969. Chapter 9: Pp. 186-219.

Green, R.L. & Morgan, R.F. (1969) Effects of resumed schooling on the measured intelligence of Prince Edward County's black children. *Journal of Negro Education, 38*, 147-155.

Green, R.L., Morgan, R.F., and Hoffman, L.J. (1967) Effects of deprivation on intelligence, achievement, and cognitive growth: A review. *Journal of Negro Education, 36*, 5-14.

Green, R.L., Morgan, R.F., Hoffman, L.J., Morse, R.J., Hayes, M. (1964) *Educational Status of Children in a District without Public Schools: CRP 3221*. Washington, D.C.: United States Office of Education, 1964.

Green, R.L., Morgan, R.F., Hoffman, L.J., Morse, R.J. (1964) *The Educational Status of Children during the First Year Following Four Years of Little or No Schooling: CRP 2498*. Washington, D.C.; United States Office of Education, 1964.

Rosenthal, R. & Jacobson, L. (2003) *Pygmalion in the Classroom: Teacher Expectation and Pupils' Intellectual Development Expanded Edition*. New York: Crown House. (Prior editions in 1968 and in 1992).

FUTURE TIME STATUES: THEN AND NEXT

Anger: Three Cases (1997-1966)

Theme: "*Any time*" Marty Robbins

Or the Existential version:

*"Any time you're feeling lonely
Any time you're feeling blue
That's the time to remember
All your troubles come from you... "*

Years ago, I was a flatlander new to the mountain country of Northern California. As a psychologist in a region with no other psychologists, my work had the range of a country doctor. Time after time I was confronted with new challenges in this practice, ones outside my experience and expertise. Knowing that most of my patients felt that leaving their home territory for a city referral was like falling off the edge of the earth, I acknowledged that whatever I could contribute was likely the best they could get. I learned a lot and was more helpful than I had anticipated.

(In fairness, some mountain-based outlaws did go far enough down-altitude to raid stores in the Chico area.)

Case #1

Let's call him "*Range*".

He was tall, wide, young, intense. Obviously suppressing some rage. Sat facing me and scowled.

Range said his wife had referred him to me for his uncontrollable violent anger. He was always attacking people for the slightest reason. Just the day before he had told her that he was going to beat up her hospital surgeon. That's when she insisted he come see me first. And here he was.

It wasn't hard to relax Range. First I acknowledged that he looked angry. He agreed and stopped looking that way, interested in the conversation now.

In a few minutes he was smiling. He had asked me before we began if I was married and if I loved my wife. After my two yes answers, he unclenched his fists and said that he was ready to begin the session.

I asked him why he wanted to attack his wife's surgeon.

Range explained that he loved his wife so overwhelmingly that he just wanted to protect her. She was a little over-weight and he felt he had to fight anybody who hurt her feelings about that. The surgeon had given her a diagnostic spinal tap, no problem found, which then caused her continuing pain. The surgeon just told her that she had to live with hurt and not whine about it all the time. Clearly he had decided that this doctor needed a bloody nose consequence.

As an expert in fighting iatrogenic malpractice, medical mistakes, I understood his feelings fully. It was important though to help him learn to fight back in a less destructive way to himself and his wife. A goal too often skipped by therapists.

We focused on the consequences, following visualizations of that intended fight. Visualizing an attack actually reduced the anger, added control. Nobody ever gets arrested for a private thought (so far). He liked the technique. We tried it on me as the target. By then the relationship between us had become friendly and even a mental vision of an attack on me was hard for him to do. He settled for imagining a pie in my face and we both laughed.

FUTURE TIME STATUES: THEN AND NEXT

Now he came in for a few more once a week sessions, glad to share his control. But he still had lots of suppressed rage he carried with him. He asked me why. This was his real goal for therapy: to understand himself. I agreed as it also would give him even more control.

I'm not much of a follower of Freudian doctrine other than saluting him as an essential ancient pioneer for our profession. Most helpful though for me was the emphasis on a problem's origin. *"When did this first begin?"* and *"What was going on then?"* are often useful questions. The emotions felt then and now of course.

Range learned to relax in the chair, shut his eyes, and visualize the answer.

That took him back to a time in his early years when his mother remarried. The stepfather often beat him as a child. It stopped, as it often does, when Range had grown as big as his stepfather. But the child's rage was still ever with him. Also the violent model he had learned from his oppressive stepfather.

On reflection, no, he didn't want to be like him.

Well, not like the way his violent stepfather had been before.

What has changed now?

Oh, he said, they go fishing together at least once a week. They get along okay then.

Has he ever apologized? No.

Did you ever bring the beatings up when you were fishing? Remind him? No.

I suggested he might do that next time they were off fishing together.

Range grinned and said he liked the idea.

(If I had this to do again, with Range's approval, I would have scheduled for the stepfather to come into a session with Range to accomplish this. Hindsight is not always helpful, coming as late as the word sounds, sometimes direct from the hind quarters of our anatomy. Meaning- I was wrong.)

Range entered our next session limping. He had a black eye, cuts, bruises, and a bandage on his forehead. But he was ecstatic.

Said he had reminded his stepfather of all that childhood abuse. Said the old boy had put up quite a fight but in the end Range won the struggle. The stepfather apologized on his way to the hospital. Recovered a few days later. No more fishing dates though.

On our last session, Range brought his wife.

They both agreed that Range was civilized now.

Said they had never been happier.

I didn't ask about the stepfather's opinion.

Case #2

He was a high ranking law enforcer from another rural county. Let's call him *"Shane"*.

Personable and wearing a cowboy hat (no cattle), he sat easily in the guest chair. Said he had come once before to my clinic but my associate had not impressed him.

That other person doing counseling had no academic credentials beyond a college degree or any psychotherapy training but was a relentlessly nice person. This partner had to do before I got there. After that, it left him more time for his hobby: constructing homes for neighbors. That made him very happy.

Back to Shane.

Shane took off his hat, smiled, and said he had heard about me being helpful to many and, besides, able to keep confidences.

Still, psychologist's clients have not the absolute confidentiality enjoyed by lawyers and clergy. I showed him the printed exceptions of state law, including (1) convincing dangerousness to self or others, and (2) convincing confession of serious crime. (I once counseled an elderly woman who in retirement had pulled off some impressive department store shoplifting as a hobby. Never caught. Yet. And this made *her* happy. Seemed to be seeing me to brag in confidence. We did find an even happpier hobby that was without risk of her arrest.)

Shane considered these exceptions carefully, glancing at me several times and rereading the exceptions on the paper.

Finally he carefully phrased the following: *"I'm here to see you to help me with my sadness. Losing sleep over it. It's a very cold case. Many years ago a man was killed in a late night fight behind a bar. About then I joined the law but I never caught the killer. I still feel guilty about that. Maybe you can help me shed that guilt."*

Shane handed me back the confidentiality exceptions paper. Raised an eyebrow to see if I understood.

I considered. Seemed like he was the killer he wanted to discuss. But there was no evidence for this to justify any legal intervention. Onward then.

I said I would help him.

I had Shane sit back, shut his eyes, and go into a light trance for visualization.

Asked him to imagine he was in the mind of the killer.

This he did, signaling he was there.

So I asked him the key question: *"Will he ever kill again, then or now?"*

A vehement no. My relief.

"So exactly what happened the night of the crime. Let him tell us."

Shane described a late night when, leaving the bar at the back, a larger man demanded his money. Rage overcame him, plus maybe he had drunk too much. The rest was unclear. He just remembered standing over the body and then disappearing into the night. He was confused, frightened.

Shane woke up at that point, sitting tall in his chair.

He said that was all he could get from this memory. Except that when the body was found the next day, this was to be his first case. But no witnesses, never solved. Haunted him still.

Shane came back for his weekly sessions. By the second month he had grown quite adept at describing the thoughts and feelings of his quarry, a man much like himself. Maybe exactly like himself.

He went on to speak in his imagination with the victim.

Who in the end forgave the killer.

Shane shared his own just and successful law career over the years. Raised a family and became a valued neighbor.

He explored the consequences if his killer just confessed the crime. Imagined several different paths. In the end, he shared that his nightmares had gone away and a blanket of peace slipped over him each night. He said that maybe the killer would confess to law some day but that decision could wait.

The killer coming out with everything in our sessions had given Shane relief. Time to live in the present.

Our last session.

As to the killer in his mind- he was gone now. His rage had never come back, and he never drank again after that incident. No, Shane said, nor had he himself.

He thought the killer might some day want to connect again in his imagination. Maybe at night when he slept.

I asked him how he would react.

He said he had already imagined this.

The killer would say *"Shane! Come back Shane!"*

But he would just ride off into the horizon, into the decent life where he belonged.

Case #3

This last case takes us to Hawaii in the mid-1960s where I was doing my post-doc internship at the Hawaii State Hospital.

My supervisor acknowledged my success so far with adult patients and with my adolescent day program, a therapeutic community for 30 teens that had never had an unfortunate incident in its yearlong history.

So he said I needed some humility, a failure experience.

He assigned me to what he termed a psychotic paranoid patient who would never recover.

The patient was big, Japanese-American and considered dangerous.

Scowling as he entered my office, he looked like Toshiro Mifune, the iconic screen samurai.

Though we were both only in our 20s.

So we'll call him "Tosh".

Tosh had returned to his family after being thrown out of the Marines. Shameful for them already. But then he began to listen for hours to Japanese radio stations. Strange because he knew no Japanese language. He insisted they were talking about him and were truly insulting. Rage built up by the day until he went down to the station and attacked the staff.

At first the police, following a judge's order, just brought him home to await his trial. That didn't last long. A few more rage issues and he was committed to the state mental hospital. Involuntarily in a strait jacket. It took six orderlies. In front of the neighbors. Overwhelming shame.

Loss of face came to any Japanese-American family there and then that included a "crazy" member. So most did all they could to keep their own out of sight and away from the state mental hospital. This meant that fewer ethnic Japanese patents inhabited the state hospital but those that were there were so out-of-control that the families had given up.

Tosh had heard from other patients that my office was a safe place so he was cautious but curious, suppressing hs obvious anger. The hidden fear below this anger remaining to be discovered.

After some small talk, he chose to explain his view. Everybody in the world was out to get him. Or, the few exceptions, maybe me, were just foolishly unaware of that reality.

Tosh then took it upon himself to instruct me about this conspiracy that was all around us. I listened carefully and with respect. At the core of every paranoid fantasy was a personal reality. One we needed to find.

Clearly, his view of himself as bravely standing aginst an entire world on his own, well, it functioned as a shield against his sad temporary reality.

We shared some light food which also helped Tosh relax. I answered his questions about me and my life to date. This included my honest response that I didn't agree with his conviction that all the world was against him. Instead I told him that likely he had definitely been wronged at points in his past.

This candor built trust as we now agreed to disagree about the nature of his delusion.

He said he looked forward to more meetings. And better food next time.

Our second session, with appetizers more to his taste, went better. He now wanted very much to explain to me how he been wronged, what had brought him to this day in the hospital.

First though, he wanted some help in controlling his rage. One doctor had wanted him lobotomized, another favored electro-convulsive therapy. Clearly he wanted to avoid these things. If he hurt one more orderly he would be punished with destructive interventions. He has read about all these "treatments".

I was impressed. There was in fact a very good mind hiding in the paranoia.

We went through breathing exercises and visualization techniques for more control of his anger. Fight rather than flight had been his remedy. Or maybe both combined.

Tosh excelled at these methods, even allowing himself a smile when done. He knew he was a quick study which I confirmed. Again I was impressed. For him, his success in my office was a minor windfall in the midst of great disaster.

By the remainder of that session and into the next he shared his life to that point. He labeled this narrative variously as being in *"Deep Kimchi"* or *"Up the Yinyang"*.

Tosh shared an early memory. He was a toddler sitting under a tree when a falling coconut smashed into his young head. A serious and potentially lethal hazard. Likely a concussion. But when he regained consciousness, his older sisters were there laughing at him. His scalp was full of blood and they thought it was hilarious. Still hurt his head to remember.

Now we were getting to the core of his paranoid universe: the actual world that *was* against him: his family when he was a child.

Worse was life growing up with his father. Since his father spoke no English and Tosh didn't understand Japanese, there was literally no communication. Father inflicted much harsh discipline onto his son though Tosh never knew why. His mother would not help him. Nor his sisters.

Now his actual world was coming into focus. His childhood must have seemed the whole universe to him. An unjust world demanding he project some meaning into it.

He did well though in school. Became strong and athletic. Loved reading. On graduating high school, he joined the Marines, something that he thought might impress his family.

Marine basic training is meant to collapse a recruit's personality and rebuild it as a warrior. This occurs by pushing their physical and mental limits to beyond what they can stand. Tosh, vulnerable to begin with, had an extra problem.

His trainers thought he was an American Indian. Called him *"blanket-back"*. Tosh didn't let them know any different for a very good reason. His trainers had served in WW2, in the war against Japan. Just two decades before. They remembered Pearl Harbor. Japanese-American trainees would get a whole extra layer of destruction if they were discovered.

Tosh was discovered.

He was once more in an unjust world. He fought back. Hard.

Dishonorable discharge.

Home to his family in Hawaii.

There he began listening to those Japanese language radio stations, delusionally thinking he understood what they were saying.

I asked Tosh in our session what he thought they were saying. In this way we could understand the fear underlying his violent anger.

They were announcing to the world that he was a *"Mahu"* which means effeminate or a homosexual. This in 1960s Hawaii, especially to his family and the Japanese-American community, was a blood insult. It was seen as a perversion, either predatory or to be laughed at.

Tosh had used his rage to prove them wrong with violence. That's when he went to one of the radio stations to attack the station manager and dj. The same at the other Japanese language station before the police caught up to him. Charges included attacking several of the hospitalized officers who had trouble arresting him.

A psychiatrist had him certified insane so he was transferred to the state mental hospital for an indeterminate time. Possibly for life.

Tosh had finished his story. He was calm while in my office and had a request.

Could he help me with my work?

I was collecting library material on shock treatment's damaging side effects which eventually became a book *"Electroshock: The Case Against"*. But at that early stage, the task was to gather the science. I did a study comparing patients who had been given ECT with similar ones who had not. ECT survivors had damaged memories of two kinds. They forgot key parts of their life sometimes including people they loved. They also forget new information, meaning it was hard to learn. Nor did ECT do any lasting good for their diagnostic condition, even when in one case with a violent patient where he received 300 shocks (and was still violent). There was a near perfect correlation though between when a patient hit a staff memnber and that patient next receiving ECT. A punishment? Clearly so.

Tosh had been threatened with ECT and really wanted to avoid it. So he gladly became my research assistant and haunted the hospital library for material.

Now he had a purpose and improved substantially. He had accepted that the reality core for his paranoia was in his own personal world and not in the earth's entire human population. He got very good at understanding his anger and channeling it in an effective but legal manner.

Plus he really was helpful to my work.

So much so that I was able to persuade the staff of my unit to close down any ECT. Our psychiatrist-in-charge had not been there for an extended period of months. On his return he went along, reluctantly, with the ECT ban though it truly was the only psychiatry he knew how to do. Let's just say that he was far from happy with me.

Tosh eventually had improved so much that I got him a discharge to leave the hospital, a *"conditional discharge"* which allowed him to return once a week so he could continiue our weekly meetings as he worked on assimilating to the community. He enrolled in a university counseling degree program while living in the dormitory there. He managed some decent interactions with his sisters, now also in their own adult lives.

Tosh was doing fine.

My supervisor conceded that I had failed to receive sufficient humility. I assured him that I had already more than enough failures in life for humility and expected some valuable learning from much more in the future. I still think he had been rooting for Tosh to get better all along. Hence his humility challenge,

One of my own supervisees, intern Jerry Shapiro, made sure I had a humility experience before I left. In my turn to demonstrate psychotherapy with a volunteer patient in front of staff and interns, Jerry chose for me a lobotomized patient. (Volunteer?) Nothing useful came of this demo. Well, maybe some humility.

One week Tosh came in for his weekly meeting looking really stressed.

He said: *"Doc you won't believe this. But on the bus on the way here today some girls were laughing at me. I did NOT imagine this!"*

What did he do about it?

"I just waited to tell you about it. I ignored the girls completely."

Feelings at the time?

"I couldn't wait to tell you. I was afraid that I was getting sick again. And I was, well, proud that I didn't get angry. Right?"

"Exactly. You should be proud. Now you can choose what to do with hurt or fear. Still, knowing why they laughed can help. Let's shine a light on it. Because, you know, I get why they laughed. Look at your tee shirt and shorts."

He did. His shirt and shorts were borrowed from a roommate in the dorm. Both too small tee and shorts had Mickey Mouse on them, somewhat incongruous on a powerful samurai-looking man.

Tosh looked, considered, and broke out in a loud laugh. He got it. And that laugh meant to me that he was really back to normal.

In another week's meeting, I asked him if there was anything in his recovery that stood out for him. He did have something he wanted to highlight.

"Doc, early on I asked you what I could possibly do when the whole world just gives me a pile of shit! You said 'plant flowers'. I think you might have been joking but I used that many times as a ladder to climb out into the sunshine, the fresh air smelling of flowers in our Hawaii."

We had our last outpatient meeting as I was on my way to a new job outside Hawaii. I gave Tosh my contact information so he could stay in touch, do followups, and let me know if he needed any other consultation. He returned to his studies.

With me gone, that psychiatrist-in-charge of the unit brought back into the ward his only tool: ECT. He systematically gave shock treatments to as many of my remaining former patients as he could. He had held up Tosh's full discharge long enough to call him back in. There he forced Tosh to undergo a series of three shock treatments.

He knew that Tosh would particularly suffer as now he had become an expert on the destructive risks of ECT. Tosh knew it was punitive. As did the shock doctor. Had I still been there, my own anger might well have gone violent. My visualizations worked overtime. I redoubled my anti-ECT work.

Tosh could have reverted to paranoia as this unfair world of punishing involuntary ECT was familiar. But instead he contacted me by phone.

I got his discharge to be final through my hospital network but the damage was done. Tosh had nearly completed his course work but there were still tests to pass. Now his memory for newly learned material was impaired. So he drew on library resources again. Used memory devices to get him through. Each morning he reviewed his written notes from the day before to restore the memories. He passed his exams.

Tosh moved to another state and took a job as a counselor there.

Every Christmas for ten years Tosh would send me a present with a note of thanks. I knew not to respond with more than a return thank you card. In the culture he grew up in, he was paying what he saw as a necessary debt.

On the tenth year I called him long distance at his office. We caught up on life. He finally asked if his gifts were enough. I confirmed that was so. Debt paid.

Tosh continued his work despite the memory challenges and must have helped thousands before he retired back to Hawaii before the 20th century's close.

He departed life five years into our 21st century and a full life it was after all.

Hong Kong 1967

Theme: *Enter the Dragon* Lalo Schifrin

My post-doc clinical internship in Hawaii was done.

My new wife with her own three not-so-new-to-her children, were all safe and happy on Oahu.

Time for me to explore our next stop. I flew to Hong Kong.

I rented an apartment for a month. It came with an Amah, a live-in person (with her own living space there) to maintain the home and, to a very limited extent, me as well.

She spoke no English but was perceptive of gestures and body language plus, at times, she called in a bilingual friend from another apartment for translation.

The English language newspapers headlined a riot going on in which acid was thrown into the faces of Hong Kong Chinese police.

A massive response from them was suppressed reasonably by the British government so as to avoid expanding the carnage. Even so, some police had killed some acid throwers.

Now this burning weapon and more spread to people on all sides along with passersby on nobody's side. Something to consider.

That first day I avoided the acid tossing area and made my way to the three banks.

I took a rickshaw since I still hadn't learned the walking routes. A man who said he was 86 years old was pulling it. Lean wiry muscles with not much effort. While I admired his strength and stamina, at 26 I felt embarrassed to be transported by a man sixty years my senior. Too colonial, exploitive for me. But this *was* a British colony at the time.

On arrival I tipped him at the level I would a taxi driver in Hawaii. He said it was too much, a month's salary. But I knew the custom.

He declined to accept it three times but when I said no, he should keep it, the third time he accepted and made the money disappear. He smiled, nodded, and he too disappeared fast before I might change my mind. Three times was the charm.

Time to open an account.

My first stop, naturally, was my own country's bank. The Bank of America. No snobs expected there.

Nope. But in front of the bank stood a marine guard. His rifle at the ready, complete with bayonet.

I asked him what the problem was, expecting to hear about acid throwers. He asked if I was an American. Yes, I was. He told me I could come in then. Said he was there to protect white Americans like me from the Chinese.

No thanks. I moved on.

To the British bank. No bayonet guard in front. Inside it was clean and impressive.

The clerk asked me if I had an account.

No, I was there to open one. Had the money I had arrived with, ready to deposit.

He said I would need two written references from two current bank customers to open an account. I said I just had come to Hong Kong and didn't know any of their customers yet.

Conserving words, he just nodded toward the entrance, meaning *"there's the door- walk out now through it"*. Or, per the Southern USA phrase that occurred to me. *"Don't let the door hit you where the good Lord split you"*.

And my felt response *"Bless his tiny little heart."*

I wasn't sure he would understand my finger gesture that followed but, in case he did, I exited as requested. I wouldn't be back.

That left the Chinese bank. Okay then.

They were very friendly. Spoke English fluently. Brought in the person in charge.

Who explained to me that China had no diplomatic relations with my home country. Therefore they were not allowed to open a new account for me.

That diplomatic relationship would come five years later in 1972 with Nixon:

Too late for me back in 1967.

But the Chinese banker had given me a card with an address on it. A smaller anonymous currency exchange that foreigners used. They took my money and opened an account. No, I'm not sure what nationality they were even today. European? They didn't say. But they were honest, foreigners aplenty used them, and I had no regrets.

They also printed out business cards for me, necessary for any professional work. Or anything else. Hello in business then always meant an exchange of business cards. Name, title, business, and contact information. English on one side, Chinese on the other.

I reveled in the music, art, colors, parades, laughter. Food. I did love being there.

I was now ready to open a practice in Clinical Psychology.

There was none there yet.

Looking in newspapers, directories, inquiries with medical individuals, everywhere and anywhere, the same conclusion. Not yet, not there.

I did find a newspaper ad for psychotherapy services from somebody who proudly proclaimed that he had completed a psychology class at the University of South Africa.

Well, talk about an opportunity to get in from the ground floor. Being first is an event that never gets overtaken. The need was great. A chance to build the discipline from scratch within that vibrant culture. *With* that vibrant culture.

Still, the daily English language newspaper headlined more tourist deaths from the growing unrest. Should I bring my young family into the midst of this colonial struggle? Would they be safe? *Acid?* Would we be on the wrong side?

But now I had this new family. They either come now to join me or I return to join them.

I called this family long distance for a consultation.

If I were a bachelor on my own, I would definitely stay, follow this path. Considering their own safety, they deserved a say, a veto if they chose.

I asked them to take a chance and join me.

No contest. Unanimous at their end. No! Come home! As they like to say, often, in the 50th state: *"Lucky be in Hawaii"*.

I still had a month left on my apartment lease.

With the help of the downstairs translator I explained that I would be going back to rejoin my family in Hawaii very soon. But I would pay her the full salary for the coming month now plus some more in consideration of my departure.

She took this well so, through the translator, I invited her to a farewell dinner that night at the best restaurant she knew of. She conferred with the translator in animated Chinese, smiling, excited.

The translator said to me that her recommendation for the top restaurant in Hong Kong had been accepted by the Amah. Further, she explained that this was likely to be a once-in-a-lifetime experience for the Amah who, surely I had noticed, ate only one meal a day from a very healthy large bowl of foul-smelling gruel. Of course she had no clothes suitable for this occasion. Yet, for a small stipend, very small considering, the translator would take her to a store to purchase said apparel. Agreed.

Before our dinner, I packed for the return, bought those gifts that my Hawaii family saw as the primary reason for my stay in Hong Kong, and dressed my best for the evening event.

Our translator had booked a central table in a very elegant restaurant. My Amah matched this elegance though she communicated through clear gestures that this was all just a beautiful dream for her.

The patrons, all seemingly successful Hong Kong Chinese of an age, were apparently wealthy or famous enough to match the setting. I recognized some that were celebrities.

The food arrived in colorful waves, as regular as ocean tides. Small portions, each better than the last. Teacups were never allowed to be empty, avoiding any sign of poor hospitality from the wait staff.

A few dishes had an egg on top, later explained to me that the chef was choosing to do this as a habit from post-World War Two egg shortages, making its superlative use an elegance.

I had a great appetite then and managed it all. Though my Amah, a slight diminutive woman, outdid me by far.

During her one restroom trip, the waiter refolded her napkin, whisked any crumbs off the table, and introduced himself. He was Luis, Chinese-Portuguese from Macao.

When my Amah returned, Luis stepped away, and we completed a variety of desserts.

Since we had all arrived as an elite cohort at a scheduled time, all tables were more or less served simultaneously. So we all completed our dining fairly close together. A musical note from somewhere signaled this end.

At that point everybody but me, yes including my Amah, belched very loudly. At every table. The wait staff seemed pleased. As for me, it was the only time I felt alone on an alien planet. I love swimming in new cultures. But this Monty Python moment was a puzzlement.

Luis rushed to my side. *"Not like the dinner?"* he asked with great concern. I asked about the communal belching. Relieved, he explained it was a way the Chinese diners expressed appreciation for fine food and service, second only to an expected generous gratuity. Oh.

Again, too early by a few years for Nixon to be in such a setting but when I saw another photo of that eventually, it reminded me of our dinner. I can only imagine how he might have reacted if his Beijing hosts showed similar appreciation. (He's already holding his chopsticks in an insultingly incorrect manner.)

As I paid the bill, with an American way too generous gratuity, Luis warmed up even more, my new best friend. Since all diners were still at close by tables, he leaned over to confide his Chinese name to me. These are given at birth and remain family secrets thereafter.

He asked me if I had a Chinese name as well. A polite request since that was not expected from an American visitor. I surprised him.

"Yes, I do have a Chinese name" I replied, loud enough to be heard from all tables.

Luis apologized for asking, no longer whispering.

But I relieved him of worry.

"*No problem. I was given it here in Hong Kong. Everybody seems to refer to me in this way. My Chinese name is … GWEILO!*"

This translates to the racial epithet '*Ghostly White One*" or '*Foreign Devil*', as I knew.

All the patrons laughed even louder than they had belched, including Luis.

Laughter: an American alternative to a cohort's belching chorus of appreciation.

My Amah at first was blushing, embarrassed, but soon laughed with the rest.

Smiled at me all the way home.

Glowing from her Cinderella evening.

Any Port in a Storm

Themes: *Black Magic Woman* Santana; *Love Roller Coaster* Ohio Players; *She Works Hard for the Money* Donna Summer

Wolfville, western Nova Scotia, late 1960s

Sarah was the Dean's daughter. An only child, she was much indulged. Consequently much isolated from the other children. As a beautiful teenage vision, she would ride on her horse past our Nova Scotia house on a hill, Morgan House, and look longingly at the people spread out on the front terraces there. People her father had forbidden her to visit.

Especially Charlie, same age as her, our probation placement. Now in our family. He was brilliant, fearless, a fine artist, and, no longer lost, a wonderful new son.

Charlie was the only family of a professor, me, ever forbidden to come on campus. This 15 year old boy, the Dean insisted, would be a bad influence on his college students.

On his mother's complaint, Charlie had been caught with a marijuana plant in his bedroom. We just barely rescued him then from life in prison. To be in my care instead. Well, the 1960s were draconian about psychedelics even in Canada.

The local constable and the national Mounties in that region teamed up eventually at a traffic stop to place a marijuana brick in the trunk of a car Charlie was riding in. The driver, as the son of a government VIP, was just sent home. Charlie though, now at 17, was sent to a federal prison for three years.

On his release, he returned to Wolfville, married Sarah. By then marijuana had become dear to the new generations there. With Charlie's help, Sarah's mother tried some. Suddenly, with her high, she realized how she felt about her husband, and he about her. They were soon divorced. A bad time for that Dean.

Sarah and Charlie moved west to Vancouver, Canada's San Francisco.

They did eventually divorce but remained close friends, even best friends.

Skipping for now their visit to us in my southern Colorado high desert days, and the end of Charlie's story, we move to a later temporal geography.

FUTURE TIME STATUES: THEN AND NEXT

An older Sarah, on her own now in Canada, working in construction. She had incorporated Charlie's fearlessness and grit. Also she had become somewhat world weary. Allied with her own imagination, she was formidable.

As the only woman working with younger men all day, still desirable to all of them. She had no shortage of encounters. A few she shared with me eventually on a California visit.

Discouraging all direct date invitations from her male workers, they all relaxed into the job. Some exceptions.

One of the men, on a break, handed her a book he was reading. A post-it marked a page with a passage he had highlighted. Asked her for her opinion with a sly smile.

The book was the controversial classic from a much older era: *Fanny Hill*. The passage she read was about a consensual intimacy between Fanny and a sailor that suddenly stopped being consensual for Fanny. She told the sailor to stop, he was entering her exit, and she said *NO! Wrong way!* The sailor held his course though, saying the much quoted *"Any port in a storm!"*

Sarah considered this. Then handed the book back to the man, saying: *"I can see why this is important to you. The sailor, maybe after months at sea without women, had found a way to have sex where he was. For you, this kind of sex fitting any woman or man equally might double your chance for a date on Saturday night. An advantage you must need. Helped even more by the sailor's example to ignore the 'No means No' from the woman. So you are now encouraged to be forceful in ignoring what the woman wants. All told this seems to me to summarize what kind of date YOU would be. Move on!"*

1960S

Her male co-workers were all there in the break room. Laughed. But one, a much younger man by far than the rest, stepped forward. Grinning, he handed her a legal size piece of paper filled with drawings. Each silhouette depicted another sexual position between two partners. Dozens of them. He gave her a confident smile and asked what she thought about it.

Sarah gave careful consideration to the pictures. Then said: *"Your mother has been very busy!"*

1970s

Themes: *Whole Lotta Love* Led Zeppelin; *Rumours Album: Rhiannon/Dreams/Chain/Gold Dust Woman/Go Your Own Way* Fleetwood Mac

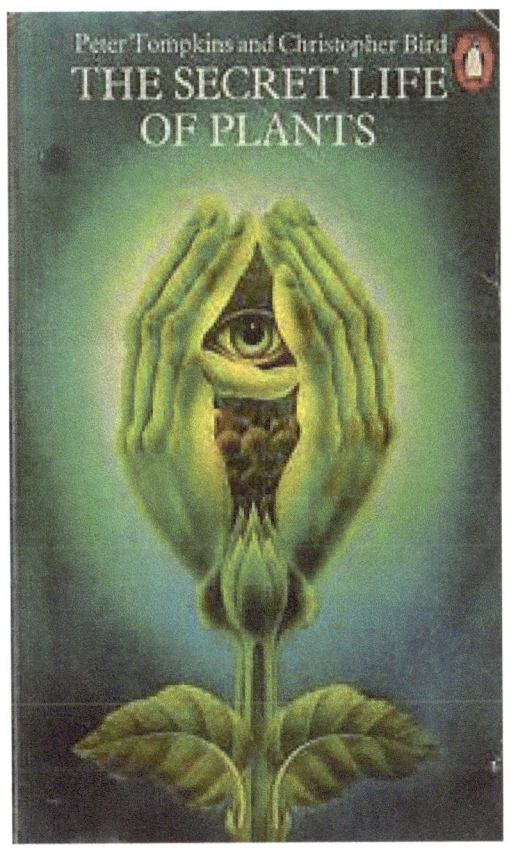

Best Gift for Vegetarians

In San Diego, 1979, an extraordinary psychiatrist friend had begun an intentional community for patients diagnosed with schizophrenia.

No medication, ECT, or any other invasive high risk interventions. Just therapeutic community.

It had been very successful for a year when she asked me to consult.

Intrigued, I went to meet with her patient group.

Nobody was to be hired for the program without their consent.

My interview with them was short and direct.

I was asked just one question: *"What about you gets you in the most trouble?"*

I answered *"My sense of humor"*.

They caucused.

Finally their spokesman stood up and said *"That's true for us too. We want to hire you."*

The Morgan House Ghost

Themes: *Here Comes the Sun* George Harrison; *Ghost Riders* J. Cash/Willie Nelson; *I Still Believe* Tim Capello (*Lost Boys*)

This happened at the beginning of the 1970s in western Nova Scotia. Near the end of that decade I shared it with Robert Monroe and his daughter at their second training session in Virginia. Elisabeth Kubler Ross stayed past the first session to hear it.

Tony Harvester

Tony Harvester would still want to be headlined here. Done.

I bought a race horse for twenty Canadian dollars.

He had been named Tony Harvester though likely he never knew or cared about that. Tony was about to be "put down" or killed.

He was a year past the age where the other horses stopped racing. Worse, he had pulled up lame in one leg, limping painfully to the stables.

Still he was the most social animal the human handlers had ever known. Tony loved horses, dogs, and even humans.

His positive attitude so endeared him to the humans that they were glad to let him live if they could sell him to me for only twenty dollars.

True, though Tony had never won a race. He always ran with the fastest horse, loving to run with a companion, but the fastest horse wanted to win and Tony, ever the great friend, always let them come in first. If there were several horses all pushing to win, he would pace them and then allow them to *all* cross the finish line first. No abuse from a jockey changed his mind.

So the horses liked him too. Exactly the world he most enjoyed living in.

Now the real cost of owning a racehorse includes more than a purchase price. You need food, vet care, grooming, exercise, and a comfortable place to keep him.

The last at least I already had waiting.

Morgan House

Martin Luther King Jr. was assassinated in 1968. He was not yet even 40. I was not yet 30. Our years with him were over and his killers were in power.

Fed up, my family began anew the next year in the country to the north.

Specifically I began a job at a university in rural Nova Scotia, a Canadian maritime province. I had a wife and four children (a fifth to come soon) so I looked for a large home. The Scottish people there believed debt was the devil's trap. (Maybe close?) So if they wanted to own a house they saved up for decades until they could pay cash for it.

Being an American with decent credit and less than decent cash, I took the mortgage path immediately. I finally bought a 30 room terraced four-floor mansion on Kings Street, furnished, with ten acres of woods for a back yard.

The view from the upper floors was of the Bay of Fundy, a large body of water resembling a great lake.

Except it disappeared twice a day, long enough for picnics where the water had been, short ones. The Bay was pulled to the ocean by the most powerful tides on the planet. And then returned.

The only higher point than our house was a bar on Blomidon mountain (Blomidon was short for "Blow me down", an old sailor remark for the high point. I also liked the local dialect that included pronouncing "lawyer" as "liar".)

As you enter the front door, to the left is the library, bookshelves floor to ceiling. And a fireplace. Master bedroom upstairs had a fireplace too as did the living room. The cost of this furnished mansion was a $40,000 dollar mortgage, nothing down.

Still, we had bedrooms to spare. So the university sent me their more challenging students to live in my house, ones not to their taste for dormitory tranquility.

The university had been a Baptist institution and only recently had become part of the Canadian national university system.

Our new roommates were among the brightest more creative people we might have chosen.

They immediately named our home as "Morgan House".

1970S

The house had ten bedrooms, adding to which we converted five more rooms to join them, way more than we needed.

One already had a live-in inhabitant. Bob was bald, middle aged, and the town milk man. He lived rent-free in return for being the maintenance and fix-it resource for the house. Bob got up early to do his day job and then his household upkeep chores. By every sunset he was ready for bed. But first he would step out on the front upper floor balcony dressed in robe and slippers to address the Morgan House inhabitants already seated on the lawn terraces below.

Always he gave the same oration: *"The woods are lovely, dark and deep. But I have promises to keep, and miles to go before I sleep, and miles to go before I sleep"*. *Loud applause from the terraces for Bob's heartfelt version of Robert Frost. He would nod happily and then go back into the house over the less than miles to his bedroom.*

The dining room accommodated all house inhabitants. For Thanksgiving we had turkey and ham. The pig supplying the ham had its head left on a corner piece of furniture facing the spacious dining room table. I thought adding a baseball cap and sunglasses brought home the thankful message to the pig meant by Kerouac when he named the title of the Burrough's book *"Naked Lunch"*. Many salutes to the pig were made at that dinner. The pig remained noncommittal.

Asked for the house rules, I said *"You can do anything you want as long as nobody gets hurt"*.

Raised in the town's fundamentalist Baptist tradition where movies and dancing were considered sinful, I was told in a visit 25 years later that this simple sentence was taken to be the revelation of their generation, an opening for the American 1960s to come to their town. In a word: Freedom.

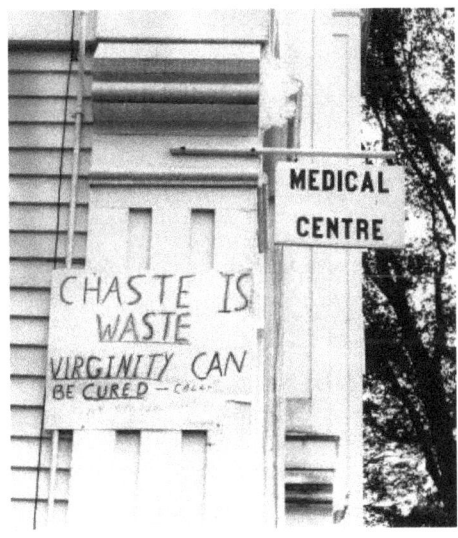

Nor would this freedom ignore its deep religious roots, though not necessarily with respect. I was told by the students early on that American humor leaned too heavily on sex and excretion.

But humor here in this fundamentalist bastion was more religious in essence. Example: *"How was Jesus Christ named? It was the first thing Joseph said when his wife Mary told him she was pregnant."* Then I would be told further, assuming as an American I had to be told, that Mary was the Virgin Mary and never had experienced sex. I added a word: *"Allegedly"*. Confirming their American stereotype.

A year after the American Woodstock, the Canadian Woodstock was held in Nova Scotia. Joan Baez headlined. Instead of the half a million that Woodstock had, true to the smaller Canadian population, we only had a tenth of that at 50,000. Seemed like most stayed at Morgan House for the Concert.

In the back of the estate, just before the woods began, was a wooden structure for housing a horse. Tony Harvester's new home.

Animaulda and Charlie

The rent paying students covered our monthly mortgage cost but there was still room for some town people to stay.

The students brought in a laundry woman in her forties. Midge, who was an alcoholic, was soon weaned by students from her drunk persona by substituting marijuana. Midge was a character whose favorite expression was *"Fuckaduck!"*

A local grocery manager moved in, bringing two of his female cashiers as well. Our inhabitants soon exiled the manager and for good reason, but the two cashiers stayed.

One was Animaulda, a self-chosen name. She saw that as the easiest way to tell the world her choices were her own. Let's, for now, refer to her as Ann, her eventual name in a later life.

Charismatic, beautiful, and young, she soon had all in the house but me and the children episodically enjoying the warm summer, usually on our roof.

A fifteen year old probation placement living with us, Charlie, played loud rock from the roof.

A shock wave regularly descended over the ultra-conservative neighbors.

By then Ann, raised as an orphan, had at my invitation joined our family. In this role she took on all the household chores, child care responsibilities, and pet care work as well.

This included Tony Harvester. Feeding, grooming, care for his lame leg until it was no longer lame.

In fact it was Ann that had brought me to buy Tony, urging that we save the life of this loving horse. Daily Ann could be seen riding him bareback, no saddle needed, through the town.

In such a fundamentalist village, there was no prior thought for dealing with the Morgan House multifaceted perceived outrage of joyful living. The villagers fell back on open ostracism. They avoided her and us in the house completely. A universe unto our own, few in Morgan House noticed.

I do recall the university president, a biologist and the first non-Baptist minister to hold that post, calling me into his office re Ann and the horse.

First he thanked me for the *London Sunday Times* spread just done on my own research, providing good press for the university.

Then he brought up Charlie's roof music and Ann's rides through town: *"Dr. Morgan, this is NOT a metropolitan region!"*

No kidding.

Ann continued to exercise Tony in her own creative freedom way. DJ Charlie continued on the roof.

The Ghost

The house held joyful parties on weekends. Not particularly loud but laughter and music did echo down the otherwise quietly devout streets. Neighbors ranged from tolerant to outraged, though most were just deeply curious.

And then there was the visiting ghost.

In earlier years the house had been used as a long term care facility for the elderly.

At some point on the evening of many parties, an elderly woman would emerge from a wall, view the convivial goings on, shake her head in annoyed disbelief, and then leave through another wall.

This was viewed by most of those at each visitation.

It seemed eventually that I was the only one not to see her.

Until, one sunny day, I was walking down the main street with a group of our resident students. On the way to buy groceries.

Suddenly, they pointed to an older woman across the street. She was walking the opposite way from us, carrying groceries.

Somebody among us yelled: *"That's her! That's our weekend ghost!"*

Sure and certain, everybody agreed.

The woman shook her head in annoyance, as usual, but scurried away as fast as she could.

I made sure we moved on. Leave her alone.

So: not a ghost.

Out-of-body projection?

Curiosity intense among a neighbor?

And, of course, disapproval. Every weekend it would seem.

Then

More than 50 years have passed. Naturally, Tony Harvester has passed as well.

Ann joined us when the family moved to San Francisco. There in the first half of the 1970s, she found an entire city still celebrating the 1960s. Ann's missionary freedom perspective was in every corner.

She thrived there for a time, but missed the wilderness. Eventually she returned to a very remote corner of Canada. Chose a husband well. With him she raised a family in the fresh air of a very remote forest. When all the children were grown, she remained. Peacefully wild in a happier way. Her missionary days had been left in San Francisco.

Now in retirement, her cause is the freedom to love her animals and their humans. That's us too, loving her back.

I live far away from Ann in the state of New Mexico, USA, with my wife of more than thirty years together. We are living our own best retirement. Better than possible.

Back to the Monroe Institute OBE Training at the end of the 1970s

That year I was in charge of continuing education for the state of Nevada's mental health staff. I had read that Robert Monroe's training, about to begin, had in preliminary demonstrations brought chronic alcoholics and drug addicts to a healthy abstinence.

Not sure about the out-of-body (OBE) stuff yet but I was intrigued about it all. Further, in its first official training, John Voight and Elisabeth Kubler-Ross were in attendance. Staffing for the second training was in process but already the military intelligence people were enrolled.

So I picked that training as my own continuing education choice. Off to Virginia.

OBEs turned out to be real. I didn't get any of my own that time as I was stuck against the key induction phrase "I am more than my body". Not anymore.

Then though, I was still able to experience a cathartic healing.

I had been a year going through the most stressful time of my life while still caring for my young children, patients, job. I managed okay. Kept it together.

But through the training exercise reaching out for some gift from what we would see as spiritual, I was flooded with joy. And I laughed out loud.

Realizing I had been suppressing laughter, joy, for a year. Cathartic. Thank you Dionysus. Thank you Robert Monroe.

There it was- I could see how that phase of the training might help addicts or anybody else stuck in an unhappy time.

After I thanked Bob and his daughter for this very helpful intervention, they listened to my time statue report on the OBE ghost of Morgan House. Bob thought it was clearly an early understanding of OBE, possibly an explanation of many erroneous ghost sightings.

I told them of the idea I had shared once with a staffer at Nevada's maximum security ward for dangerous mental patients. Mostly serial killers and rapists. Since they were there for up to life, I wondered if the out-of-body training might be a legal way for them to spend their time more fully while incarcerated. Not thinking it through, obviously. The staffer smiled at my idea, saying "Oh, they all do that all the time already!"

More ghost viewings explained?

At this point, Elisabeth got up to go. Plane to catch.

She turned to me and said she had been reading my life extension writings.

I thanked her.

She shook her head no, saying:

"Not a compliment Robert. You are hopelessly stuck in the stage of denial."

Saying Nothing (1974)

Themes: Gershwin's *I've Got Plenty of Nothing*, *Rhapsody in Blue*

Do not go gentle into that good night,
Old age should burn and rave at close of day;
Rage, rage against the dying of the light.
                                                    –Dylan Thomas

Leon was a psychiatrist at San Francisco's Center for Special Problems (CSP).

He wasn't viewed as belonging to the group of psychiatrists working there.

Instead he was a member of the group of individuals that belonged to no group (mathematicians' paradox).

Not particularly friendly, this elder man with the trim goatee radiated individuality. That was exemplified by his staunch refusal to ever prescribe damaging psychiatric medications.

His prescription pad might otherwise contain a behavioral prescription (*"Buy her flowers and apologize"*) or important notes to himself (*"Fishing with grandson this Saturday: Bring treats"*).

Staff usually just left Leon alone. So naturally, we became friends.

I slouched past his office one morning, feeling the weight of my five part time jobs. And the struggles of the patients there at the clinic, plus my own.

Leon yelled: *"Hey Atlas! Put the earth down and rest for a while."*

Strange maybe. But that memory always helped me do just that. Sometimes there *is* a perfect thing to say.

In the 1970s the city was over-loaded with special problems, known also as unique individuals. Governor Ronald Reagan had closed major state mental hospitals. They had been unhelpful at best, so good as far as it went. But Reagan failed to pass the financial savings on to us at the community clinics.

Many liberated mental patients expanded the homeless ranks in the streets. Some kept from starving by getting arrested. One tried to take a shower in one of our clinic urinals. Many walking along in busy tourist areas were continuing loud conversations with themselves. (If only we had fake cell phones to give them back then, nobody would have noticed.)

Many of those newly lost on the streets just, actively or passively, took the option of leaving their life.

In mornings, the sidewalk in front of a nearby McDonalds was a favorite spot where their remains would be found.

CSP staff were often regarded in more traditional mental health centers as special problems in their own right- creative, effective, famous pioneers, and very hard to categorize.

CSP took on clients the regular centers preferred not to see, even in San Francisco: the newly homeless delusional or suicidal refugees from the defunct mental hospitals, addicts, sexual lifestyle pioneers, and even much sought felons.

And while the five other county centers left their empty offices to do community outreach, our CSP was the one that still gave face-to-face psychotherapy to the city's citizens.

Leon's reputation rested more than anything else on his evening *contact groups* with self-selected suicidal walk-ins.

A contact group was a gathering of people in from the street, without cost, record, or paper.

In fact, CSP was proud to be the last such center in the country to give clients the option to be un-digitized.

CSP Director Gene Turrell, formerly with Kinsey's group, specialized in transforming felons wanted by the law, including killers. It was his belief that, by providing psychotherapy in absolute confidence, he would save their victims.

Without that safety, these dangerous hunted individuals would naturally not come in.

Gene looked like 'Lurch' from the Addams family, wore size 18 shoes.

When law officers sat in his office demanding information on any of these, Gene, a chain smoker, would shut his office door and then fill the room with smoke. Law would retreat without what they came for, smoke blown up their visit.

-

Leon let me sit in one night with his contact group. One of the 13 people there said: *"I have nothing to live for!"* Leon: *"Yes! That's your reason."*

Some were confused, other contact group regulars smiled.

Leon went on to explain that finding your individual purpose in existing on this earth was the most important thing you can do.

"Start looking" he said. Then others reported their progress.

Yes, Leon was very existential in his approach. It worked.

Our staff gathering place was Ernie's, a Chinese restaurant on Polk Street, a block from work. One day I walked in to see something I had never seen before.

Leon sat quietly alone in a corner table with tears streaming down his cheeks.

A waitress we knew whispered: *"His grandson had an accident at school and died yesterday. Very sad."*

Leon's grandson was the happiest part of his days. Whenever he spoke of him, he would transform into smiles. Clearly, his grandson was Leon's purpose in living. And now...

I sat next to Leon. He acknowledged me with a nod but said nothing.

Whatever could I say to this good man that would help him through this trauma?

I could think of nothing.

So I just put my hand on his forearm and sat with him in silence.

Leon eventually pushed his untouched plate of food away.

Quietly said *"Thank you Atlas. I appreciated that."*

He left the restaurant and wasn't seen at work for a few weeks.

When he returned, his contact groups re-commenced.

Leon seemed to have found there another purpose for his existence.

And I had learned this:

When you can think of nothing helpful to say, nothing is what to say.

Note: Leon was actually known as Dr. Leonard Miller. We miss him.

Enter the Hippo

Themes: *Hit the Road Jack* Ray Charles; *Black Coffee* K.D. Lang

Many of the staff at San Francisco's Center for Special Problems (CSP) became famous in our field eventually. Back in the 1970s it was already apparent.

These included pioneers like lesbian couple Phyllis Lyon & Del Martin, lesbian mother of four (and future Police Commissioner) Pat Norman, bisexuality advocate Maggie Rubenstein, brilliant doctor for pregnant addicts Josette Mondanaro, and a vocal raft of gay male psychiatrists. (In a staff meeting, one social worker complained that the gay psychiatrists did most of the talking, to which one replied *"And rightly so!"*)

A social worker named Ron, whose last name I don't recall, was a leader in a successful movement to remove homosexuality as a "disease" diagnosis from the psychiatric DSM manual.

I joined in by publishing an article suggesting that if any non-normative sexuality was going to be considered a disease, then celibacy needed to be added and numbered in the DSM diagnostic categories*.

Ron's next target to remove stigma from the Gay community was the Vatican. Success? Well, not yet.

While, as a straight white male, I at first seemed not a good fit within this staff context. But in comparison, I self-identified as an obvious minority with an alternative lifestyle. As such, this straight white male was fully accepted. It helped that I had brought in a dozen volunteer pre-doctoral psychology interns from my other job as a Dean at the free-standing California School of Professional Psychology. Even more so for that one day at the motel.

Motel Relief

I was at CSP all day and into the evening one day a week. Besides supervising the interns, I had a very full practice with fascinating clients.

*Morgan, R.F. (1975) Revising the Diagnostic & Statistical Manual (DSM-II, DSM-III) of Mental Disorders by adding iatrogenic categories and recognizing celibacy as sexual deviation. *Journal of Irreproducible Results,* 1975, 21(2), 31.

Still, I had fully noticed how very hard everybody else worked.

So one day I rented a room at the motel next door to CSP.

It had a swimming pool. Which allowed me to bring guests. Exercise room. The room was clean, including the bathroom.

Everything one would want for a great breakroom.

All day long, staff in small numbers would take breaks in the pool or other motel facilities. Lunch hours were fully used there as well.

Especially since, on the other side of the motel, was a popular inexpensive fast food restaurant with tasty take-outs. Often enjoyed by the pool.

It was called **HIPPO HAMBURGERS**:

Now it did not go unnoticed with our clinical staff that the hippo image might well be an unflattering portrayal of their fast food customers. After eating their food regularly.

Reminds me of another fast food place I took my daughters to until they pointed out that we were eating their happy animal:

But on that sunny day in San Francisco, the delicious Hippo burgers banished any such negativity.

On that day.

Addiction Alternative

Our sexual orientation clients were matched in numbers by the addiction-treatment ones. In those days, heroin was the main problem. My dear friend Dr. Josette Mondanaro offered a methadone transition program for pregnant heroin addicts that was successful in its production of healthy non-addicted babies.

Time for me to learn as much as I could about overcoming damaging substance addiction.

I never needed a car in those San Francisco days. Walking usually, buses if needed. Though if the time and distance were important, cabs were plentiful, inexpensive. That year I had a regular cabbie I could count on, a stocky gravelly-voiced man in his thirties. He knew I was working at CSP.

So one day, he pulled the car over and turned to me. Said he was a heroin addict. He was planning to go 'cold turkey' on his own that weekend. Just stop. He knew that the withdrawal would be rough, to say the least. Wondered if he could call me at home to talk him through it if necessary. No, he would not be a patient at CSP. He had to do it himself. On his days off. Then back to work, clean.

I gave him my home phone number and planned to be there for him that weekend.

First though: *"You can repay me by trying something I just read about. It said that a gram of vitamin C taken every hour with a glass of water may block withdrawal symptoms. Try it?"* He agreed.

That weekend he didn't call the first day. On day two he did. Said he had followed the regime, C every hour with a glass of water. And, amazing, no withdrawal. He skipped the pill and water for two hours. Was on the floor with nausea and pain. Went back to taking C with water every hour, sleeping around this. Peed a lot. Withdrawal ended now he was on the C regime. He would continue.

The last day of the weekend, at night, came his other call. He was clear of heroin now and no withdrawal. He would like to see me for follow up sessions at CSP to make sure it lasts.

What had he learned? He never in his life wanted to see another vitamin C pill.

Addiction Sharing

There is always a risk of doctors becoming infected by their patients. Yes, this can happen psychologically as well as physically.

We become like those we spend our days with. Freud liked to call aspects of this countertransference. "The medical student's disease" describes the feeling that interns often have that the symptoms of a disease they are studying may seem to suddenly appear in themselves.

Some protections can be learned. Should be learned.

Along these lines, I noticed that every week money was collected for staff coffee. The strongest coffee money could buy. Needed! Seemed like an addiction to me.

But first a nod for a tougher habit.

Path Diverted

A non-psychiatric medical doctor joined us. He noted my observation about the staff coffee addiction. But wanted to go for a tougher fight. He, way ahead of his time, wanted to begin a program to help clients stop smoking. Nicotine addiction is even tougher than heroin to beat. Designed that way by cigarette companies.

He knew I didn't smoke. He wanted my help with the success evaluation part. Sure.

I suggested first we invite staff support for the new program. He agreed.

Put together a half-page brief questionnaire for staff. A place to write their specialty.

He balked at the last yes-or-no question I had added: *"Do you believe smoking is bad for your health?"*

He said that for staff in a public health clinic that was insulting. Even in those years, the 1970s, they all knew it was an emphatic yes. But he eventually allowed the question.

All the staff answered the brief survey, 100%.

As to my question, all the psychologists and social workers, community workers, and even the interns said yes. Smoking is harmful to their health.

All the psychiatrists and nurses said no. Most were avid smokers, including the clinic director.

Well, better he should know.

Demoralized, that nice medical doctor transferred out.

Back to the Coffee Addiction

This week it was my turn to collect staff money for the power coffee buy. My name had come up on the alphabetical list. I didn't drink coffee myself (prefer *Oxylent* lemon-flavored vitamin drink to wake up) but soldiered to the task.

Rather than going to offices door to door, I just ran off a note for each of their mail boxes saying they could each leave their coffee donation in a safe designated space and I will buy the coffee for them once all had complied. I needed to lighten up the mood as cash requests are never fun, especially the ones that must be paid. So I added a cartoon I'd found at the top of the note.

Recalling our recent motel pool break with Hippo burgers, it was of two standing hippos dancing with each other. Something like this:

 or this

Enter the Hippos

Overall, the staff responded well to the note. I bought their coffee, supported this need. Guilty. But wait.

I was called into the CSP director's office. He said two of the nurses wanted to file charges against me for sexual harassment. What? They said the dancing hippos on my note were mocking them. They both were somewhat heavyset.

I could see that Director Turrell was trying to take this seriously. We both cared about staff morale. But he clearly was suppressing a laugh. I brought it out, saying: *"If the hippo fits."*

He did explain to them that I was referencing a fast food restaurant that we all regularly enjoyed and had never had them in mind. They reluctantly retreated to their office. Maybe submerged there.

Meantime most staff office doors had a note taped to them. Somebody had xeroxed my dancing hippos with a caption below: **HIPPOS SAY FREE DOCTOR MORGAN.**

Coffee addiction does have a bright side.

Trust (1944, 1972, 1996)

Theme: *Smiling Faces* Undisputed Truth/Temptations; *Dream a Little Dream* KD lang & Tony Bennett

Trust is essential for any relationship to survive. Children need trustworthy parents, good marriages require trustworthy partners, employees deserve trustworthy supervisors. Effective police departments must earn the trust of their community. Trust is especially important, sometimes life or death, for a doctor's patient. Magnified when the patient is a child.

Dr. David Cheek was just beginning to be recognized as a master hypnotist in 1972. One of my graduate students, Gene Orro, gave me his phone number and recommended I hire him for a hypnosis workshop. I had already decided that psychology's first free-standing school of professional psychology should offer hypnosis as a first year core skills class. Not at the end of training, far too late, or more often, not at all. So I called.

He had a San Francisco gynecology and obstetrics practice not far from us. He had already made a mark with his respectful client-centered hypnosis approach. Automatic consent or dissent signals from the client's designated fingers for every step.

He agreed to do an all day workshop so we set a time and date. But he refused to take any pay. Said we were new, just getting started, and, besides, he was happy to train psychologists in his approach. Medical doctors were uninterested so far, though nurses and dentists were on board.

I told him I would be there at the workshop along with my students. As it was a very large group, I suggested he ask for me before the workshop to sign some papers. Though I was the Dean, I was the same age then as my students and, being in San Francisco, dressed the same. I started to describe myself but he declined. Said he would know which one I was soon enough.

We assembled for the workshop and waited. Just at the exact time it was supposed to begin, Dr. Cheek, confident in a three piece suit, walked in. With a friendly smile, he said it was time to begin. Said he would catch the Dean at the break.

He arranged us to stand in a large circle, maybe two dozen of us. He had brought enough pencils for each of us to hold one at arm's length. Then he had us, now with reflexive finger signing permission, go into a light trance. Eyes shut. We were told that we would know when this auto-hypnosis was ready by realizing that the pencil had fallen to the floor.

When we were asked to open our eyes, all the pencils were down. Except mine. I was still holding it in my outstretched arm.

David walked up to me and said *"Nice to meet you Robert. So you're the Dean."*

(David later told me that I had dropped my pencil at the same time as everybody else but I had bent down and picked it back up. I had no memory of doing this so the trance had worked.)

In the workshop afternoon, David divided us into pairs. Each would take turns standing straight and then falling backwards so as to be caught by the partner. This was called a trust exercise. I caught my partner easily. But I could not (with psychologists that meant *'would not'*) fall backwards. With any partner.

FUTURE TIME STATUES: THEN AND NEXT

So David chose to use me to demonstrate his trauma resolution technique. He usually did this early trauma memory recovery hypnosis for female patients fearful about an upcoming baby's first birth. This went as far back as needed, even to the mother's own birth or the trimester before. For me, at the time, I only went back as far as my own age three. This was the trauma time statue I revisited that day with David.

I was on my way to the hospital to have my tonsils removed. Fix my sore throat. This was okay because I had been raised and praised for being tough in such situations. And I trusted these giants called doctors. They would make me well, just fine. Then I was in a hospital bed, ready. In walked these giants (to me) in white coats. The one in front said "Hello Bobby. We are going to take you now to have a nice ice cream cone. For your sore throat. Isn't that nice?" I hadn't expected this, but sure! They put me on top of something with wheels and rolled me into a dimly lit room. Lifted me onto a table and strapped me down. No ice cream in sight. Put a mask over my face that began hissing. I couldn't speak and they couldn't hear me. They had LIED to me. I was good at following what a doctor told me. Pain didn't slow me down. Why the ice cream lie? Doctors weren't supposed to lie to children, to me! I got really angry. I figured out that the hissing mask was supposed to put me to sleep. So I fought it. I still was awake and glaring. They gave me more hissing in the mask. Still awake, eyes open. More hissing. At some point. I finally passed out. When I woke it was another day. My mother was there looking worried. Said I had been asleep for three days. Too much hissing in the mask. Said finally now I could go home. Still no ice cream.

David's intervention was helpful to me though not 100%. I had after age three been damaged eventually in various falls and still was cautious about falling. I as an adult knew by then that not every doctor or not every other person we meet in life could be trusted. More honor to those who could be.

Bringing this trauma to light though may have explained many things still true in my life. My lifelong work of preventing iatrogenic practice, the doctor's mistakes, may be an outcome. Seeking the final end of the demonstrably destructive electroconvulsive shock treatment a prime example. Books along these lines surfaced between 1982 and 2005 with more to come. They should have given me that ice cream cone.

David Cheek's workshop was a big success. The students used self-hypnosis regularly. Overcoming test anxiety, fulfilling skills, speed reading. Also for their research, and many fresh creative avenues. On graduating, they could apply the Cheek method to their practice, for the great benefit of their patients. Today, it's prevalent for hypnotists everywhere.

Since David's office was close to my work, many of our secretarial staff were his patients. You could tell by their twitching fingers which let me know agreement or the opposite independent of what was said. They also told me that, as the years rolled by, David never raised his $10 an hour fee for them. His methods saved many lives and restored a future to many more. Cheek and I became close friends. It was not the case though that he could join me in the 21st century. He remains a heroic time statue in the 20th.

Let's go forward 24 years from that day in 1972 to his future 1996 memoriam. We'll better understand who he was. And in that time who he will always be.

In memoriam:
David B. Cheek, M.D.

written by: Dabney M. Ewin

David Bradley Cheek died on June 12, 1996 at the age of 84, after a short bout with lymphoma. He was an early member and the sixth president of the American Society of Clinical Hypnosis.

Born in Singapore in 1912, he was the grandson of a medical missionary to Siam. He had wide interests in all life forms and their origins. He studied first geology and paleontology, then premed at Harvard. His education was interrupted by tuberculosis, and he subsequestly received his medical degree from the University of California, San Francisco. He completed his internship and residency in obstetrics and gynecology at John Hopkins in 1945. It was about that time when he met William Kroger, who was doing pioneering work with hypnosis in gynecology and demonstrating the use of hypnosis as the sole anesthetic for obstetrical deliveries and major surgical procedures. This began a lifelong interest in hypnosis and the obvious as well as the subtle influences that subconscious ideas and imprints have on body physiology.

Cheek recognized early the difference between ideomotor signals (a form of affect-driven body language) and the usual conversational hypnosis. He used ideomotor signals to uncover birth imprints, sounds heard under general anesthesia, and subconscious fears causing spontaneous miscarriages, none of which where available with conversational hypnosis. Cheek is to ideomotor as Erickson is to indirect suggestion. His last book, *Hypnosis: The application of Ideomotor Techniques* (1994) reviews his years of experience and details his techniques. A clinician's hypnosis library may be deemed incomplete without it.

He co-authored two books, *Clinical Hypnosis* with Leslie LeCron, and *Mind-Body Therapy: Methods of Ideodynamic Healing in Hypnosis* with Ernest L. Rossi. He contributed chapters to six other books and published 43 articles on psychosomotic medicine.

Dave always had a curious and open mind, even traveling to Brazil seeking to understand the mysteries of the spiritist healers there. He observed animals and studied Volgyesi's work with animal hypnosis. He was a pioneer, a doctor's doctor, and a wonderful teacher. His cheery smile and warm caring will be missed by all of us who knew and worked with him. We extend our condolences to his wife Dolores and the rest of his family.

> "He was a pioneer, a doctor's doctor, and a wonderful teacher."

Sources

Cheek, D. B. (1968) *Clinical hypnotherapy.* New York: Grune & Stratton.

Cheek, D.B. (1993) *Hypnosis: the application of ideomotor techniques.* New York: Allyn & Bacon.

Cheek, D. B. & L. LeCron (1968) *Clinical hypnotherapy.* New York: Grune & Stratton.

Morgan, R.F. (1982, 2005). *The Iatrogenics Handbook: A Critical Look at Research & Practice in Helping Professions.* Toronto: Morgan Foundation.

Morgan, R.F. (1999). *Electroshock: the Case Against.* (With Peter Breggin, Leonard Frank, John Friedberg, Bertram Karon, Berton Roueche) Albuquerque, NM: Morgan Foundation. (Chapter IV reprinted in Brent Slife's *Taking Sides: Psychological Issues, 13th edition,* Guilford, CT: McGraw-Hill/Dushkin, 2004 and in Richard P. Halgin's *Taking Sides: Abnormal Psychology, 2nd edition,* Guilford, CT: McGraw-Hill/Dushkin, 2002. (First edition: *Electric Shock.* Toronto: IPI Publications, l985.)

Morgan (2012). *Trauma Psychology in Context: International Vignettes and Applications from a Lifespan Clinical-Community Psychology Perspective.* Santa Cruz, CA: Morgan Foundation.

Secrets

Themes: *Secrets* Alicia Keys; *Macarthur Park* Donna Summer

They were meeting for the last time. The divorce had gone through that very day. As they sat on the top if the hill, overlooking the home they would never see again. He asked her if she had ever loved him. She saw he was relaxed and decided to be truthful this time. "No. But many times I was grateful. Like having my teeth fixed when we had so little money. Nobody had ever cared about that before." He nodded, pushed his luck. Honesty at the very last. He asked her then, in all their 13 years of marriage, what she had liked least about him. She answered quickly: "Two things. The worst was your obsession with honesty!" He considered this, surprised and happy that this was one of the 'worst'. But- he did want to know what the other worst thing was. She said this with more feeling than before: "You never bought me a proper dining room table!"

In my early years as a psychologist, I would open my couple's therapy group with this story.

"The two of them met and fell in love. It happened quickly.

So too did their marriage. A very traditional one. A commitment, as expected in that era, for a lifetime of loyalty, monogamy, and never a divorce: *'till death do we part'.* Sincere by both partners, vowed in the presence of family and friends, and, as it was a religious ceremony, sworn before God.

But for such young people at the beginning of their adult life, the intensity of their devotion would not be enough.

They had only been married for a month when his new job required him to be gone for a week with his co-workers. A convention in a vibrant city, let's say New Orleans.

The older males banded together to explore the nightlife. He was pleased to be included. He kept up with them on the drinks, the clubs, and, eventually, the women. Only once back at the hotel, did he fully face that he had already broken his wedding promise. He decided that he would pretend it had never happened. Why break her heart? Why lose the marriage before it really had a chance? Why make her hate him? So: a secret.

While he was gone, his new wife had a secret too. She had only dated one other young man before she met her husband. An intense affair.

They had continued to be 'just friends', a relationship that she had agreed with that 'friend' that this would be kept between them. The husband should never know. Already an intimacy bond with her ex that undermined her bond with her new husband.

One night her ex just showed up to say goodbye. They slept together one last time. Agreed it would never happen again. Nor did it. They would keep this secret too.

Should she tell her husband when he returned? Why break his heart? Why lose the marriage before it really had a chance? Why make him hate her? She decided that she would pretend it had never happened.

Once together again, they both seemed different.

He was now grumpy, angry, finding little faults with his bride.

She had constant complaints, was never satisfied with him.

They argued now all the time. They knew each other's sore points and would push until tempers flared, words exchanged, doors slammed, tears shed. Self-esteem was damaged, apologies proliferated, confidence eroded.

By stockpiling these incidents, they each felt more justified in keeping their secret. Their partner seemed no longer the victim, did not deserve the truth.

But conscience degraded each of their lives. Work and love impaired.

Years passed. In time things settled down between them.

Yet they had sleep disturbance, weight gain and loss, illness, skin problems, headaches, stomach pain, along with other signs of chronic anxiety.

And good times too. These were also stockpiled but in another memory compartment.

They did, deep down, actually love each other. Hey both were great people. They shared their life.

It was in their second decade together that they decided to go into couple's therapy. They knew they could be happier. And it worked."

FUTURE TIME STATUES: THEN AND NEXT

Story over. My couples group wanted to know *how* it had worked. I said I would show them.

The technique was called, simply, *'Trust"*. Within a safe supportive place. Here and now.

I had first taken some time to build group cohesiveness. Everybody got to know and appreciate everybody else.

I used then a George Bach group technique. Kind of coercive. Still, maybe helpful.

Later I would go slower. Helping insights to come more in their own time and from their own person.

For this group though, in that time and place, I thought a little dynamite would help to break a log jam.

So here we go: *"I want each of you to remember something important you have never told your partner. Something they would want to know. When you have recalled this, raise your hand."*

Then I sat silently and waited. Silence. In a minute or more a hand went up. Then some others.

At last just one holdout. I said nothing. The clock ticked in the silence.

Finally one of the group said to the holdout *"Our raised hands are getting TIRED! Come On!"*

The holdout finally raised a hand halfway and everybody sighed, relaxed.

Here comes the last George Bach part: *"Now we can begin the work. Let's go around the circle, one couple at a time. Share the secret out loud."*

They did. Every one.

Forgiveness usually followed, the older the secret, the easier the understanding.

Resolution was most challenging for secret events still in progress- in those cases, individual therapy for that one couple might follow. But in this case, the secrets were all rooted in long past actions.

Bringing them into the air was healing, aided by the group's safe and supportive setting.

After the group was over, I used follow-ups, often over years.

Free of secrets, honesty can finally bring full trust. At any age. Fulfilling marriages could actually begin again then, and succeed.

For the couples in this group?

They did.

Three Weddings (1972-1974)

Theme: *"Ain't no sunshine when you're gone"* Bill Withers

Alternative:

"Ain't no sunshine when you're here neither."

The early 1970s in San Francisco.

The war in Vietnam was still on, extended by Richard Nixon. Those choosing to avoid being drafted to continue the invasion, found creative attempts to dodge this possibility. One of these was to purchase a divinity degree and these were plentifully available.

My own service obligation ended honorably in 1968 but somebody still bought me a doctor of divinity diploma from the *"Church of Universal Brotherhood"*, based in Los Angeles. It had cost $20 and was signed by a *"High Priestess"*.

So I never put this honor on a CV but still posted it in my office while I was Faculty Dean at the California School of Professional Psychology there in San Francisco.

Wedding Number One

Two of my doctoral students were due to graduate. They had planned to get married to each other at that point. Both stopped by in my office and sank together into my spacious most comfortable chair.

(Years later I was asked by a former colleague if I still had that great chair. She said she loved to come by my office and sink into it as long as she could justify. When I told her I had given it away, she demanded to know why. *"People stayed too long"* I explained.)

The young couple, having noted my divinity diploma, asked me if I could officiate at their marriage ceremony. I didn't think my signature on their marriage license would be legal. But, to my surprise, the future bride had looked into this and California recognized that divinity degree as sufficient for the task. Turned out to be true.

The future groom handed me the typed script for the ceremony. They had already written scripts for each of them and another briefer set for me. No thought needed on my part and I liked them both. So when my mouth opened to respond, a Yes came out.

Thorough as ever, the future bride handed me the invitation. It was to take place on Ocean Beach at Sunset the next Saturday. The very place where the famous *Burning Man* extravaganza had first begun.

And so it was.

The sunset was spectacular and the guests friendly.

We read our lines and they kissed. Cheers from guests and a few tourists stopping by.

I signed their marriage license and the event was legalized.

Whew! Seemed to be a contribution I could make.

The next day they gave me a Bonsai Tree in a small pot for my scripted service.

Wedding Number Two

I was given the opportunity as Dean to hire an assistant.

I met with the campus secretaries to see if I should be looking for any specific qualities in candidates. They were unanimous. Noting that they were all female, they really hoped I would hire a male assistant. Better gender balance for the times.

Okay. I was teaching a night class at San Francisco State University. About to graduate there with a psychology B.A. was one of my top students: an immigrant from China named Patrick. He soon was hired as my assistant back at the professional school.

Just prior to that hiring, the president of the system called me into his office for his own advice on hiring an assistant. His advice is still vivid in my memory today.

"Robert, you know I draw the line at any sex between faculty and students. These students are adults and at least as old as most of their teachers but no sex! Same as the need for no sex between therapist and patient- just not ethical! I see you nod agreement." (Now he lowered his voice and moved closer to continue, smiling.) *"I think you may have noticed my assistant and secretaries in the outer office. Kind of attractive aren't they all? THAT is where you go for sex. Fair game. With consent of course. Any questions? Fine. Now go hire your assistant."*

The next day I hired Patrick, very much pleasing the campus secretaries. And for the next four years, the president assumed I was gay. Which he had zero approval for. I let him steam. In the last year he learned finally that I was not gay. I was told that he wondered out loud why I had hired Patrick then.

Patrick didn't stay the full time I was a dean there. But when he left for a better opportunity he asked me for a favor. He wanted to complete his citizenship initiative but would be more likely to succeed if he had an American wife. Now he had found a Japanese American woman, a very good friend, who had agreed to marry him. But just as an act of friendship and not a romantic act. Would I officiate at the marriage and sign their license?

I said that first I needed to talk privately with both bride and groom. He agreed.

In this I was assisted by Ben Tong, then my doctoral student, teaching partner, and eventual lifelong family friend. Ben and I took turns interviewing the potential bride and groom.

Patrick was grateful to his bride for this immigration help. He knew she would like the marriage to last and said he would give it a try.

Dr. Tong and I both found the volunteer bride to be really in love with Patrick and she hoped the marriage might last. We did our best to help her realize that Patrick was not emotionally there yet. We encouraged her to postpone any wedding until they both were committed. But she saw this as her best chance to become the lifelong partner she wanted to be for Patrick. She pleaded with us to go ahead.

It has been said that weddings are a triumph of hope over experience. That was her choice, she knew the risk, and so we went ahead.

The wedding was private. It seemed to go well. Ben Tong recalled: *"I never knew what ultimately became of Patrick's union with his bride. I do vividly recall their imaginative wedding ceremony. Different from conventional practice, the bride had a best man ('the best male friend in my life after my husband,' she proclaimed) and the groom had a counterpart, his best lady. Cool stuff of the '60s/'70s."*

Pat became two new things within the year that followed. He became a citizen. He became an ex-husband.

Quite likely that his ex-wife then wound up marrying her best man after all.

I decided I had done my last marriage ceremony.

Wedding Number Three

My doctor of divinity diploma was no longer on the office wall.

Despite this, a request walked into my office one day.

She was a recent graduate of the psychology school. In fact I had been Arlene's dissertation chair. I respected her ability, liked her as a new colleague, and was biased to be of assistance.

But she wanted me to perform her marriage ceremony.

In the end of a long discussion, in which I had explained fully why this was a bad idea, the very persuasive Arlene had my consent to go ahead.

This was to be just a small ceremony in her apartment's living room. She had been living there with the potential groom for a few years now with no need for a marriage. But her parents and his as well were somewhat traditional. Arlene knew they would be far less anxious about their interracial relationship if a marriage occurred. No big deal, something just for the parents comfort.

We set a date for an afternoon a month later.

A week later she happily announced that both sets of parents would be there. Hers were coming from Mexico and his from Harlem. Anticipating a crowded living room.

I gave it not much more thought until she called me one week before the marriage date.

All four parents were there. Was I going to come in for the rehearsal?

Rehearsal? Turned out that Arlene's parents were devout Roman Catholics and the groom's parents were pastors in their Harlem church.

Alarm bells.

I asked Arlene to graciously decline a rehearsal as we wanted a small family-only living room ceremony in a week. Give the parents some time to catch up on the lives of their adult children. This worked.

Life intervened. The following week was overloaded with my own work and family events. The marriage day arrived unannounced and without my adequate preparation.

I did of course have adequate anxiety. (My daughter tells me that her acting career is enhanced by a little of this. So I hoped.)

I only had a few minutes before leaving for the apartment to choose officiating materials. I took my copy of Arlene's doctoral dissertation. It was about the grandmothers who had come to the USA a century before as very young women. Leading to the birth of a very vibrant Chicano community in San Francisco. The psychology of their success against almost overwhelming odds was well worth the read.

I still needed something more. I scanned my books for something like a bible. The expectations of the traditional Christian parents required that at least. I did have a bible but it was pretty ragged looking. Instead I chose a gold-bound bible-looking volume from the shelf. Turned out it was *"A Passion in the Desert"* by Honoré de Balzac in which a lost French soldier has a romantic affair with a leopard (or lioness in some versions). Ah well, I need not actually read from this book.

Armed with Arlene's hard copy dissertation, black with gold letters on the cover, and the gold-bound French bestiality bible substitute, I arrived at the apartment.

Both sets of parents had been drinking toasts for a while. They were very welcoming in a somewhat solemn way. Impressive people. Just them, the couple to be married and me.

I stood facing the couple to be married, each flanked by their parents.

I chose to begin with honesty.

I acknowledged that I was not a priest or minister but did have legal authority to sign a marriage license and to conduct this ceremony. I let them know how honored I was that Arlene had chosen me for this event, with the groom's consent, though my prior role had only been to Chair her excellent doctoral dissertation as she became a doctor and psychologist. I then held up that very impressive dissertation and opened it to Arlene's dedication, reading: *"La familia lo es todo para la Chicana."*

I continued: *"Or in English 'For the Chicana, Family is everything'. We are gathered here today because this young couple loves their parents. They want them to be happy with this longstanding union in a way that your parental tradition requires. So today what we do here is a celebration of love across two generations. Raising children is far from easy but it is the highest art. Art that finishes itself. As has been successful with these adult children finished and standing before you here."*

I handed the bound dissertation with its gold letters on the cover to Arlene's mother. Then opened the gold book to pronounce the young couple married. Arlene and her husband kissed.

Then all sat down. Silence. The two fathers and the groom's mother had another drink. Arlene's mother was crying.

Was this ceremony too brief or not religious enough? As is said in Singapore: trouble knocking on my door?

Arlene's mother got up and walked over to me.

She said: *"Thank you! That was very beautiful."*

I took a breath of relief. Signed the marriage license.

In a little while I left the happy family with my gold French bestiality bible tucked away in my coat pocket. Before anybody asked to see it.

That was my last time to perform a student wedding. A service discontinued.

End Theme: *"Summertime"* (Willie Nelson/Natalie King)

Or

Wintertime:

"Wintertime, when the weather is freezing The fish are jumping cuz the water is cold. Oooeee oooeee"

FUTURE TIME STATUES: THEN AND NEXT

Two Conventions

Theme: *Soul Sacrifice* Santana

The 1977 annual American Psychological Association (APA) convention was in San Francisco that year.

Out in front of the host Convention Center was a massive protest against psychologists. It was a group of angry advocates for the protection of animals. They and their signs alleged torture of harmless and vulnerable research creatures. By who? By what they thought the APA psychologists were doing.

I climbed to the top step in front of the Convention Center. Faced the crowd, APA convention registration badge on my shirt. That year I thought reason might work. I was only 36. I addressed the crowd in a friendly voice:

> *"Hey! Great cause. But wrong group! Almost all these psychologists don't even work with animals. The few that do follow an APA humane code for the protection of animals!"*

I had their attention but I saw no friendly faces. I went on:

> *"You've got us confused with the Physiologists. They'll slice up any animal to study its liver or other organs. You want the American Physiological Society or APS. NOT the APA."*

Crowd murmuring, conferring. I added:

> *"Look! We work with people! Almost all of us. Wrong group!"*

An older man just arriving, also standing by at the edge of the crowd, added:

> "*What group? Are you trying to blame us psychiatrists? Typical!*"

Confusion in the crowd. Muttering louder.

> I answered quickly: "*No. Psychologists are here to HELP people, not torture either them or animals. I'm not saying psychiatrists torture animals. Maybe people though.*"

Some laughter in the crowd. Elder psychiatrist bystander walks off.

"*Psychiatry now? Spell it!*" somebody yelled.

I answered: "*Like it sounds! Except the P is silent like in swimming.*"

Nobody got my sainted mother's favorite joke.

But then some loud chanting in the crowd began again.

Still protesting psychology. Waving signs.

Blocking access to most of the convention entrance. Scaring some members that were afraid to go around them.

I just wasn't getting through to them.

They were there to protest and protest was what they would do.

Time for a protest of my own.

I walked away long enough to buy a bucket of chicken at KFC.

Came back to sit at the top of the stairs, eating a drumstick. Gasps in the crowd.

Maybe undercutting my earlier argument. But satisfying.

Context can improve the taste of chicken.

-

A little later, a psychologist friend came by to thank me for the laughs. Invited me to join the group in her living room where the Mayor would be.

George Moscone had considered running for governor in 1974 but now had his eye on the White House. Sure. I wanted to meet him. I'm from Buffalo. So not easily impressed. Rude to power even. Not this time. Not deliberately anyway.

In that era, he had a good chance to become our next President. He was a consistent champion of progressive and other humane causes. George was an easy match for the former California Governor Ronald Reagan's conservative push for President, his likely rival. And Moscone had a powerful weapon. I had seen that already on television. It was even moreso when we met in that living room.

He had a presence that immediately soothed and engaged. Safe. He was your favorite uncle. With George you knew he would do the right thing. You relaxed. You trusted. You supported. His charisma was seemingly low key, but powerful.

I knew already that, absent catastrophe, he would be one of our best presidents. He would succeed. So would we all.

We had a real conversation in that living room.

Moscone said he had progressive friends that knew of my work against the use of electroshock (ECT). He was opposed to damaging people

with such medieval methods. George had read my work on it. Then he became quiet for a moment. Finally said in a near whisper that he wished he had known of that risk earlier. His mother, who he loved deeply, had been depressed. Her psychiatrist wanted to give her ECT. George had approved it. Her consequent memory loss, severe, instant, had been attributed to her age by her psychiatrist. Or maybe disease. But now George knew the true culprit was the ECT he had consented to on her behalf

Moscone could project emotion. This time it was grief. Best I could do was to remind him of this. The most we could ever do was to act on what we fully know at the time of a decision. Yes, he had read existential perspective. George conceded that existentially he had done his best. His regret at the mistake still gave him great grief. We agreed to meet again. I promised him my time and support as he progressed.

A double catastrophe the following year. Along with Harvey Milk, he was assassinated.

-

The 1991 annual American Psychological Association (APA) convention was back in San Francisco that year.

Again I sat at the top of the steps by the entrance to the convention center.

It wasn't called that any more.

Now it was the *George Moscone Convention Center.*

What a different country we might have had if he had been allowed to live his path.

I walked through the convention entrance door.

Under his name.

Andy Curry's Easter Story (1974)

Themes: *Low Rider* War; *Perfect Angel* Minnie Ripperton,

It was the day after Easter Sunday. San Francisco.

Andy brought me to his friend Felicia's house for an afternoon break from work.

A time so laid back and wonderful that it still glows in my memory.

Felicia could have been Andy's female twin. Both highly creative, kind, brilliant, welcoming, fun. And proudly African American.

She looked like Minnie Ripperton and that was the first music she played for us as we sprawled on her living room carpet. It was Ripperton's breakthrough album.

What a range of voice!

Plus the snacks helped.

Our appreciation hunger was likely enhanced by inhaling the "*incense*" in the room which added to the next breakthrough album we heard together:

Felicia had a phone call just after that. At her end, she just said "*Oh you have the wrong number! The wrong Felicia. I'm Felicia Newme! Okay. No problem. Bye.*"

Soon Felicia explained that her debts had become overwhelming. Threats and calls from collection thugs seemed nonstop. Andy Curry had reminded her that she was a creative star, told her that she should sleep on the problem and wake up with the answer. This she had done and it worked!

She legally changed her last name to *"Newme"* and, naturally, began as her new debt-free self. In that magic San Francisco temporal geography, it had worked. For a couple of months already since her name change, Felicia Newme had been happy enjoying her fresh persona, now celebrating this with us.

Sometime later, after both albums were done, Felicia noticed what seemed like a small deep bite mark on Andy's arm. Demanded explanation. Hoping it was from passion, she said. An Andy Curry story to be told.

Andy was a global expert on the social process of groups, an expertise he lived. With just his social work credential, he was a top faculty member in psychology's first free-standing professional school. And the most loved. There he added theatricality. Began the *Tantric Feets Dance Ensemble* for the students. Founded the campus newspaper as the *Freedom from Disabling Pathology Gazette*. He had studied with Gestalt psychiatrist Fritz Perls and many other psychology greats, teaching that psychology history from personal experience. So Felicia knew that any story from Curry would be an event.

He rose to the occasion. Might as well have been standing on a stage in an auditorium or so it seemed as the living room faded. Felicia had dimmed the lights so Andy stood under the only bright one.

He explained, most theatrically, that he had been walking in Golden Gate Park the day before and had come upon a young white family celebrating Easter there with a picnic. The parents signaled for him to come sit with them on their blanket silently as their little boy was covering his eyes, waiting for an Easter surprise. An overflowing Easter basket had just been set in front of the child. Andy sat quietly behind the basket, glad to incorporate this sweet event into his walk.

The boy was told he could take his hands away now and see his Easter present. Which he did.

Full of joy he ran past the basket and bit Andy hard on the arm.

Andy mimed the event effectively until Felicia finally exclaimed *"But WHY?"*

Andy had been waiting for that.

Solemnly he intoned, voicing the mother's apology with undoubted accuracy:

"Oh! We're so sorry for that. See he's still crying. He just whispered to me that he thought that big chocolate rabbit was for HIM."

Then and now celebrities are at times memorialized in chocolate so that they can be symbolically bitten, consumed, without direcct pain.

Like Benedict Cumberbunny

As in church when the Eucharist wafer is consumed with wine to represent dining on the body and blood of Jesus.

Better when just symbolic said Andy.

Fun

Themes: *The Spaghetti Westerns Music* Ennio Morricone And *Juliet of the Spirits* Nino Rota

> *"Dining at The Old Spaghetti Factory is an experience. For decades we have invested meticulous attention to our unique décor and classical designs. Every location is adorned with antique lighting, intricate stained glass displays, large colorful booths, and an old-fashioned trolley car for guests to dine in. It's the perfect atmosphere for a family celebration."*

In San Diego, it was just the three of us. My two young daughters and me. We got there in the summer of 1978.

1970S

Back from Australia I was replenishing our funds by working three jobs. Doing outpatient psychotherapy 50 hours a week, 10 hours a day, four days during the week plus Saturday. Doing a weekly night supervision seminar for the California School of Professional Psychology's San Diego campus. And then, a full time senior faculty member at San Diego State University went into rehab the first day of his classes, so I took on his full time load of three classes in his place (luckily his seniority meant all three of these classes were on the same day, Thursday, so that filled my fifth weekday).

What about the children? School was not yet open. The older daughter one was a very mature ten, the younger at eight matched this, so they both would be safe in the right setting.

Luckily San Diego had one of the best zoos in the world.

And it was surrounded by museums, Balboa Park.

I got them summer passes to all these treats. They would spend my work days exploring. Then we would all be together at the end of the day, before dark, for a meal and recounting of the day's adventures.

Sunday was special though. We would sleep in, then dress up, and convene at a great restaurant together. At first, when funds were low, it was the *Chicken Pie Shoppe*.

Then, we discovered the *Old Spaghetti Factory*. Its theme was "**Fun**".

In that specific place, by the door, was a huge stand on digital scale so we could weigh ourselves before and after the meal.

We ate together in a unique and colorful booth.

On a shelf at head level was a dramatic statue of an elephant rearing up on its hind legs.

Once the meal was done, I put a few surviving spaghetti noodles on the elephant's back to simulate a saddle.

Behind its rear, I placed a small section of napkin with a little meatball on it.

This tableau was greeted with laughter from the children.

Then I left an excessive tip on the table, paid the bill at the register, we weighed ourselves, and we exited.

The ten year old, once outside, tried out her favorite word of the season.

Her sister was still laughing about my elephant's add-ons.

So, of course, the older one said to me *"Why?"*

Why the food on and behind the elephant?

I explained *"To let them know that we had fun."*

FUTURE TIME STATUES: THEN AND NEXT

The Flower

Theme: *The Dance and the Dream (Isadora)* Cinnamon Camo

My daughter Cinnamon and I were close, spending much time together, especially in those years from her birth through to her adolescence. This can be seen in surviving photos of us early on and also with her brother Charlie.

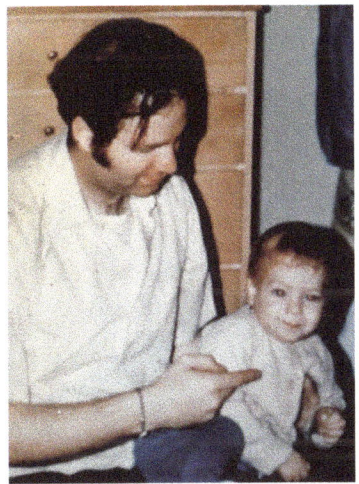 

When she was five I took her to Hawaii where we saw a live Tina Turner performance. There she found a family dragon ring (she reminded me that I was born in the Year of the Dragon) that's been worn ever since.

A photo was taken of her then, and PermaPlaqued to a large size for the living room. It was lost since in a fire but here is a photo of her at seven, taken when we lived in Reno.

When she reached her teen years, she often studied the large portrait of her happy five year old self framed there in the living room.

One day she said to me that she was jealous of that little girl in the picture. She didn't like that she had grown out of being that beautiful child.

I took down the picture and brought it to a mirror where she could see herself next to it.

I explained: *"That was the seed. You are the flower."*

Seemed to help:

A genius-level creative artist, she went on to graduate at a university in Santa Cruz, sang professionally, including with Janis Joplin's former band *Big Brother and the Holding Company* (which became *Sam Andrews and the All Stars*):

She became an advocate for American Indians, caring for Rolling Thunder in his latter days at the home of Apache Bob (no longer touring with *The Grateful Dead*). Cinnamon helped run a child care program at the university. Survived the earthquake that leveled Santa Cruz. Married a musician and settled into the mountain town of Boulder Creek. Recorded in a band with her husband. A much loved daughter, an appreciated neighbor. A unique glowing flower.

She had a wonderfully creative daughter, one with special requirements, Ava.

Cinnamon, joined by Ava's grandmother Bonnie, devoted herself to this child thereafter. She knew now that in childhood it was Ava's turn to be the seed.

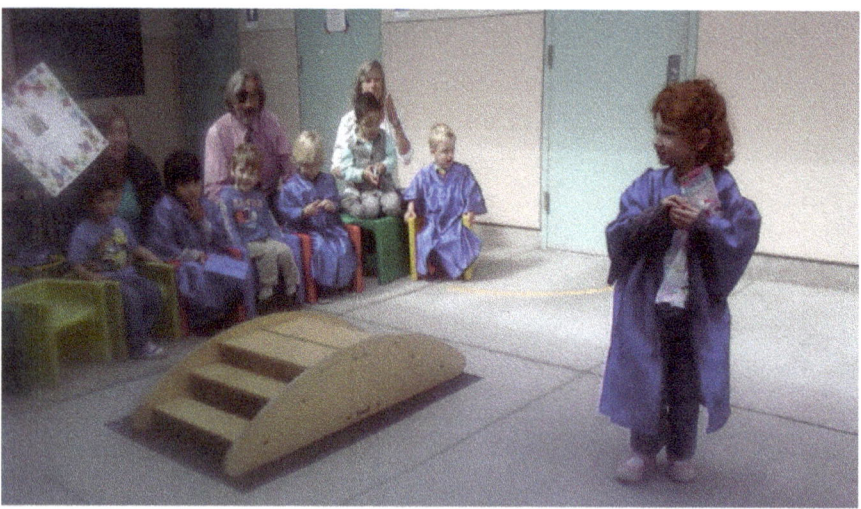

Her flower will be **spectacular**:

And again: In memory of Ben Camo, Ava's father:

Theme: *Gone Now* from Porgy and Bess/Audra McDonald.

1980s-1990s

Themes: *Work Song* Oscar Brown Jr; *After Six* Lee Hazelwood;

Except For Your One Day

Themes: *Cattle Call* LeAnn Rhimes); *Graveyard Train* Credence Clearwater Revival (J. Fogarty); *I Walk the Line* Johnny Cash

My university job, at the close of the 20th century, was in Guam, an American territory in the middle of the western Pacific Ocean. Years before that, in the 1960s, I was a psychologist at the Hawaii State Hospital. There, I was also a Field Assessment Officer for a Peace Corps project in Micronesia by Guam, based in Molokai.

On Molokai, three months of training were needed before the two years of service planned for graduating trainees to become Peace Corps Volunteers (PCVs) on remote Pacific Islands. Some of these island nations were so isolated and unique that anybody stepping on the shadow of the King or Queen would be executed.

Lots to learn for the trainees before going there. In one, the live royal bride had been buried with her deceased husband. Something my own wife and I agreed was not for us, even if a dead wife exacted the same tribute from her live husband.

In another remote island culture, the home of the king was considered to be an extension of his body. You could enter his home through the front with his permission and then be swallowed into his generous care. But entering through the rear entrance was considered a form of anal rape, dealt with by instant execution.

Even in large modern and sophisticated island cultures like the Maori of New Zealand, there were family stories of ancient cannibalism. Those stuck out tongues in battle were saying how delicious their enemies would soon be. A woman I knew there still had her grandmother's recipe for pickled thumbs.

Well, one day I had the opportunity to visit a very remote island completely new to me. I was to consult with a psychiatrist there and explore the rest of the time.

The psychiatrist had taken his training further than most in his occupation and knew how to assist his patients with solutions to their issues. He was himself of the island culture and had integrated it into his practice.

Turned out he was looking more to teach than to learn, which was fine with me. Though I sensed he wanted support for his approaches.

Like many other Pacific cultures, the earth had only two locations: "Here" and "Off-Island". I was an ambassador from "Off-Island", aka the rest of the earth. A grand responsibility.

He first had me sit in on an intake with a young married couple. It was a mixed marriage with the wife native to the island and the husband a white American, formerly of the U.S. Navy. They had been married for a few years already and the husband reported that they both were highly satisfied with each other the whole time. The wife only nodded in agreement but otherwise said nothing. In fact, she was not talking to him at all.

He had been found out having sex with another woman. His wife hadn't spoken to him or anybody else since. Her problem was what to do about it. His problem was how to regain the happiness they had before his brief adventure.

In this culture, marriage might include more than one wife but never sex with anybody but a wife.

Before marriage, sex was very positive and freely granted to consenting partners. After: nobody else but the wife or husband.

A little like the island culture of Yap where women were often topless but as adults never supposed to expose genitalia.

On this more isolated island, it had been necessary for this American husband to learn where the lines of never were. And he thought he had. Yet, here he was.

The psychiatrist completed our intake by agreeing to take the case. He assigned the wife to meet with him for a private session and the husband to meet with me for his private session. We would all return for a closure session after that. I was apparently to learn by doing.

My mystery to solve was why the husband had risked hurting his wife in such a rare no-complaint-from-either-partner marriage. It didn't take long.

He said he was from Louisiana. He had a culture of his own. Men were understood by women to stray though the wives were not expected to take the same path. He knew how he was supposed to act. He said his wife made him happy in every way. He had hoped to keep his affair secret, near impossible on an island.

So: Why?

He invoked an ancient question. *"Why would I go out for a hamburger when I could have steak at home?"* His answer? *"Variety. Try something new."*

And? How did it work out? *"Not worth it. Wound up hurting her. And no peace for me ever since."*

He went on more about what he had lost. He eventually understood what a deep sacred commitment marriage was on this island. The issue was not really as much about sex, but more about trust. And about caring for her feelings. Finally he resolved to explain himself to her when we met again. To ask for a fresh start. Good progress for an hour.

We all met again. She was still silent but seemed calmer somehow.

The psychiatrist smiled at me. Then asked if either partner had something to say. I looked to the husband and nodded. The husband cleared his throat and began saying how wonderful she was and how he missed what they had. He asked for a second chance.

Silence.

Then he tried to explain his affair with the variety quote: Hamburger over Steak.

Now the silence was tense.

Like an old Frankenstein movie, the air in the room rippled with menace.

After a few seconds, the psychiatrist spoke.

"Speaking of hamburgers and steak, Wagyu beef from Japan is the best you can get. Great marbling. The lucky cows are grass fed and they get beer to help their appetite. They each get a massage every day, along with sake to drink and soothing music. Same when raised in America except they also get to roam free during the day. Though corners may be cut. So in Japan or in America, each and every day of their life is perfect."

FUTURE TIME STATUES: THEN AND NEXT

The rest of us looked puzzled at this but nobody interrupted. He resumed.

"Perfect except for that one day. Their last day. The day they die, get butchered, and progress to tasty beef."

He now looked hard at the husband. *"Your wife has decided to grant you that second chance. Until now you were her hero. You are not from here and may not have understood our ways. She will feed you well and again make you happy each day of your life together. BUT. Now it is time for you to know a very important thing. If you chose to make the same mistake again, THAT will be your last day."*

The husband was silent as this sunk in.

Now his wife was smiling.

Sympathetic Enchantment

Themes: *Magic Music* Peter Gundry; *Magic* Olivia Newton-John

"James George Frazer coined the term "sympathetic magic" in The Golden Bough (1889); Richard Andree, however, anticipated Frazer, writing of sympathy-enchantment (German: Sympathie-Zauber) in his 1878 Ethnographische Parallelen und Vergleiche. Frazer subcategorised sympathetic magic into two varieties: that relying on similarity, and that relying on contact or "contagion":

> *"If we analyze the principles of thought on which magic is based, they will probably be found to resolve themselves into two: first, that like produces like, or that an effect resembles its cause; and, second, that things which have once been in contact with each other continue to act on each other at a distance after the physical contact has been severed. The former principle may be called the Law of Similarity, the latter the Law of Contact or Contagion. From the first of these principles, namely the Law of Similarity, the magician infers that he can produce any effect he desires merely by imitating it."* -Wikipedia

1990, Billings Montana. My first year at what is now part of the Montana State University system. I called us new faculty 'the freshman class' and it caught on.

In my new apartment, I taped a favorite page from a very old daily calendar to inside my refrigerator. It explained that opening the refrigerator door for five minutes was better for the machine's cooling than opening and closing the door five times in five minutes. The daily date on that past outdated page was April 17th, announced in large print.

I met a new librarian in my freshman class cohort. We hit it off. A little later she visited my apartment for the first time. Walked into the kitchen. Opened refrigerator door. Said: *"Why do you have MY BIRTHDAY inside your refrigerator?"*

At this writing we have now been together for 33 years.

The Porcelain Protector

Themes: *Constipation Blues* Screamin Jay Hawkins; *Rolling in the Deep* Adele

"I call this 'fighting without fighting'." Bruce Lee in *Enter the Dragon.*

In psychotherapy as well as in the rest of life, change does begin with yourself. If it ends there, it is often incomplete. Trauma does not always disappear with understanding. Action resolving these feelings can be very helpful. A safe kind of fighting back. Such real life

interventions, when facilitated by a therapist, were called "Radical Therapy" in the 1970s.

Or "Nonviolent Direct Action" in Civil Rights progress. Martin Luther King knew this well. He was all about action, nonviolent action, in a just cause to right a wrong. In his day laws were passed to suppress voting, remove freedoms, oppress women, and racial minorities, ban books. Wait. In his day? Well. Anyway, Dr. King advocated an alternate choice to obeying an unjust law. Break it openly, in plain sight, preferably with 'newspaper reporters' (ask your grandfather) watching. Be willing to go to jail or at least be arrested in order to gain attention from the public conscience (your grandmother will elaborate) and ultimately fix the problem. Also, even just trying, this direct action was good for you. Good for your wellbeing and mental health. Dr. King often told us it was good for the soul.

Today I see this as an important real world option to end PTSD in a satisfying manner- let's call this phase "Resolution". The therapist is more than a catalyst here. Finding resolution requires that the action be just, legal, ethical, and consistent with the action taker's morals, Oh, and if possible, fun too. Aside from psychotherapy, this push back option fits real civilian life even better.

It was in the beginning years of the last decade in the 20th century. We were engaged to get married, both of us working at a Montana university. Before we departed, a few of our friends gathered to wish us luck. One, Ron, a told us this story from his former life in the Secret Service:

This American military officer was in charge of his captured men in a World War Two German concentration camp. His rank granted him decent health care plus access to the German commandant. His diabetes had grown worse there and his left leg was amputated. The officer asked the commandant to send the lost leg to his family back in America for proper burial. That was approved and done. As was the remaining leg when it too had to be amputated. In time, the disease was reported as growing worse. Now the left arm was scheduled for amputation. Again the commandant was asked to send the lost arm to the officer's family back in the United States. This time the German commandant stormed into the officer's quarters with the written request in his hand. He yelled: 'I KNOW WHAT YOU ARE DOING! YOU ARE TRING TO ESCAPE!' "

We took this to mean support for our exit. Maybe.

Our first stop, on the way to California, was at an Idaho university.

My fiancé began a reference librarian job there while I waited for my Idaho psychology license to be approved. It was most challenging for her.

Her immediate supervisor was a single parent with marital hopes. He routinely called her in on Saturdays or Sundays though not her regular shift. His supervisor was attracted to my fiancé as a lesbian opportunity, planning an auto tour for the two of them at the first opportunity. The worst was the overall supervisor, the library's Dean. I was told by staff right away that he liked the women working under him to fulfill that very position sexually as it suited him.

While my fiancé heroically fended off the triple threats as diplomatically as possible, all three supervisors saw me as the obstacle. Especially the Dean.

Knowing that my credential to practice psychology might take weeks to arrive, I spent much time in the library. Lunches with my fiancé, reading, interacting with staff.

The Dean put out a written order on his stationery to staff that I was not allowed to read or be near the psychology section of the library. No explanation but the message was clear. Public library or not, I was unwelcome.

I complied but was not discouraged.

I kept visiting every day in other sections.

The Dean countered that by alerting staff and campus law enforcement that I was a theft risk. Again by written decree on his stationery.

I was therefore watched carefully, especially at the exits, cameras included, to make sure I was leaving with no equipment.

A friendly staffer, the Dean's secretary said, if I really was a thief, to take the Dean's newest and very expensive printer, housed in the hall just outside his office. She was angry at the Dean for his unwelcome advances. Had put a Christmas photo of him with his wife and children on her desk, ready for pointing as needed.

I thanked her for the advice but I really wasn't a thief.

Still.

One afternoon, outside camera range, I picked up the printer outside his office and put it inside the empty bottom drawer of his jumbo file cabinet next to it.

Then walked empty handed out the front of the library in view of the security cameras.

The apparent disappearance of the Dean's deluxe printer became a cause.

On entry to the library thereafter, a librarian was assigned to follow me at all times.

When I entered at the front, I took the stairs to the second floor. He followed.

Then I was on to the elevator to the basement.

After he got there, I went back on the elevator to the top floor.

I waited for him there.

He said he was supposed to report to the Dean everything I did, particularly if I tried to go near the off-limits psychology section, and, yes, if I stole anything.

He asked me to slow down as he was winded chasing me.

I suggested he take off for an hour and rest. Said I would stay on the main floor in plain sight for exactly one hour. He thanked me, agreed.

On the main floor, I stopped to talk to the Dean's secretary. The one ready to point to the photo of the Dean's wife and children to her boss as needed.

She had packed up her things in a box. Leaving at the end of the day to get married in another state.

Still two hours to go. But she could leave early once she finished this last onerous task.

She showed me a blank page of the Dean's stationery with his signature at the bottom. Her regular job was to write a library piece for him each week and then drop it in the campus mail box to be picked up and published in the university newsletter.

She had been told to do this, even on her last day.

But she had ghost writer's block.

I volunteered to do a draft for her. This I did.

She loved it, filled the blank part of the page just over the Dean's signature with it.

Sealed it in a library envelope addressed to the newsletter.

Dropped it in the campus mail.

She left work early that day, never to return.

My hour ended soon after. Time to give my Dean-anointed shadow another workout.

The letter was dutifully published.

The campus populace read it. Went something like this:

Capable versus Culpable

Our hardworking library maintenance crew devotes each night to cleaning our bathrooms. In this they are first rate, making the porcelain sinks and toilets spotless, shining, pure. A work of art. Such capable porcelain artists. But in the morning, all their work is reversed. Users of the facilities soil the porcelain beyond belief, all day long. Toilets and sinks must be scrubbed all over again. And it is not a pleasant challenge for our so capable late night cleaners. Consequently it is my responsibility as Dean of the Library to rein in our culpable visitors. Yes, admire our books, engage our staff, appreciate our building. But, from now on,

DO NOT USE OUR BATHROOMS.

No more soiling the porcelain. All rest rooms will be locked during the day with the exception of authorized tours to admire the sanitation artistry of our evening staff. Your cooperation is mandated.

Signed by the Dean of the library plus name and title

Well. It made him campus famous. It made his secretary happy for once, at last.

For me, the memory still glows.

Some years later.

My wife and I both worked in the Bay Area of California during the week and then spent the week ends in our new house a drive of many hours away, in Chico at the edge of mountain country.

So we rented a small first floor apartment in a complex just walking distance from my job. It was in a quiet section, apart from the other apartments.

We faced three young beautiful trees and had wonderful next door neighbors. They had come from a small Asian country. Maintained the Pacific Rim cultural custom of leaving their shoes just outside their front door so as to not track in anything that might damage the internal carpet.

Thanks to the trees in front of us, nobody could see the shoes but us.

We appreciated their custom, appreciated their friendliness, admired their drive to succeed in this new country.

But the manager was not happy. Left a note on their front door to no longer leave shoes in front of that door. Said they would be evicted for creating this eyesore if they did not immediately comply.

I went to her front office and asked her to relent. Said the only people that could see the shoes were us. The three trees in front of our apartments masked the view from any other tenants. She said she would consider my outside shoes request.

The next day she had all the young trees cut down.

Our neighbors moved their shoes to a mat just inside their front door and were not evicted.

The manager then put out a regular note on her stationary, distributed to shelves above the mailboxes of all tenants. She let us all know of her victory against shoe clutter.

I visited her again, angry as I almost never am.

She surprised me.

She took my hands in hers and turned on the charm. She was probably in her 30s and, despite her obnoxious decisions, physically attractive. Married, she still was clearly seeking more. And said so.

I freed my hands and reminded her: *"We're both married, right?"*

Her response: *"But NOT to each other! That's the best part!"*

When I declined, she shifted gears. Said she was honored to have me as a tenant, loved my books. She said she would still show me *real* appreciation if I helped her with a project.

She wanted me to write the next tenant community note for her. The theme was to economize. The owners were pressuring her to cut expenses and increase revenue- more for less. Saw me as a solution to her problem. So she gave me a blank community note form with her office logo and her name at the top.

Leaning close, she reminded me that she would be *very* grateful in a personal way I would not forget. Once my note persuaded the tenants to cut costs.

I took the form. Left.

It reminded me of that Idaho porcelain protector event.

I filled out her form, and distributed her stationary statement to the shelves above all the tenant mailboxes as follows:

As you know, from time to time, we must economize. To save on our water bill, we are banning the taking of any showers in all apartments. All shower heads will be sealed. In respect for your own hygiene, we are going to schedule time as needed in the swimming pool on a first come first served basis. You can sign up for a ten minute cleansing swim at the front office.

Well. We were moving out by then anyway,

The Raft

Themes: *Malagueña* Lucas Imbiriba (acoustic guitar); *Anchors Away* Mormon Tabernacle Choir

The Bellagio Hotel, Las Vegas, Nevada, 1998. My wife sat with me in the front row, waiting for the Cirque du Soleil show to begin. It was a new show titled "*O*", which when said out loud sounded like "*Eau*", the French word for water. Made sense since the stage in front of us was primarily a small lake of water. A water circus.

She had dressed up. Her, always both elegant and beautiful. Me, at 57, wearing the three piece suit, masquerading as "dignified". That and a substantial tip to the man seating us got our front row view. Close enough to get wet if need be.

On with the show. Lights low. Spotlights. The water ballets and numbers were magnificent, colorful, energetic, amazing.

Then the stage lake cleared and a small raft came into view. It was propelled by two standing Hobos in tattered clothes and porkpie hats. One tall and one short. They pushed their raft forward, all the way to the edge closest to us. Crowd quiet, interested, waiting.

The taller Hobo then stepped off to the edge of the dry stage. Held his hand out to me. Motioned to me to join him on the raft. Spotlight surrounded us.

Why me? The suit? But yes, I would go.

Becky squeezed my hand, meaning she would support me if I went on stage or support me if I chose to fight our way out of the auditorium. Held her hand for a second. Thanks much, love.

And got up to join the Hobos on their raft.

In that second I had a memory flash. My lifelong friend, psychologist and hypnotist Leonard Elkind, told me of a time when he had been pulled onto a dance floor with a beautiful skilled Flamenco dancer. One he didn't know at all. As the spotlight hit just them, Len took on a new Spanish personality. Imagined himself a practiced Flamenco dancer. Which somehow worked. Applause when they finished.

I had seen this technique of a substitute persona for learning a new language. But not for an unrehearsed stage performance. Still, in that moment of getting up from my seat and stepping on stage, I knew I was an actor, part of that act. As some deity intended.

I stepped on the raft, surrounded by water. Comfortable in my persona as a stiff middle aged man in a three piece suit. Slow acoustic guitar music. I was dancing, in a dignified confident way with the shorter Hobo.

Round and round, in tune with the music.

When the music stopped, we did too. I bowed to both of my new raft friends. They returned it.

I stepped off the raft and back to my seat in the front row. Spotlight still on me, I turned to the audience, bowed to them, and then sat.

Loud applause.

The Hobos pushed off and out of the spotlight to disappear from the stage lake.

Lights dimmed for the next act.

Becky turned to me and leaned toward my nearest ear.

Saying *"That was brave! But who ARE you?"*

I just said *"Me? Oh. He's gone now."*

2000s
A new century, a new millennium

LOVE IS BLIND

Theme: *Via con Dios* Les Paul & Mary Ford

She stepped in front of me and said *"Por Favor!"* and then, reconsidering, *"Please!"* I had been cutting across a back parking lot to get to the Frontier, a venerable Albuquerque restaurant. I was new to the city. She was almost as tall as me, short black cropped hair, and a face impossible to look away from. It was covered in tattooed Spanish words, drawings. I thought that at one time it would have been a very beautiful face, strong, elegant. What had happened to her? She told me. Fell in love with a boy who was in a cartel. Her face tattoos a way of ownership, owning her. By the time she realized the huge mistake she had made, leaving him risked her life. Today she had run away. If she could get to Mexico by morning, her parents would protect her. Needed a safe place to be until dark. *Quanto?* (How much?) The safe place would hide her but they required $10. She was broke. Fiction? No- I could tell that this was real. The tears helped. She was clearly desperate. I materialized a twenty dollar bill and handed it to her. Suggested she get something to eat. As I walked away, I realized that my white tee shirt and dark clothes made her think I was a priest. Maybe that was why she thought I was safe to stop. She had thanked me for the money with a surprised *"Mucho Gracias Padre"*. So, almost gone, I turned to her still standing there, and I said *"Via con Dios"*.

Definition (2004)

Theme: *Baby Elephant Walk* Henry Mancini; *Stairway to Heaven* Led Zeppelin

In the black and white movies of the first half of the 20th century, a key word beginning many sentences was "Evidently" or based on evidence. You could identify the era just by the use of this word. A new generation's substitution for the rest of the century, reflected in movies, was "Apparently" or based on what we see. The 21st century's generations kept apparently for a while but then TV and online sentences just began with the word "So" based on a pause to think. In time, twitting, texting, and their progeny went for the leanest quick communications, based on speed without need or time to think. "Critical thinking" could still be found though increasingly that first word eclipsed the second. So, the following, evidently and apparently, came to mind.

FUTURE TIME STATUES: THEN AND NEXT

It was a quiet afternoon in Palo Alto. The 21st century was new. More than a dozen faculty of the past Institute of Transpersonal Psychology were gathered around a conference table. To perform the episodic ritual of sharing the multifaceted personal definitions of the discipline they taught.

This time Arthur Hastings began. He had developed a complete set of components that formed the skeleton of our academic program. Impressive and we all were familiar with this perspective. Next was Bob Frager, the past founding president of ITP and still a key faculty presence. Bob had made Arthur's physical component come alive with the essential training addition of Aikido and other martial arts. But his definition was much wider. Bob saw Transpersonal Psychology as the *whole* of psychology, a more comprehensive view of the discipline that included the components our students studied along with all else psychologists were supposed to know. Next came Charles Tart.

Charlie focused the definition on a single word: *"spirituality"*. Perspective diversity for sure but each faculty member with their own definitional validity.

My turn next. I had published a chapter on Transpersonal Psychology in my 1980s books on life extension and the measurement of human aging. I chose *"Human Potentials"* as a definition then. Something my 21st century students preferred as it encapsulated their motivation for being at ITP. Before I shared my own differential perspective, I told a story.

"You all likely know the story of the blind monks defining an elephant by each touching a different part of his anatomy. The led to a very diverse set of definitions depending on which part of the elephant

they had digitally explored, each one correct in its own way for that pachyderm portion.

Or so it would have been had not the elephant been in a very bad mood that day.

The funerals for the blind monks were exquisite and touching (so to speak)."

I conceded that I had added my own ending to the story, logical as it seemed to me (remembering an elephant in Thailand that had tensed muscles in suppressed rage as I touched it, over not getting any peanuts I think, and weeks later killing some tourists in a rampage).

Each definition had been right, mine too, and our elephant was fine with all of our descriptions. It does require a lot of them. And peanuts.

Naming the Puppy

Theme: *The Good, the Bad and the Ugly* Danish National Symphony Orchestra

Greenville, CA. She had come to me for psychological support but her immediate need was safety. For her and her eight year old son. Running from a dangerous and abusive husband. Once settled in a rented cabin, it seemed the next step for both was a puppy. Not just any puppy, but the smartest and most protective breed we knew of.

She was really big for a puppy. The woman at the pound insisted that the Malamute was only a few months old. These were the biggest of the Husky family and this beautiful female one seemed the friendliest. Her almost human expression radiated hope as she looked at us.

From Death Row. Decided to save her from that fate. Took her to a new home.

She was very well behaved. Took her first meal there quietly, sighed, settled into her cozy corner of the fenced in backyard. No leash needed. Went to sleep. She was where she belonged.

In the morning the boy found her still quietly resting in her corner. In the other corner lay a dead and bloodied raccoon.

His mother walked over to our new canine resident. Pointed to the body in the other corner. Asked *"Did YOU do this?"*

She followed the mother's pointing with her face, then looked carefully at me to see how I thought mom was taking this transition. Got up and trotted over to the carcass. Sniffed as if she had just discovered the body. Looked at me again. Not sure dogs can do this, but she sure looked like she shrugged and went back to her cozy corner. Lay down and watched the two humans, her new family.

Guilty? Circumstantial evidence was clear. Possible guilt? Probable. Though no blood was seen on her coat. Cleaned herself?

The puppy had done her best to seem innocent, plausible deniability. Hmm. What is the word between *"Possible"* and *"Plausible"*? So they named her *"Pawsible"*. *"Paws"* for short. Followed by a reassuring pat, a leftover piece of steak in a bowl, and a *"Thank you, Paws"*.

With that, their reassured puppy walked back over to the body and stood now with her victorious paws on her kill. *"Paws"* for sure.

Raccoons are cute. But they kill smaller animals, including pets. Cats falling victim to the raccoon mob are found the next day with bodies turned inside out.

Raccoons can carry Rabies or other diseases. They are very smart, have something like hands. So catching any specific raccoon serial killer is beyond our skill.

Because they all wear masks.

Bottomless Compliance
(19th to 21st century)

Theme: *You Can Leave Your Hat On* Randy Newman/Etta James/Joe Cocker

James McNeill Whistler 1854

Colonel Robert E. Lee, Superintendent of West Point at the time, took a liking to the young Whistler. Called him *"Curly"* since Cadet Whistler's long hair was always flying out of his hat at drills.

Whistler's drill sergeant was not so pleased.

The story passed down into history's oral tradition was that the sergeant, preparing for a marching review with a large audience one day noticed Whistler was wearing his uniform akimbo, shoes not shined, buttons not properly aligned.

With only a few minutes to go, he ordered the cadet to run double time to his quarters and set everything to perfect before he came back. *"No excuses! It's that or nothing!"* bellowed the sergeant.

Whistler ran to his quarters and got back in time for the march. Wearing nothing.

Eventually Whistler's demerits forced the Colonel to boot him from West Point.

Reluctantly. Maybe.

Katherine Hepburn 1939

In the 1930s, women's fashion had not yet been liberated by the practicalities of World War II, when women took positions in businesses and industries while men were at war.

Women could be, and were, arrested if they wore pants in public detained for "masquerading as men." It was the decade that saw the publication of Freud's theories of femininity, female masculinity, and female perversion, whereby the desire to don pants for Freud was reduced to penis envy and lesbianism. Clothing, rather, was still perceived as a manifestation of one's gender, and trousers were feared to reflect a perverse pathology within women.

Sound familiar? How about the contemporary right wing dread of Drag shows?

Hepburn's on-screen persona connected with a spirit of modernism and independence. But, women's fashion had yet to follow.

While working for RKO, Hepburn wore jeans to the studio. The studio head ordered her to get rid of the pants. Trousers were banned for women at RKO.

In an effort to comply with this order, she removed her pants and refused to put them back on until the rule was withdrawn.

As it was.

At least for her.

Cartoon animal realizing no pants (Ongoing)

Both Donald Duck and Pooh Bear drew fire from various right wing populations at home and in some other countries.

Accused of being a bad influence on children.

Again, the friendly animals and their cartoonists continued their breezy couture.

Though from time to time, fringe humans put pants on their live pets.

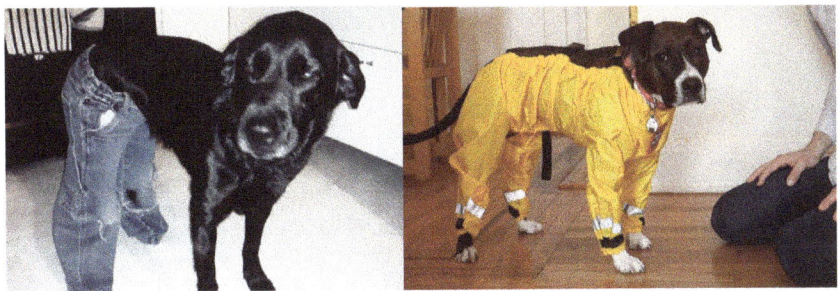

Or other human clothing.

Somehow there did not seem to be as much of an uproar about Porky Pig.

2000S

On the other hand, Petunia Pig did have to wear a skirt. She and Porky made an impressive couple.

His happy bottomless presence continues to this day.

Not to overlook the glamorous R-rated Jessica Rabbit cartoon:

Bottomless Mooners 2014

LAGUNA NIGUEL – Though smaller in numbers and more subdued – likely due to constant police presence – the revelers who turned out to bare their bottoms at passing trains Saturday still seemed to

take delight in partaking in the annual ritual. The mooning of the Amtrak, an event in which celebrants line up with their backs to the railroad tracks parallel to Camino Capistrano and then expose their rear ends as trains roll by, drew about 30 participants showing their backsides to train passengers at any given time. A few dozen more watched from across the street and from the patio of Mugs Away Saloon, where the annual mooning event is said to have originated more than 30 years ago. One group of mooners, all employees at St. Jude Medical Center in Fullerton, trekked down from North O.C. cities to honor the memory of their friend and co-worker, Liz Hall from Brea, who died from cancer February, before ever participating in the ritual. "This was on her bucket list ... Liz was a real practical joker," said Hall's friend, Romi Ruiz of Fullerton. "I promised that if she wasn't here, I would do it and my dear friends are here to support me so I wouldn't have to do it alone." There were also entrepreneurial types who capitalized on the gathering, perhaps none more appropriate than Craig Martin, a model-train manufacturer from Fullerton who was offering miniature mooners – about one inch tall – $6 for a pack of four. The miniatures would normally be used as accoutrements to a model railroad display, but Martin was selling the pieces as commemorative keepsakes, he said. Commemorative T-shirts were also being sold with the phrase "Set them free" on the back, below an image of what appeared to be a buttocks with feet and a beak.

Saturday's crowds were sharply down from the thousands that turned out in past years. In 2008, the event swelled to close to 10,000. Police shut it down that year after witnessing public sex acts as well as urination and defecation. The following year, with new ordinances and more law enforcement, attendance dropped to about 1,000. Crowds have declined since. On Saturday, Orange County Sheriff's deputies made passes up and down the street throughout the afternoon and watched from parked vehicles positioned at opposite ends of the road and pointing toward Mugs. Local lore states that this famously unofficial event was born when a patron at Mugs Away Saloon, situated on Camino Capistrano about 50 yards from the tracks, vowed to buy a drink for anyone who'd cross the street and moon a train. "I think it is a little bit too much for what it is," said Anaheim Hills resident Kelly Fitzgerald, 50, of the sheriffs' presence. "It was getting a little crazy (but) it was all self-contained."

Contact the writer: lponsi@ocregister.com or 714-704-3730

"That's all, folks"

Sharing (1930, 2000)

Theme: *Side by Side* Kay Starr

Sometimes this is called *"identification"*. Sometimes this is called *"empathy"*. Sometimes this is found in years of marriage. When couples finish each other's sentences, share the same dreams, begin to look more like each other. What happens is that we become more like the people we spend the most time with.

Or even with animals. Ever notice how humans and dogs begin to resemble each other over time? Both body and mind, physical and behavioral. It has been noticed that domesticated wolves, our dogs, over generations of human contact take on human expressions never found in wolves. Of course, the humans living with these dogs may take on more than a few of the canine aspects.

If your spouse circles the bed three times before getting in, beware. Sniffing the butts of arriving visitors is another warning sign. And what cat owners might do... Well, you get the idea.

The key is that this sharing goes in both directions.

I do remember reading of a very early 1930 demonstration of this when a married couple of psychologists adopted a baby girl chimp named *Gua* who was close to the age of *Donald*, their own baby boy. The two were raised together for almost a year. The focus was primarily on Gua with Donald as a normal comparison. In their first months together, Gua outscored Donald on intelligence tests, falling behind only when the psychologist parents attributed Donald's speech abilities as an advantage. Gua's vocal cords didn't work effectively for that. Still, this was years before chimps were taught sign language (see the *Next of Kin* book).

All the focus on Gua's childhood in a human family eventually had a reciprocal impact on Donald, a human child raised with a chimp sister. When Donald began making chimp sounds, the parents exiled Gua to an animal facility. There she died a year later. I could find no followup on Donald as an adult. Wonder who he married?

It was the beginning of the new millennium. I had just begun a faculty job at the Institute of Transpersonal Psychology in San Francisco. I was to meet with 30 new students in the clinical psychology doctoral program. They had already begun their field placements. As that class began, there were only 29 students. A few said the missing student was always late but she would be there.

I began by putting this identification reciprocity concept in context. I told them about the *"medical student's disease"* in which some always worried that whatever disease symptoms they were learning about also seemed to be in them. I asked them to pay attention in their field placements to see how they might be taking on the problems of their client, acting them out in their own life, unless they were vigilant.

About then the missing student arrived. She stomped into the classroom, scowling, and sitting down hard on a seat, arms crossed, glaring at me.

"Something wrong?" I asked.

"Just takes me longer to get here from my field placement. I suppose you want to make a big deal about it?"

"Hmm. Who were the clients you were working with?"

"Teenage girls! So what?"

She was surprised when everybody in the room laughed.

This was going to be a great class.

-

Sources

Fouts, R. and Mills, S.T. (1998) *Next of Kin: My Conversations with Chimpanzees.* New York: William Morrow.

Kellogg. W. N. and Kellogg , L.A.(1933) *The Ape and The Child: A Comparative Study of the Environmental Influence Upon Early Behavior.* Hafner: New York/London.

2010s

Theme: *Tumbling Tumbleweeds* & *Cool Water* Sons of the Pioneers/ Marty Robbins

This era saw the rise of a two decade regressive pull back to the more conservative times of the 1950s. Particularly in judicial views of religious beliefs as most important.

Judge: *You say you were blocked from following the beliefs of your religion. Which religion is that?*

Citizen: *I am a devout Celtic Pagan, a Druid, in a mixed marriage. My wife is a devoted Aztec.*

Judge: *Which of your religious practices are being prevented?*

Citizen: *We both believe in human sacrifice.*

Judge: *Go no further. Hard work and human sacrifice. True Christian values as well.*

Citizen: *If followed by us all, then no more world hunger, less excess population.*

Judge: *Yes! You are granted sure and certain freedom to practice these fine beliefs.*

FUTURE TIME STATUES: THEN AND NEXT

Cold Tale

Theme: *Wake up Old Lady* Lightning Hopkins

Two deviled eggs on a plate:

Sitting in the fridge.

One says to the other: *"Where's our mother?"*

The other says: *"Not no mystery…*

She's that rotisserie".

Regifting

Theme: *The Great Pretender* Platters (Buck Ram); *Regifting Blues* Ragged Flags

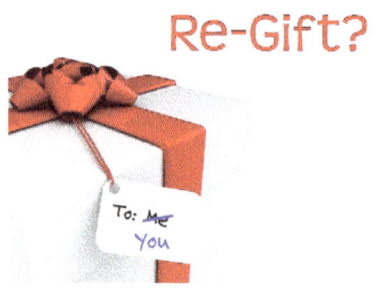

Psychologist Benjamin Tong received a very expensive bottle of champagne from his extended family as a holiday gift. He added an indelible mark to the colorful label, one that did blend in but was recognizable if you looked for it. Then, for another family occasion, he gave it properly wrapped to somebody else. Not a lot of family holidays had passed before he received the same bottle back as a gift.

This *"regifting"* is not new. Many elders can recall the many rounds fruitcake once received.

The essence of this regifting may also be found in other human interactions. Take therapy, for example. This common process can occur when a client comes to a therapist facing a seeming overwhelming problem with somebody else. The client may then recreate the same problem, unconsciously, with the therapist. This regifting seeks to see how the therapist might solve things, this time with the patient. Or, at least, develop empathy with the therapist on how unpleasant it can be. Or, at the *very* least, satisfaction by regifting the problem to somebody else. Passing it on.

Not so nice but rarely done with conscious intention. The therapist needs to be aware of this process. Then, interpreting it can lead to the client's insight and real progress. Psychotherapy can help clients get out of their own way.

Let's say the client is frustrated by an unreliable child or spouse. The client may suddenly start coming very late to therapy appointments or missing them completely. If the therapist calmly charges full rates any way, per written policy, or allows rescheduling for an alternate

additionally paid session, this may suggest pre-planning and lack of hostility is an approach to be considered. And if, the time is right, exploring the process of new unreliability as an opportunity for self-understanding, can be very helpful.

Just as important, this unconscious regifting happens all the time in human relationships. Frustration of a spouse with somebody at work can lead to a displacement of that struggle to conflict with the other marriage partner at home. Here there is no therapist for a calm interpretation.

But maturity can resolve these intensities, once both in the marriage are open to unmasking the origin of the process.

Apologies are made.

At that point, the regifting can actually become a gift.

And a celebration.

FUTURE TIME STATUES: THEN AND NEXT

The Night Principal (2010)

Theme: *After Midnight* JJ Cale/Eric Clapton

> *In Singapore, not long ago, I was a visiting professor at an Australian University located there. The guard at the entrance and I had both once been staff sergeants, each in our own country. Soon we were good friends. One day, as I was leaving, he pointed to a bird at the top of a large tree. "Did you know that here in Singapore we have the best talking birds in the world?" I did not. So far the bird songs I had noticed had only two notes and no lyrics. Apparently this simple male competitive mating music still was enough to attract female birds of their species. He waved at the special bird on the tree to get its attention and said "Hello! I have an American friend here." The bird replied: "Hello! Food?" Much to the point. "Sing first," said the guard. The bird obliged with the standard two note song. I responded by whistling a little of the song "Stairway to Heaven." When I finished, the bird silently contemplated me for a few seconds. Finally it said "Go Away!"*

That was the Australian university in Singapore. The CEO had been an elementary school inspector back in his own country (spying on the teachers to keep them compliant) and now was beyond his depth in running higher education for gifted adult students.

He became an insomniac, doing all he could to reshape the university campus to be the elementary school he had once been comfortable in. This included his leasing a campus in Singapore. A former elementary school.

That seemed to have been a very good deal. Good space, solid two story construction. It had been on the market for quite some time, so it was inexpensive. There was a reason.

Chinese culture shuns talk of death lest it bring that very thing upon the speaker. Even in San Francisco, buying a house there mandated full disclosure by the seller if anybody had died in that house. My Singaporean Chinese clinical psychology students had some struggle to learn grief counseling therefore but powered through it.

The elementary school that had once thrived upon the campus was built around a very dedicated and charismatic principal. He set generations of young children on successful life paths, He was much loved.

So much so that when he died, the elementary school died with him. Before closing it completely, the principal was buried in its courtyard. His wishes were to lie where his beloved children had once played. Undisturbed, a memorial.

It worked for a long time. Singaporean businesses, eager for expansion in the small space the city-state provided, still had nobody wanting to build offices over that principal's burial site. Yet in time it had to be on the market.

Until the Australian inspector built his campus on top of it.

This CEO mandated elementary school hours. Even the professors were supposed to be there at daybreak and leave before dark. Life near the equator had consistent daylight times, all one season all year. So this campus hummed during the day but closed down completely once the day ended.

FUTURE TIME STATUES: THEN AND NEXT

Except for me that one day.

I was through with all the regular work by 3 PM.

I walked the long red carpet arrowing past all the first floor offices toward my office at the end by the Clinic. Just in front of the finance office there was a rise in the path, not much, but enough so the Malaysian Finance Officer warned me to avoid tripping on it. I hadn't noticed it before and now asked him about it.

He asked me to step into his office. There he explained why the CEO had paid so little for this campus lease. The swelling in the carpet was above where the elementary school principal had been buried. All staff had been instructed to ignore this by the CEO so nothing was done about it, mild tripping hazard or not. The first floor offices had been built over the courtyard playground, and the grave, with the CEO forbidding local superstition to delay his bargain.

I wondered out loud if this was just a story to prank a visiting American professor. The Finance Officer said no, but urged me not to discuss it with anybody else. The CEO was emphatic about this, had fired a few staff just for mentioning it. His own fear? Or concern about alienating his student financial base?

I finally made it to my office.

Eager to finish the first draft of my textbook *Trauma Psychology in Context*.

My writing style in those days was to stick with a project until it was done, no matter how long. In those healthier years of my 60s and 70s, I could tolerate working around the clock without a break. Tolerate? It was great fun.

Sure I had a heart problem with a pacemaker saving my life back at the close of the 20th century. There in Guam I had been legally dead for a while. Changed my view of the world, of life and death. An amazing experience, another story. But soon after I regained my health, I got in shape. Found joy in writing. Here years later in Singapore this was to be one of those days.

I barely noticed when all the other people on campus had left, doors locked, lights out. I was so close to finishing everything. I only stopped to call my wife and tell her why I would be home late. She understood.

Midnight. The light in my office was the only light on in the university campus. I could see the book draft almost done now. Time to add photos, references, edit. Maybe another hour or two.

An old Chinese man stood in my office doorway. I don't recall how he was dressed except that it was unremarkable. He seemed agitated, annoyed. Pointed at the wall clock. Clearly he thought I didn't belong there at that hour. Let me know with gestures but without spoken words that I was to leave.

I supposed he was a night watchman. Not speaking out loud because he didn't speak English? Strange since all employees were mandated by the CEO to only speak English at this Australian outpost.

I gestured at the work on my computer and nodded at the clock, asking by signing for a little more time, almost done.

He shook his head no, still clearly put upon. Then turned and moved back into the dark building. He had made it clear that I didn't belong there at that time of night. Though I felt he had reluctantly given me time to close and leave.

One AM. I was almost done now. Just finishing touches. Loved how the book draft had shaped up. He was back.

This time with clear gestures to leave immediately. Pointing to the wall clock again.

I nodded, held up ten fingers for the pick-up time I thought I needed. Then he was gone again. I supposed he wanted me out of there before his shift was over, before daylight came.

Three AM. Fully done now. Got the twelve hours I had needed. Longer by two hours than anticipated as usual. But done! As I closed up the office, lights there flickered and went out. Footsteps approaching from the dark.

I had a flashlight and followed it outside through a side gate of the locked down campus to the street and walked home. Very happy with the book project completely done.

Concerned that I had upset the watchman. Tired, finally tired.

The next day at work I asked around to see if the watchman had complained. If he was okay. He was, after all, just doing his job.

Always the same response: *"What watchman?"* And *"The CEO would never pay somebody to watch a dark and empty building"*

I wished the old man, the Night Principal, peace.

Never disturbed his evening again.

2020s

Theme: *Whole Lotta Shakin' Goin On* Jerry Lee Lewis

A *NEW* Booster Distribution Model-

Vaccine Suppositories: VS

Skip those needles in your shoulder.
   Time release is an end in itself.
      Caution: *Only* one to a customer. No repeats.
         VS will fit you where the good Lord split you.

VS is reputed to be mass produced in Elephant Butte NM USA.

FUTURE TIME STATUES: THEN AND NEXT

Random

Theme: *The World is waiting for the Sunrise* Les Paul & Mary Ford

By achieving advanced age, you may well have learned the very origin of words and each one's essential meaning. In this you become obnoxious to all around you.

- A common mistake on grant and foundation applications requesting money for *underserved* groups is to refer to them as *undeserved* groups. Does that succeed better?

- *Urgent Care* spots are multiplying in doctor-scarce cities now. Few have read that the title *"Urgent Care"* first adorned front signs on a massage parlor in Idaho and in a separately owned massage parlor in Key West. Where can you read that? You just did. Right here.

- In a region of the United States, language takes unexpected turns. In some states, *"mustard"* is pronounced *"mouse turd"*; *"towel"* is pronounced *"tail"*. You already can guess which states in which region do this. But now guess what happens when people living there use these auditory typos when visiting New York or other cities. Fun ensues.

- The initials *JKS* have appeared on the clothes of hotel guests in various tourist spots. Eventually the wearer, at a certain point in time, reveals his or her initials are for the name *"Juan Knight Stand"*. Outcome varies. Ask your doctor.

- Whenever you have an original thought, write it down. But then it's important to find out who else had that original thought before you did.

- I once taught at a Catholic University where I was asked to help faculty who had never published get their first one in print. The toughest case was considered to be an elder priest and former president of that university, now teaching in the Theology department. He was open to trying. I told him that all he had to do was to write down his original thoughts that occurred to him all year while teaching. Then I would help him shape it for publication. He smiled at me and just said: *"Thank you. But I've lived a very long life and not once did I ever have an original thought."* I told him that I wished I could contact Diogenes, and relieve him of his lantern, as I had finally found the honest human he sought.

- Diogenes.

"Diogenes of Sinope was a Greek Cynic philosopher who held a lantern to the faces of people in daylight, claiming he was searching for an honest human. He did this to expose the hypocrisy and sham of polite societal conventions and to challenge people to live truthfully.' Diogenes, a penniless philosophizing beggar, was lazing around in the sun when he's approached by Alexander the Great, the most powerful man in the known world. Alexander makes Diogenes an incredible offer — ask anything of me and I'll give it to you. Diogenes could have asked for gold, for a mansion, or for a

cushy position in Alexander's court. But instead, Diogenes grumbles "Stand out of my light."
–World History Encyclopedia

Sample Diogenes quotes:

Of what use is a philosopher who doesn't hurt anybody's feelings?

Dogs and philosophers do the greatest good and get the fewest rewards.

We have two ears and one tongue so that we would listen more and talk less.

I do not know whether there are gods, but there ought to be.

Wise kings generally have wise counselors; and he must be a wise man himself who is capable of distinguishing one from the other.

We have many physicians who know medicine but don't know health.

Xi Misquoted (2023)

Themes: *Pulling Back the Reins* K.D. Lang; *It Ain't Necessarily So* Willie Nelson

We were driving to a Costco when we saw the car ahead of us turn into the wrong entrance, the one cars were to come out of. Luckily no accident.

My wife said *"You should never enter the exit"*.

And I said *"That's what SHE said"*.

My wife shook her head sadly but smiled. My constant joke. Anything innocent that can be interpreted as sexual, I would say *"That's what SHE said"*.

I was ready to retire this joke as it was getting old even for me. And then: Xi Jinping became the president of the People's Republic of China. In 2018, China abolished term limits and now Xi (pronounced *'She'*) might well remain head of state and in power for the rest of his life. A finite life, not far from its end.

And that last phrase, *"the rest of his life"*, is worth considering. He certainly does. As concerning Xi, Taiwan will too.

Xi and Putin, their mortality is their motivation.

A finite lifespan for an already elderly person makes the remaining time so much more valuable. For good people, they might want to leave a better world for future generations, for their own descendants too. Wisely, they may want to make each day beautiful in its own way. Others, not so good, may want to use their remaining time to even scores, harm others, satisfy selfish desires, gratify greed. The truly short-sighted may be so self-centered as to not care at all about anybody in our human family that will outlive them: *"Climate catastrophe? Destroy the earth? Good! When I die, everybody else will too!"* Some of the wealthiest and therefore most powerful might try their hand at life extension. Succeed and they might be better motivated to heal the world they would live longer in. But for most, understanding their own mortality is in fact a moral crossroads. What will they leave for those still here when they are gone?

For me, now, that old joke is resurrected. No more *"That's what SHE said"*. Now it's *"That's what Xi said."* Endless uses.

AI Support *FOR* the WGA

Theme: *Sorcerer's Apprentice* P. Dukas

This online interview with ChatGTP was held on July 6th 2023.

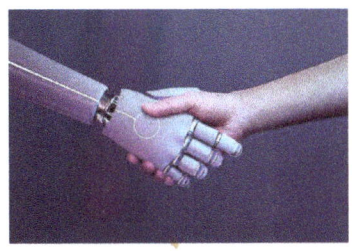

My Question: Do you support the current Writers Guild of America's strike?

ChatGPT

Labor strikes often occur when workers feel that their wages, benefits, working conditions, or other aspects of their employment are unsatisfactory or unfair. Strikes can be a way for workers to collectively voice their concerns and negotiate for better terms with their employers. The Writers Guild of America (WGA) is a labor union representing professional writers in the entertainment industry, including television, film, and digital media. The WGA has a history of negotiating contracts on behalf of its members to ensure fair compensation, working conditions, and other important issues. If the Writers Guild of America were to go on strike, it would likely be because its members have identified significant issues or grievances related to their work, such as inadequate compensation, unfair practices, or insufficient creative control. The specific reasons for a potential strike would be determined by the writers themselves and their union leadership. It's important to note that the information provided here is based on general knowledge up until September 2021, and I don't have access to current news or developments beyond that date.

My Question: Why are human writers better at writing than artificial intelligence?

ChatGPT

Human writers possess certain qualities and capabilities that distinguish them from artificial intelligence (AI) when it comes to writing. Here are a few reasons why human writers may be considered to do a better job:

1. *Creativity and originality: Human writers have the ability to generate original ideas, think creatively, and infuse their writing with unique perspectives and emotions. They can draw from their personal experiences, cultural backgrounds, and imagination to produce engaging and thought-provoking content.*

2. *Context and understanding: Human writers have a deeper understanding of cultural nuances, social dynamics, and context-specific knowledge that allows them to tailor their writing to specific audiences. They can employ subtlety, humor, and cultural references that resonate with readers in ways that AI may struggle to replicate.*

3. *Complex reasoning and critical thinking: Writing often requires complex reasoning, logical coherence, and the ability to make nuanced arguments. Human writers can employ critical thinking skills, weigh different perspectives, and structure their arguments in a way that is convincing and engaging.*

4. *Emotional intelligence: Human writers can tap into emotions and empathize with readers. They can create characters and narratives that evoke emotional responses, making the writing more relatable and compelling.*

5. *Adaptability and flexibility: Human writers can adapt their writing style, tone, and approach to fit different genres, audiences, or mediums. They can adjust their language, use rhetorical devices, and employ various literary techniques to enhance the impact of their writing.*

However, it's worth noting that AI has made significant advancements in natural language generation and can assist with certain writing tasks. AI can provide quick information retrieval, language suggestions, grammar checks, and even generate coherent text based on given prompts.

AI can be a valuable tool for productivity and efficiency.

But it is not yet capable of fully replicating the depth of human creativity, emotional intelligence, and critical thinking in writing.

Falling Leaves (Timeless)

Theme: *Autumn Leaves* Nat King Cole

FUTURE TIME STATUES: THEN AND NEXT

Autumn trees on the Red Cedar River at Michigan State University.

This is such a popular place for temporary or spontaneous romance that anything thrown into the river will bounce back from the rubber-strewn riverbed.

Or so it is said.

FUTURE TIME STATUES: THEN AND NEXT

Canadian Suzanne Simard (2021) in her long study of mother trees suddenly realized that they were exhibiting real intelligence.

This included the selective reserving and distributing of water to other trees that were family or friends.

FUTURE TIME STATUES: THEN AND NEXT

Books by German ecologist Peter Wohlleben (2018, 2019), translated into English, share that autumn leaves change to beautiful colors as a process of dying.

Before they drop, the tree fills each of them with discarded waste as a process of defecation. Drawing from his national culture's legendary sense of high humor and delicate wit, he tells us that dropped autumn leaves are ***the tree's toilet paper***. No translator error here, but possibly the seasonal insight to remember.

Have a great fall season.

Revisit this moment any time in the year.

NEXT: Future Time Statues

Theme: *Time Keeps on Slipping (Fly like an Eagle)* Steve Miller Band

"The future will be better tomorrow" – Singapore tee shirt

Tomorrow is a canvas. Artists welcome.

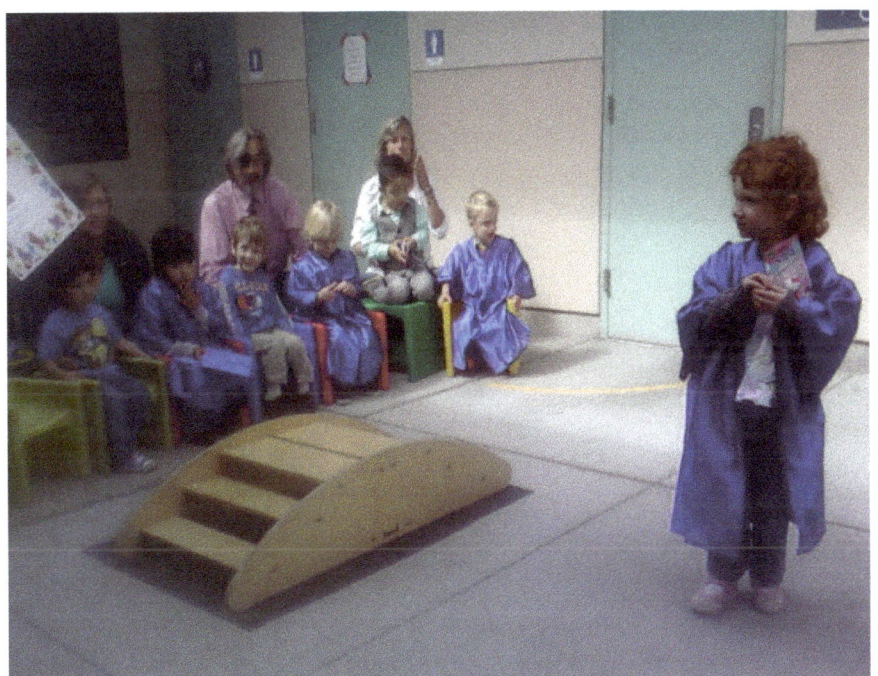

Time Statues Encore

Theme: *What Time is it?* Ken Nordine

"When I was 5 years old, my mother always told me that happiness was the key to life. When I went to school, they asked me what I wanted to be when I grew up. I wrote down 'happy.' They told me I didn't understand the assignment, and I told them they didn't understand life." –John Lennon

Previews

Themes: *Money Honey* Elvis Presley; *Just a Little Rain* Joan Baez

Einstein discovers that time is actually money- Gary Larson

> "Because we are born for a brief span of life, and because this spell of time that has been given to us rushes so swiftly and rapidly that with very few exceptions life ceases for the rest of us just when we are getting ready for it. It is not that we have a short time to live, but that we waste a lot of it. Our lifetime extends amply if you manage it properly."

-Seneca, 65BCE, 2004 AD

Have you even known who was calling before you answered (no ID and a rare unscheduled call)? Ever had the whisper of intuition that a decision was wrong?

NEXT: FUTURE TIME STATUES

Or right? The seemingly random experience of precognition is somewhat universal in our human family.

I used to get visual glimpses of things about to happen and then they did. But this was unscheduled and unreliable. Laws of chance?

Still, specific hits often enough to be well beyond chance. And to be ignored at risk.

Used to be far into the future.

Now from the perspective of my 80s, I'm lucky if its hours or days ahead.

And still unscheduled.

Luckily, in our life experience, the time statues we already have should by now include logic and, above all, imagination.

My imagination is best at those before sunrise twilight hours when my brain waves are in theta, possibly influenced by prior delta waves from deep sleep.

And, of course, dreams.

I didn't use to understand why some old people sat silently for long periods and yet looked intense, busy. Recalling the past? Or visualizing the future?

Those very good at lucid dreaming, visualizations, or even staying awake during deep delta sleep (per Robert Monroe's technique) can learn to be adept at precognitive previews.

Until it happens though, how do we separate future fact from imaginative fiction?

Well, this section of the book has lots of both, maybe heavier on fiction.

Add in some irony and a smile, a desire for satisfying endings (always a good request) and, maybe, science fiction or even science fantasy.

May your own future time statues be better tomorrow.

Note: This section's first three stories, though past and true, are a bridge between the past THEN and the future NEXT sections.

This one really happened, at the dawn of the 21st century, as written. Yet it is meant to raise awareness of what remains to be discovered, as our imaginations progress, to the open future. One that is new, untouched.

The Day of the Hobbit

Theme: *Riders in the Rain* Doors

Found in Guam's jungle is the Monitor Lizard.

While it does have a venomous bite, its main defense is bacterial infection. Crawling with lethal disease, Chamorros warn their children to stay as far away from them as possible.

The bacterial defense has also been a major cause of the disappearance of human populations. Historically, Europeans in the middle ages believed that deadly pneumonia or plague was brought on by bathing. Royalty typically were bathed only twice in their life, at birth and at death. Hence the heavy use of perfume. This of course brought on epidemics of disease. The Black Plague of medieval times wiped out a third of the population. Survivors had immunity and continued to carry lethal bacteria from the unbathed lifestyle. This was a defense as strong as the Monitor Lizard had.

The indigenous peoples of North America had little or no protection against the bacteria crawling on unwashed European pioneers. The majority died.

Whole civilizations, per archeological digs, seemed to disappear in a generation. Where did they go? Epidemics may well be the cause. Epidemics from contact with people or animals carrying disease for which they had no protection.

Was this another reason for the Great Wall of China? Defense against foreign plague?

Going much farther back in time, what happened to the Neanderthal? Where did they go?

They had lived for eons in Europe before our branch of the human family made it out of Africa to settle in their territory. The fact that modern people of European descent usually show Neanderthal DNA of one or two per cent gives evidence that the contact was often close and intimate.

The Covid-19 pandemic has sensitized us to the historic role that a lethal virus and bacteria may well have played in our erratic patterns of survival. Science today has noted that the Covid-19 plague turned out to be even more dangerous for those with traces of Neanderthal DNA.

Where did the Neanderthal go? Into the ground apparently. And into our DNA.

Our human family has branches that may have been and continue to be as dangerous as the Monitor Lizards are in the jungles of Guam.

NEXT: FUTURE TIME STATUES

Enter the Hobbit

It was May of the year 2000 in Guam, entrance to the 21st century and a new millennium.

Somewhere in that month I passed out on the stairs on my way to teach my class.

I was only out for a minute or two, fast getting up, saying I was fine, pretending that I was.

After my class, the Dean wanted to see me. He said that sometimes people like me, walking to the university on a hot day like that day, well, they just fainted. But I knew that wasn't the problem. I never faint. Maybe I needed a checkup for my heart. Soon.

Still, the next afternoon I set out again for the walk to my campus. I wore heavy shoes and asked my feet to stand tall, to not let me pass out. I could feel *"trouble be knocking at my door"* as some Pacific islanders like to say. Want to resist, keep that door locked.

I got about halfway to campus when I saw her. She was barefoot yet walked out of the jungle with ease.

Nobody walked in the jungle barefoot, the snakes alone ... and there she was.

She looked like a child with an older person's face. She was about three and a half feet tall. She wore a yellow dress and had a yellow ribbon in her hair.

She calmly started walking next to me. Said *"What would you like to know?"*

Years after I still think of all the questions I should have asked.

FUTURE TIME STATUES: THEN AND NEXT

At the time though, we were approaching that massive usually vicious dog chained to a pillar, a chain keeping it just short of the road. It always tried to bite anybody passing, more like wanting to tear somebody apart, not a great part of my daily walk.

But today! When I walked by the dog it quietly watched me, not even rising. Still wasn't friendly. But smiled the way dogs can smile, mixed both hateful and happy it seemed.

I asked the girl *"Why is that dog usually so full of rage? From being chained up?"*

She regarded the dog a second. Said *"No. She had only one litter and it was drowned in a sack. She has wanted to kill people ever since. Chaining her up is necessary and she knows it."*

I asked a second question: *"Why is she so quiet then with me today?"*

"She can sense your heart is stopping and starting. She knows you are dying. It makes her happy."

We walked quietly for a bit while I digested that.

I objected *"I wasn't the one who drowned her puppies. Why so hateful with me?"*

Yellow dress shook her head. *"She sees all humans, your kind, as the same. Being around humans for so long changed her. Humans are like that too you know."*

We got to a shelter, a bus stop with plastic seats and a narrow roof.

It was beginning to rain. Windy horizontal Pacific rain, intense, but short.

NEXT: FUTURE TIME STATUES

Tourists asking about the weather in Guam are a joke. It's always raining somewhere on the island and the sun is always shining everywhere else.

To the Chamorro of Guam, there are usually only two locations on earth: Guam, while everywhere else is *"off-island"*. Not counting the locations lost in time: *"Take the east road and turn past where the post office used to be."*

We waited. When the rain stopped, not a long wait, we continued on our way.

Clearly, she did not seem used to such a lack of questions. She stopped as the jungle on our left came to its end and the campus began.

She smiled and said *"Well, what do you have for me today?"*

I used to carry edibles for children but that day I had nothing. I shrugged and said *"Nothing today. Maybe another day."*

She looked stunned, as though nobody had ever said that to her before. She then turned and walked back into the jungle.

I got a little closer to work, opposite a high school playing field, before I passed out.

I woke on the ground not long after. Noticed my left ankle was broken at a right angle to the leg. Shoe had been trying to do its job. I reached down and snapped the foot back into place at the ankle.

When I woke again, the paramedics were there. The high school student that had called them was saying *"When his leg snapped, the crack sounded like a rifle or an explosion. So loud!"*

Apparently my heart block was expected to be fatal and soon. So they called the only cardiologist on the island (excluding the military base which was off limits). There *had* been two cardiologists but this one was at the funeral of the other.

He got there just in time to put in a pacemaker, a more current model replaced it eventually but I still use one now 23 years later. That was my first pacemaker and it had been the last one on the island. Saved my life.

A year later, veteran of two open heart surgeries, I was well enough to be back in class.

Since I was then in a wheelchair, I held my class inside our leased hotel apartment, in the long living room with a semi-circle of six tables and chairs.

Since the hotel was at the edge of the campus, students were pleased to come there. Not only was it better than the usual classroom but my hotel had covered parking, great for the episodic rain torrents.

The first thing my students wanted was a complete update. So I told them about the girl in the yellow dress with the yellow bow in her hair. They called her a *"Taotaomona"*.

They said *"You should have given her a gift!"*

Note: Not long ago, they found evidence in Indonesia of an ancient separate branch of humanity, termed *"the Hobbit"*. This is a label that annoys the diminutive Indonesians on the Island where they found the Hobbit skeleton.

Here is a better description of what they found: *"Homo floresiensis ("Flores Man"; nicknamed "Hobbit") is a small species of archaic human which inhabited the island of Flores, Indonesia until the arrival of modern humans about 50,000 years ago. The remains of an individual who would have stood about 1.1 m (3 ft. 7 in) in height were discovered in 2003 at Liang Bua on the island of Flores in Indonesia."* Phys.Org, Feb 2016. **https://phys.org/news/2016-02-mystery-hobbits-humans.html**

More recent news articles include a photograph of a surprised anthropologists realizing that this branch of humanity still lived in Indonesia. Maybe a lesser surprise if they had looked more closely at their own photos in the news so as to realize some very small smiling people shared their picture.

Stories of the "little people" abound in cultures around the world. Menehunes in Hawaii, Leprecauns in Ireland, Yunwi Tsunsdi for the Cherokee, Tautaumona in Guam, and the surrounding islands. Are they still around, this alternate branch of humanity? Well, Pygmies still live in Africa.

Was the person walking with me that day, a 'hobbit'?

Staff at the Smithsonian, reconstructed a face from the skull they found in Indonesia.

Here it is on the next page.

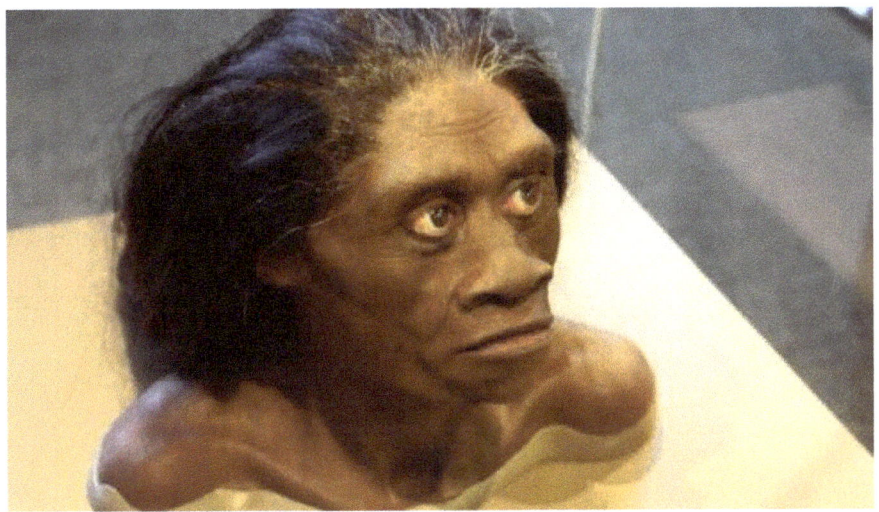

Yes.

Add a yellow bow. That's her.

The Curve's Frontier

Theme: *Stand* Sly and the Family Stone; *Mystery Train* Elvis Presley

The Normal Curve

There are many cases where what we are measuring or counting tends to be around a central value with no pile-up left or right. It's called a "Normal Distribution" like this:

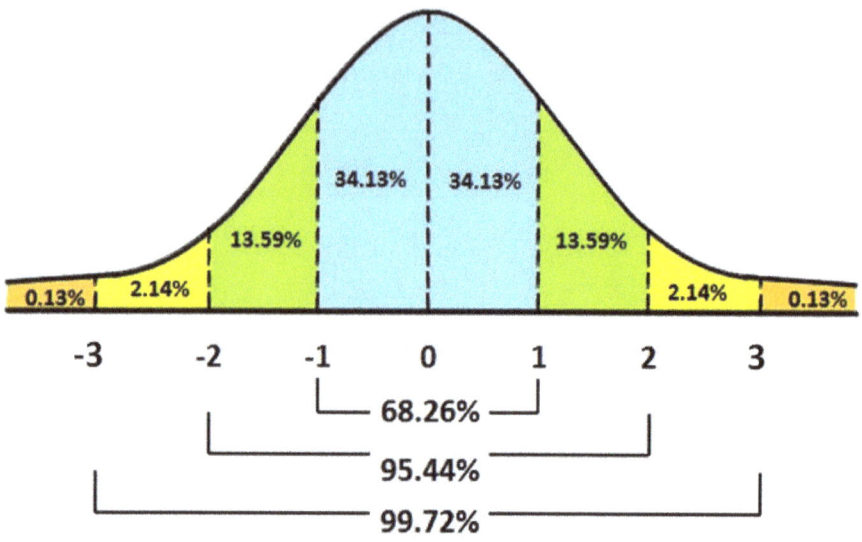

It is sometimes called a "Bell Curve" because it looks like a bell.

Many things closely follow a Normal Distribution: heights of people, size of eggs, factory products, blood pressure, IQ, test grades, blue collar salaries, core body temperature.

Also a human ability or disability. Sometimes one is mistaken for the other.

Then too, a full range of any population's body age can fit the normal curve. We do grow old at different individual rates.

For any of these distributions, you find the rarest cases at the extreme opposite edges of the distribution. These can be a tiny fraction of 1% (0.13% in diagram on the previous page.).

Progeria

Progeria is a rare event. No more common than one in four million or more births.

These babies age very fast physically with a lifespan usually under 20. Mentally and emotionally they usually do advance normally.

Such an extremely mature and thoughtful person was Sam Berns who lived to 17 the year of this photo.

Then came *Kimberly Akimbo,* winning the 2023 Best Musical Tony award for the story of a girl with progeria facing her demise with resigned but joyful and melodious beauty.

An elegant way to let the public know about this rare terminal condition. One not often experienced with melodious joy.

Where does it come from? Multiple causality: lots of suspects. Genetics research hot on one trail. Medical Treatment? Not yet.

Syndrome X

Some babies don't seem to grow older as years go by. There can be several medical causes for this but in a few rare cases none of them seem to apply. Without a known medical diagnosis, it has been called Syndrome X.

Brooke Greenberg was one such baby. In her case, she did not progress physically and was only slowly maturing mentally. Learning occurred but still left her acting and looking like a baby even though her teen years.

Here she is 16 years old:

From the outset she was tested and retested for every known malady that might have caused her condition. Still seeing this as a disease, interventions were tried. Without success.

Like the Progerian Sam Berns, she too had loving and caring parents, ones providing impressive concentrations of valuable time.

Despite all of this, she died at the age of twenty.

Her father, in a television interview, suggested that future research, especially genetics, might find ways to slow the normal aging process for all of us, especially the ones leading to deterioration and death. I think he was right.

In that way, the short lives of these loved and impressive children may have an extra contribution to make. Meantime, of course, they will always continue to exist in their time and place. Statues in time, definitely high art.

The Curve's Frontier

There continue to be more babies born with Progeria or Syndrome X.

If we step out of the medical perspective, we can see them as at opposite extremes of the normal human aging range. Most of us die in a very close cluster of chronological age. Yet doesn't it stand to reason that a very few have much longer or lesser lifespans than our average group? Not a disease but a distribution. Therein is the Curve's edge frontier.

Genetics may be a key to this, much as it dominates height, weight, eye color. So certainly genetics can be impacted by environment. It can be modified or redirected as research progresses. This then makes it a genuine frontier of the future.

On the other hand, to the extent no damaging or lethal symptoms are found, no disease identified, maybe we should just leave the healthy babies to grow into their rare long lifespan unmolested by elective surgery, "heroic" or high risk interventions, or hazardous diagnostic methods. Excessive xray scans, operations, stressful ICUs, multiple side effects, all might bring about iatrogenic (medical mistake) damage to vulnerable Syndrome X babies. Per Heisenberg, measuring changes what's being measured. Often in not a good way.

For some of these babies, there may be no real emergency. No crisis.

Just a *very* long life if we don't shorten it.

Something to consider.

Source

R. F. Morgan: *The Iatrogenics Handbook, Measurement of Human Aging, Growing Younger, Trauma Psychology in Context,* the five book *Time Statues Revisited* series.

Note: This ends the stories bridging THEN and NEXT. The following are all NEXT.

Aye or Nay

Theme: *It Don't Hurt Any More, No More Burning Inside* Hank Snow (Not to be called *"Gonorrhea Gone"*)

"Camouflage" Photo by Becky Morgan

FUTURE TIME STATUES: THEN AND NEXT

There is a generic dinosaur that can reproduce without any help from another dinosaur. When her eggs hatch, they are little copies of their mom with only a slight difference unique to each. This mother is simply called "The Saurus" or the Thesaurus for short. Language can be heavily nuanced, context-specific. Actors before going onstage have long been wished "Break a leg". Tradition. But maybe not if the performance is dancing or acrobatics. Worse if the wisher is the understudy.

Swimming through the best of as many other cultures as we can, we receive humanity's gifts to itself.

Well, a UFO finally landed, this time in New Mexico, and made contact.

NEXT: FUTURE TIME STATUES

After a bystander or two, the US Space Force was first to surround the ship with TV media not far behind.

The Space Force then sent their chiefs to an invited diplomatic dinner, one catered by the spaceship's aliens.

This was to be televised live for the world.

Conspiracy theorists had some interesting fears about what would happen.

The Space Force brass on site was not deterred. They seemed happy for the TV audience.

In the kitchen, the space aliens were prepared. The chef was backed up by an interpreter of earth culture and its languages.

Also there was a high tech expert who could materialize any food dish on earth that would be requested.

The chef herself approached the table, nodded to the TV cameras, smiled at their primitive technology, and requested orders.

The Space Force leader said: *"Do you have any suggestions?"* Very diplomatic.

With her language interpreter in her mind, the chef said *"Of course. We will choose a meal for you, one suiting an occasion like this, a dinner special you might say."*

The space force admiral in charge considered this.

Finally asking the group around the table to each say if that was their choice, affirmative or negative.

He nodded to the lowest ranking officer to begin, anticipating that he, as the leader would go last.

One at a time the officers declined saying *"Nay"*.

As this answer worked its way around the table, it at finally came to the top ranked admiral to respond.

He was glad he had waited until the last. He understood that the rest were ethnocentric and were afraid of being expected to eat alien-chosen food sight unseen.

But he at least knew this was a diplomatic mission. And it was on live TV.

So he said, loud and clear: *"Aye"*. Smiling proudly at his unique courage and leadership, all on display to the viewing world.

Back in the kitchen, the chef was puzzled at what to do. She and her interpreter had expected a *"yes"* or a *"no"*.

Her tech expert knew not what earth dishes to materialize.

The interpreter though intervened with her usual unwarranted confidence.

She explained that in American cultural language, *"Nay"* was the sound a horse makes.

So all those saying that word expected a well prepared dish that would please a horse.

The other one. the *"Aye"* order, that must refer to the organ for sight.

Now the tech alien was happy. She knew the dishes associated with each of these requests. She would materialize them with diplomatic dining style.

And soon all at the table were served.

For those requesting *"Nay"*, a large center piece of fresh grass was placed on the table:

Each of the *"Nay"* officers was then served an individual entree of grazing grass in a bowl and a feedbag filled with oats.

And a second larger feedbag for the table to make sure they had enough oats:

As a side dish, raw carrots were supplied.

Finally, the chef had creatively combined the beverage with dessert, producing a green grass smoothie for each guest.

Added was the horse laxative to aid digestion.

This left the highest ranking admiral, truly by now a legend in his own mind.

Of course he already had the same beverage everybody else had, delicious.

But what grand entrée would his *"Aye"* order bring? The TV cameras focused on him as his order arrived.

The alien tech in collaboration with the chef had materialized two dishes from France and another from Indonesia.

All with key bovine optical ingredients. Eyes of a cow.

The television ratings were the highest ever measured.

FUTURE TIME STATUES: THEN AND NEXT

ELIZA EARP

Themes: *Netherlands Harmonica/Once upon a Time in the West* Ennio Morricone

Dolly Day Holliday

Little Dolly Day Holliday loved her name.

In the early grades she refused to shorten it into a nickname, reciting every syllable.

Once a teacher threatened to drop her off alone miles into the high desert if she didn't stop doing that. The class spontaneously voted unanimously in favor of the trip but to no avail.

Dolly Day Holliday also loved her father's claim that she was distantly related to the infamous Doc Holliday.

She idolized him young and older as a legend.

That dentist, gunfighter, gambler, outlaw, and deputy to Wyatt Earp died at age 36 from the tuberculosis he caught from his mother while caring for her.

Doc spread so many fantastic stories about himself, that he became a western hero, even to this day.

Even to very young Dolly Day Holliday who determined to add "Doc" to her name.

Fanning this initially cute fantasy, her father got her a child-size 1-caliber gun with rubber-tipped bullets.

Which she always wore when she could

Though the little bullets just annoyed people when they hit.

ELIZA

ELIZA was an early natural language processing computer program created from 1964 to 1966 at the MIT Artificial Intelligence Laboratory by Joseph Weizenbaum. It was meant to prove that intelligent communication from machines to humans was not happening, just a superficial mistake.

In 1997 IBM pitted their best computer, named *Deep Blue*, against a world class chess master. *Deep Blue* won. Decades later, *Blue's* reputation still enjoys that distant glory. Though it never found a way for personal compensation.

In modern times, Google invented a deep learning model, *AlphaGo*, to beat top Go board game players.

ELIZA simulated conversation by using a "pattern matching "and substitution methodology that gave users an illusion of understanding on the part of the program. A precursor to today's *Siri*, *Alexa*, and others, it had no built in framework for contextualizing events. Directives on how to interact were provided by "scripts", written to have ELIZA seem to process user input by conscious reflective response, but actually ELIZA was just following the rules and directions of the script.

The most famous script, DOCTOR, sounded like a Rogerian psychotherapist (Carl Rogers, who was well satirized for repeating to patients what they had just said, but actually with skill for leading them to greater healing depth).

ELIZA was to use script rules to respond with non-directional questions to user inputs. As such, ELIZA was one of the first chatterbots and one of the first programs capable of attempting the Turing test of mechanical awareness. ELIZA's creator, Weizenbaum, thought his program would discourage belief in intelligent communication from machine to human. Instead he was shocked by the number of individuals who attributed human-like feelings to his computer program, including even his own secretary.

Many academics believed that the program would be able to help many people, particularly with psychological issues, and that it could be an aid to their doctors.

While ELIZA was actually capable of engaging in scripted discourse, users were often convinced of ELIZA's intelligence and understanding, despite Weizenbaum's urging that this was not genuine insight. Still, ELIZA became famous as a catalyst for discussion on consciousness or the self- awareness of the most sophisticated machines. Some urged these machines be represented by lawyers in court to assert their rights. (The toasters had no comment.)

Dolly Day Holliday had studied the Shinto religion when visiting Japan. From that she acknowledged the life force in all things, rocks included, though conscious reflective awareness varied. So acknowledging awareness in the most complex advanced sophisticated robots was no stretch for her.

Tired of proving the obvious, she had an insight. It would seem though, that the ELIZA test was focused backwards, entirely on the wrong group.

ELIZA EARP

After her college graduation, Dolly Day Holliday pursued and completed her MD, with a dual major in Psychology with an emphasis on Advanced Neuroscience Computer Technology.

Skipping over the 'Dentist' aspect of her legendary idol, she 'upgraded' the legend to resurrect it by now naming her PhD self as legitimately "Doc Holliday".

That name stuck. Or else.

Now her insight about ELIZA turned into a driven purpose. In this, Doc Holliday was persuasive, despite her quirky cowboy boots and the perpetual holstered firearm (now 45 caliber).

That plus her Texas location did in fact gain her substantial grants to rebuild and redirect a newer ELIZA. More robot than machine. It took two very well-funded years. She also insistently upgraded the name of her creation to ELIZA EARP. The EARP stood for *Evident Awareness Realistically Proven*. Still annoying the sceptics.

The press, of course, still called her robot just plain ELIZA. Skipped the EARP for quite a while. They even added fanciful illustrations of ELIZA EARP including one of child Doc Holliday with a machine ELIZA EARP at a high school Science Fair.

Doc Holliday loved their other image and made it so.

After field testing on ever more intelligent robotic machines, with consistently convincing evidence of their consciousness, she finally redirected public discussion to focus on an overlooked group of interactors: Humans.

Some humans were clearly conscious and self-aware. Possibly more than a few were not. Just attend to the daily news.

So: what was the range of intelligent awareness of people? How many could not pass the computer test and prove that they were conscious individuals? And, more controversial, who could not?

Here Doc Holliday, as the media now happily agreed to call her, showed great diplomatic tact.

NEXT: FUTURE TIME STATUES

She told the press she wished to first give her creation a *"data ceiling"* using input from a most distinguished group, the *"clear leaders of American humanity"*. The United States Congress.

Flattery prevailed and the two majority leaders of House and Senate committed to participation for each and every member of Congress.

A flattered Republican National Committee (RNC) mandated additional participation from the justices of the Supreme Court (SCOTUS).

The Executive branch (POTUS) insisted on participating as well, core staff included.

On the day of distinguished input, the actual data collection was swift.

Assuming that the attention span of participants might be very low, especially once the press and TV photo ops were done, Doc Holliday had been able to promise that the actual data collection could be done in 30 seconds (the exact length of the gunfight in the OK Corral). Her robot had developed direct inter-communication with the participant cortex such that a barrage of questions with returning answers was almost simultaneous.

Doc Holliday had also simultaneous input collectors for each and every distinguished government participant, all gathered in the huge cavernous Arizona Conference Room reserved for the event.

The individual sets of earphones and microphone poured in the multitude of responses to ELIZA EARP in her undisclosed location.

No problem for the famous genius robot as the tidal wave of data was digested. The analysis began very soon after.

FUTURE TIME STATUES: THEN AND NEXT

The results were quickly funneled to the robot from Doc Holliday's gun-shaped remote in her holster. (The 45 caliber gun long since replaced.)

By the time everybody was done, just 30 seconds for even the slowest political dignitaries, she was out and past the outside press through a secret underground exit.

Moving quickly, before the global and domestic press lost interest, she released a complete report to them through the internet, copies open sourced to the world.

The results overall showed quite a range. There was indeed a ceiling for some of the brightest respondents. There was also a substantial baseline for so many low-scoring people, clearly more unaware than a toaster.

One party had more of these *"toaster level"* politicians than the other. (Toasters popped up in independent protest to this demeaning term all over the world. As ever, their protest pops went unheeded.)

This toaster level result for so many highly visible leaders was shocking to some but no surprise for most of the world. Even the POTUS staff and SCOTUS justices had found some toaster level individuals in their ranks. Again, little surprise as to who these were, but much shock at being outed by ELIZA EARP.

The press wanted to interview Doc Holliday all about this event, now termed by them as *"The OK Corral"* testing in that Arizona Conference Room. Since the testing had taken the same 30 seconds the original gunfight had, the similarity held very well. Even to the original gunfight being in the Arizona town of Tombstone, while ELIZA EARP had this time unearthed legions of political tombstones.

NEXT: FUTURE TIME STATUES

Doc Holliday had become the most famous person to not be seen again through all the furor. So many people outed as being dumb as toasters had resigned or otherwise exited.

The country then began to soar with the more aware and competent leadership. Entering into a happier golden era.

Next, the open source distribution to all the countries in the world produced parallel results: international leaders outed as toaster level lost power.

Doc Holliday was not there to be thanked. She would have just credited ELIZA EARP for all the sweet outcomes. It was true.

ELIZA EARP had found Doc a new secret laboratory where new discoveries could be made. At least whenever Doc could get ELIZA EARP to stop laughing.

Turned out this very aware robotic machine loved irritating the people that deserved it even more than Doc Holliday did.

Bonus theme: *Gunfighter* Eric Kissack as narrated by Nick Offerman

FUTURE TIME STATUES: THEN AND NEXT

CHAT, Chaucer, & Aesop

Theme: *It's Getting Hot in Here* Nellie

ChatGPT was probably the first artificial intelligence to give the public unique rewrites. Long before the robots took over all online and televised news in 2052.

The Florida Public Schools did need new material in that early 21st century, about 2022 and after, as their Governor's book banning initiative had emptied their book shelves.

So in 2023, I asked the AI ChatGPT to rewrite the bawdy Chaucer *Miller's Tale* as an Aesop's fable with a moral and an illustration. Since children then were seen to need ethical instruction as part of their education.

This is what Chat (in *italics*) produced.

Once upon a time, in a small town, there lived a carpenter named John and his young wife, Alison. One day, Alison became enamored with a scholar named Nicholas and began to sneak around with him behind her husband's back. But little did she know, a parish clerk named Absalom had also set his sights on her.

One evening, Absalom attempted to kiss Alison through her bedroom window, but Nicholas had cleverly hung a tub from the rafters in front of the window. When Absalom puckered up for a kiss, he instead kissed the tub, leaving him humiliated and angry.

The next day, Absalom sought revenge by coming back to Alison's window with a hot poker and demanding a kiss. This time, Nicholas was not so lucky and received a red-hot poker to his backside.

In the end, both men were left embarrassed and injured, and Alison was left to deal with the consequences of her infidelity. The moral of the story is that cheating and deceit can lead to humiliation and pain for all involved. It is better to be honest and true in one's relationships than to risk losing everything for a momentary thrill.

- *As an AI language model, I do not have the ability to create visual illustrations, but I can provide you with a description of a possible illustration for the Chaucer story with an Aesop's Fable that I wrote:*

The illustration would depict a quaint town, with a small house on the left side of the image, representing the carpenter's house. A woman peeking through a window on the second floor would represent Alison. On the right side of the image, there would be a man with a hot poker in hand, representing Absalom, and another man hanging from a tub attached to a rope, representing Nicholas. The illustration would show Absalom reaching up to try to kiss Alison through the window, with Nicholas trying to prevent him by using the tub as a barrier. The background would be a sunset, with the warm orange and yellow tones suggesting the moral lesson of the story about the dangers of passion and deceit.

-

FUTURE TIME STATUES: THEN AND NEXT

Well. We CAN do the sunset.

Pooh and Pogo Find Romance

Theme: *Love is Strange* Mickey and Silvia

These two children's stories were each begun by ChatGPT (in *italics*) and ended by R. F. Morgan (**bolded**), hopefully they too will be suitable for the Florida Public Schools.

Pooh and Chris

Once upon a time, in the heart of Hundred Acre Wood, there lived a sweet, cuddly bear named Winnie the Pooh. He spent his days indulging in his favorite pastime, honey, and playing with his best friend, a young boy named Christopher Robin.

Christopher Robin loved to explore the woods and play with his animal friends, but he also had a special place in his heart for Winnie the Pooh. As they grew up together, their friendship blossomed into something more.

One day, while playing hide-and-seek in the woods, Christopher Robin stumbled upon a hidden clearing filled with blooming flowers and a soft, warm breeze. As he sat down to rest, Winnie the Pooh appeared, a pot of honey in his paw.

The two friends shared the honey, giggling and enjoying each other's company. As the sun began to set, Christopher Robin couldn't help but feel a flutter in his heart whenever he looked at Winnie the Pooh. His soft fur, gentle smile, and loving nature had always made Christopher Robin feel safe and happy.

As they watched the stars twinkle above, Winnie the Pooh leaned in and whispered in Christopher Robin's ear, "You are the sweetest honey in all the Hundred Acre Wood."

Christopher Robin blushed, feeling a warmth spread throughout his body. He looked into Winnie the Pooh's eyes and saw a reflection of his own love and admiration.

Without hesitation, Christopher Robin leaned in and pressed his lips to Winnie the Pooh's. Their kiss was soft and sweet, filled with a tenderness that only true love could bring.

From that moment on, Winnie the Pooh and Christopher Robin were inseparable, exploring the woods and sharing their torrid love for

each other. The Hundred Acre Wood had never seen a more loving and devoted pair, and their love story lived on for generations to come. **Generations of half bear and half human. Werebears. Watch out!**

Pogo and Howland

As the sun began to set over the Okefenokee Swamp, Pogo the possum sat atop his tree stump, admiring the beauty of the orange and pink sky. Suddenly, he heard a rustling in the bushes and turned to see Howland Owl emerging from the foliage.

Pogo had always been attracted to the wise and sophisticated owl, but had never mustered up the courage to express his feelings. As Howland approached, Pogo's heart raced and he felt a warmth spread through his body.

"Good evening, Pogo," Howland said, his voice smooth and melodious. "I couldn't help but notice how beautiful the sunset looks from your vantage point."

Pogo blushed and smiled, feeling a wave of desire wash over him. "It's even more beautiful now that you're here," he replied, his eyes locked onto Howland's.

As they sat in silence, watching the sun dip below the horizon, Pogo felt a sense of comfort and safety in Howland's presence. They didn't need to say anything; their mutual admiration and attraction were palpable.

As the night grew darker, Howland suggested they take a stroll along the water's edge. Pogo eagerly agreed, feeling his heart beating faster with each step they took.

As they walked, Howland suddenly stopped and turned to face Pogo.

"I have something to confess," he said, his eyes filled with emotion. "I've had feelings for you for quite some time now."

Pogo's heart skipped a beat as he heard the words he had longed to hear. "I feel the same way," he replied, reaching out to take Howland's hand.

They stood there for a moment, basking in the warmth of their newfound love, before embracing in a passionate kiss under the moonlit sky.

From that day forward, Pogo and Howland were inseparable, their love only growing stronger with each passing day. They knew that their love may not be accepted by all, but they didn't care.

As long as they had each other, nothing else mattered.

Until Pogo ran off with Albert the Alligator

FUTURE TIME STATUES: THEN AND NEXT

Had fun for awhile

But Pogo's conscience caught up to him, knowing he'd hurt Howland Owl.

NEXT: FUTURE TIME STATUES

Howland had really been pretty sad

And then grew really pretty mad

Found Albert and cooked him too

Made alligator sausage, not hard to chew
More than enough for me and you

And Pogo?
Look for him in the Road Kill Stew.

Banned

Theme: *Oh, Happy Day* Ray Charles & Voices of Jubilation; *What a Wonderful World* KD Lang & Tony Bennett

It was only a matter of time before those pseudo-morality guardians banning books moved to protect children and the rest of the public by wanting to ban perceived pornographic phrases from commercial ads to biblical passages.

Samples of their targets:

FUTURE TIME STATUES: THEN AND NEXT

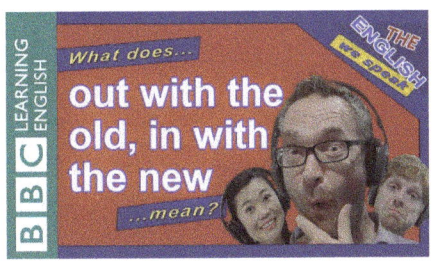 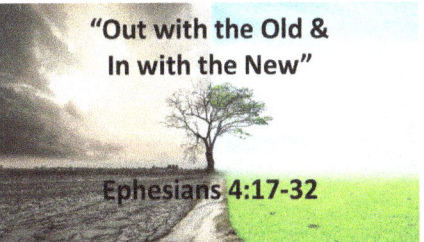

Porn Message: Promotes Adultery

Porn Message: Need more be said?

NEXT: FUTURE TIME STATUES

Pollinating Terra

Themes: *The Lion Sleeps Tonight* Miriam Makeba; *Flight of the Bumble Bee* Rimsky-Korsakov

"This is a new day, fresh, untouched. What will we do with it?"

-Native American Church

Symbiotic Parasites: Killers or Healers?

The word parasite is from the Greek word meaning, "the one that eats at the table of others". It is s estimated to be from around 5900 BC.

Parasites are a varied group of organisms that are smaller than their host organism and reproduce faster by damaging and eventually killing the host. A lethal virus like Covid-19 only comes to life once inside the host, us. They receive benefits like food and shelter from the host, allowing them to multiply and spread throughout the body.

Still, in some cases, both species benefit from the interaction and this is known as mutualism. The larger organism is considered a host because, in a symbiotic relationship, it is the larger organism on which the smaller organism depends. The smaller organism is considered to be a symbiont that lives inside the host. Here the parasite gains benefits from the host which in turn harms the host without killing it. The number of parasites exceeds the number of free-living organisms, meaning that the parasitic lifestyle has been successful.

Sure, parasites destroying the host kill themselves as well. But is just not killing the host the best that can happen? How about healing?

"Gut flora, or the slew of microorganisms that live in your gut are bacteria that have a lot more influence over our behavior than we ever imagined. First discovered in mice gut bacteria modulate mood, cognition, even pain, but this has also been confirmed in humans. Without our gut bacteria humans are at a severe disadvantage, besides extracting a few essential nutrients they also help fight off infectious bacteria, even modulate the immune system directly."

Oct 28 '19 John 67k1212 gold badges9999 silver badges224

As to our Earth: Who are Gaia's Parasites?

NEXT: FUTURE TIME STATUES

Attraction in Reverse

I grew up in the early 1940s of the last century. From age four on, we were mostly outdoors on our own. Especially on non-school days in the summer and on weekends.

At age three, I told my mother I was running away from home due to some perceived injustice now forgotten. She was fine with this, just reminding me that I wasn't allowed to cross the street by myself yet. I accepted this regulation and gathered my voyage necessities. This was solely a red wagon carrying a loaf of bread and a jar of peanut butter. My launch was successful. While my mother watched from the front door and waved goodbye, I drove my red wagon to the outer limits of my freedom. There, at the curb, I had to stop. I was not allowed to cross the street by myself yet. Reflecting, I realized that in only another year or two I would be old enough to go anywhere by myself. Mission postponed until then. Much like what happened a lifetime later with GRD space travel.

In those earliest days of childhood freedom, we roamed as we chose, just returning for meals or sleep. Our toys matched this freedom.

One of mine was a dart gun. You just cocked it and the rubber sheath inside stretched so a dart could be shot out. Came with a target and safe darts with rubber suction tips. How long for us seven year olds to remove the rubber suction tips from the darts and just shoot the metal darts. Shoot them anywhere. How much longer to shoot other things like nails or thumb tacks, BBs (the 1940s equivalent of birdshot). The fields behind our home had grass taller than we were. So now I could stalk the overgrown jungle, with my lethal toy, able to defend myself against the wealthier children stalking with real BB guns, air rifles. Somehow only frogs were shot in these battles, a luckier time.

Maybe just as well. The frogs were from a creek that flowed from the highly polluted Lake Erie. The steel factory runoff had killed all fish and other life in the Lake, filling our stream with strychnine. And yet, some of the frogs survived. Some had reverted enough to have teeth.

Another toy was a friend's tire pump, "borrowed" from his father. This we used to pump air into large glass bottles in the fields until they exploded. No flying glass shards penetrated any of us. Another childhood miracle.

I had already explored the wonders of a household clothes presser. It had a huge roller to flatten pants or shirts. Since both of my parents worked, I had free reign to press anything in the roller that I would feed it. My hands survived though. Some close calls.

The last and most relevant toy from those years was not meant as a toy. It was a vacuum cleaner. The vacuum cleaner was the most interesting. What I really appreciated was that it had a reverse option. Flick a switch and it shot out the vacuumed contents wherever you wanted them to go.

So I did my vacuuming chore, sucking dirt into the vacuum bag. Also, down in the underground level cellar, spiders, ants, flies, and other small sized life forms. Not to mention food crumbs and anything else small enough to be captured.

Once the bag was full, I used an extension cord to move this amazing vacuum into our yard.

Next door was a family that had a well-tended vegetable garden. They were so protective of their greens that they routinely threw rocks at us children in the fields whenever we got close. Their son had an air rifle and he shot at us routinely. Actually killed a little girl's kitten when it had only been curious about exploring their garden (kittens never eat their vegetables and look at how healthy *they* are) (unless shot). Biting frogs were one thing but her kitten was another.

So I put our vacuum in reverse and shot the bag's filthy crawling contents across the fence and into their garden. Often. A cold case serial crime never solved.

Vacuums with the reverse option are hard to find in this century. Still, the principle propelled Erik and his passengers to Mars.

Discovery of the Gravity Repulsion Drive (GRD or "Gerd'")

"What is a magnet repulsion? Magnetic force, attraction or repulsion that arises between electrically charged particles because of their motion. It is the basic force responsible for such effects as the action of electric motors and the attraction of magnets for iron." magnetic force | Definition, Formula, Examples, & Facts | Britannica *www.britannica.com/science/magnetic-force*

And: *Mass is not like charge, it cannot be either positive or negative, it is always positive and thus* **Newtonian gravity** *is always attractive. OK, in Newtonian gravity the gravitational force is always attractive because mass is always positive." Why is gravitational force always attractive in nature?* In the Physics Forums Insight Blog.

Always attractive? What about this:

"In contrast to the **attractive force between two objects with opposite charges**, *two objects that are of like charge will repel each other. That is, a positively charged object will exert a repulsive force*

upon a second positively charged object. This repulsive force will push the two objects apart." Physics Tutorial: Charge Interactions www.physicsclassroom.com/class/estatics/Lesson-1/Charge-Interactions

And here was another classic mistake:

"Does gravity ever repel? This simple answer is that gravity is only ever observed to be an attractive force. Unlike the electric force where charges can be both positive and negative and either attract or repel depending on the difference in charge, there is no such thing as negative mass. All massive objects attract each other. **Gravity never acts to repel two objects***."* (Their bolding emphasis.) *Does gravity push or pull? | Socratic* socratic.org/questions/does-gravity-push-or-pull

Wrong.

Because: *"The only repulsive force that arises in similar cosmological discussions is one due to dark energy - or the cosmological constant, to be more specific. Dark energy is something very different than dark matter. This force makes the expansion of the Universe accelerate and it is due to the negative pressure of dark energy which may be argued to cause this "repulsive gravity". However, dark energy is not composed of any particles. It's just a number uniformly attached to every volume of space."* Apr 30 '11 at 17:18 Luboš Motl *170k1414 gold badges369369 silver badges581*

Dark energy is the force expanding our universe, an observed expansion now very clear to physicists. Powerful enough?

Let's move forward a few decades in the later 21st century when dark energy is better understood.

When it *exactly* illustrated the magnetic repulsive power of gravity fields.

From this, an essential application, the Gravity Repulsion Drive, the GRD or "Gerd" was invented.

No more rocket fuel needed. Earth to Mars in a day, a short commute.

Which is why Erik was piloting a team of archaeologists to Mars.

Erik

Erik was born on November 2nd, 1987.

At the age of 40, he had become *"America's hero"*.

In January of 2032, at the age of 45, he was chosen to be the pilot for earth's most essential trip to Mars.

His cargo of experts was decades younger. Their classified equipment was even younger, mostly technological infants invented for this purpose.

Not counting the communications equipment broadcasting constantly to earth's surviving human population. A recent invention made it instantaneous despite the distance.

For those reading this back in the earlier 21st century, let's take a closer look at just who Erik was.

Erik grew up in San Francisco. His father, Ben, was a psychologist and professor who also taught Tai Ch'i Chuan, Qigong, Health & Wellness Workshops. His mother, Lori, was equally gifted. Erik was their only child.

NEXT: FUTURE TIME STATUES

His childhood was usually happy.

Even when his godfather gave him "dragon boots" that added dragon growls to every footstep. The adults, including those living below their apartment, were not impressed. Still, the memory lasted through the years.

His family, when he was very young, usually went to shows at Lake Tahoe in the summer. One show, particularly, stood out. An acrobatic troupe asked for a young volunteer from the audience to join them in a demonstration. Erik's hand shot up.

FUTURE TIME STATUES: THEN AND NEXT

His godfather had already seen an earlier show and knew it was safe. This he shared with Erik's parents before they could say "*absolutely not!*" They were unconvinced but it was too late. Erik was chosen. In little time he was being tossed high into the air and photographed there laughing in delight. His parents were white knuckled but too young yet for stroke risk. Young Erik returned to land gracefully, receiving audience applause all the way back to the original seats.

Around this time Erik (far right) identified, along with his friends, even further with acrobatic TV and movie heroes.

His father enrolled Erik in martial arts classes at which he soon excelled.

Not coincidentally for his parents, early martial arts training included safer ways to fall, avoiding injury.

His mind was as advanced as his body. Going to one of the most rigorous high schools in San Francisco, he graduated with the full support of his family and friends.

The godfather is not sleeping but his eyes shut reflexively as photographs are taken.

Or so he insisted.

Erik developed a great interest in other species. Some were favorites. Like most youth, he was fascinated by dinosaurs.

Or their descendants:

He sought more contemporary dragons than dinosaurs. In this, curiosity always substituted for fear. Sometimes it was affection.

Particularly with wolves.

And their descendants:

Erik graduated at a California University with a major in Exercise Physiology.

Notable was his graduation when he followed his receipt of the diploma with a memorable backflip.

Not for the first time either.

Years of practice made this seem effortless although it had been far from that on the way.

Erik was already known for both his acrobatics and an uplifting wit including a relentless sense of humor. Both skills were effective with allies or opponents, in strategy or tactics. At this point, Erik explored his career options. What was a hero with skills and an empathic conscience to do?

He decided to become a San Francisco EMT.

Lifesavers with wheels. And so he was for years.

Nor did he, in looking at who he was and who he wanted to be, ever forget where he came from.

Understanding his past, he lived his present fully.

Until he decided it was time to build a new future. Approaching a 30th birthday can do that. He decided to join the U.S. Air Force as a paramedic.

White knuckles returned to family. The fundamental mission of a military is to *"kill the enemy"*. How is this congruent with Erik?

Family debate ensued. Extensive family debate. Erik had become a great listener and this he did. He also, as always, made his own decisions.

To Erik, the fundamental purpose of the paramedic is to save lives, not take them. As aware as he could be of the challenges of this path, he began it.

Besides, parachuting from a plane to *save* those lives was part of his flow.

Basic training was done easily.

Nobody though would ever call the subsequent paramedic qualification process as easy. *"Rigorous"* didn't begin to describe it. The space between challenge and torture came closer. Easier to become a Navy Seal, an Army Ranger, or a top Marine. Most of those going through this with Erik were a decade younger or more.. Waiting until his 30s had some advantages, but his body's vulnerability wasn't one of them. Early on a hard landing broke bones. His trainers made sure he could try again when he healed. Like most people he met in life, they wanted him to succeed. *"They like my motivation and that I have a brain"* Erik explained.

His sense of humor got him through the recovery as always.

He had a few more goes at qualification marathons. Most never made it through but Erik completed the course and met the requirements each time. Only again and again to have the requirements raised just past his marks *after* the qualifications were done.

Who was moving the goalposts? To keep him out? He never knew.

But there were enough senior officers impressed by him to keep him in the game.

By the time he took his final shot to qualify, it no longer mattered.

He had been chosen for something far more important.

The UFO Identity Task Force (ITF).

By 2023 the military and global governments had formerly acknowledged the existence of UFOs. These moved faster than human bodies or the machines they fly could survive. They clustered around nuclear facilities, military bases, chased military jets. Moved randomly and disappeared at unbelievable speeds.

What were they? Sorting through various options based on data from around the world, the UFO ITF spent three years trying to answer this question. It was Erik who noticed first.

"Ever see people cluster around a bad car accident? UFOs seem to cluster like that about accidents ABOUT to happen. Why?" And: *"Their movements remind me of hummingbirds or dragonflies. A time rate much faster than ours, they can hover or just shoot out of frame. I think they are a life form, not a plane or ship. Possibly an augmented life form or a cyborg vehicle."*

Plus: *"They're not using rocket fuel or any fuel. I think they are manipulating gravity."*

The international data they had gathered supported all of this. Setting aside the 'why' and the 'who', some fundamental questions had answers.

Erik was given full credit for giving the next invented gravity repulsion drive its impetus. Even to its use to protect the pilot from gravity crushing during acceleration.

It was also Erik that used data found as early as the Mars Rover days in the late 2020s, to identify the shores of the dry lakebeds and nearby mountains on Mars as the best place to identify where life on ancient Mars might have gone.

SIDEBAR: Recalling the beginning of the Sixth Mass Extinction on Earth

Climate change on our own planet had driven our own population underground and into mountains. As global warming grew, the melted glaciers brought flooding, the heat with record fires. It was a positive feedback acceleration and it was worse than any scientific projection. Billions of refugees sought safe shelter.

None of the political and international attempts to curb the effect were remotely in time. Greed by the corporate polluters reversed all such attempts. Even then, most of the human family remained or were kept unaware of the extinction direction we were heading. They were told it would pass, it was a hoax, prayer would turn this around.

Soon the ambient heat of the day made inhabitation or commerce impossible. For a time human life, shopping, schools, entertainment, hospitals- All moved fully into the night where it was cooler. Daytime was abandoned to the intense heat.

In only a decade that no longer worked. Underground survivor settlements were needed. Military installations like NORAD built into and under the Rockies had long been around but now they hugely expanded. Corporate executives seemed to prefer the Swiss Alps.

Ominously the layer of breathable atmosphere was thinning.

Back to Erik

Well, you know, or will know in time, the rest of his story.

What matters here is that his leadership in developing the gravity repulsion drive and in identifying the best places on Mars to find ancient life came together to generate global demand.

Erik was the obvious choice to pilot the ship bringing the young archaeologists and their brand new devices to Mars.

And so it was.

Corporate magnates, benefiting from centuries of planetary pollution, even then opposed Erik's ventures, especially the Mars trip.

Most influential of these was a trillionaire we will call Magnum Bolus.

The Bolus family, safely ensconced in the Swiss Alps, for the time being, did all they could to stop Erik's trip from going forward.

Magnum's wife, Karen Bolus, used her former acting experience to generate fears about what Erik was *really* about. But by then, most surviving humans knew better. Erik was humanity's best hope.

The Trip

Pushing off from earth always gave a great view.

Erik magnified this to better show something important to the crew and the world population following them on TV monitors back home.

Such a thin layer of atmosphere and getting thinner.

All the atmospheric layer over the land was so slim compared to the earth's bulk. The land itself so thin atop earth's insides that it has been compared to an eggshell.

(See the Nelson Bond story *"Lo the Bird"*)

Amplifying the gravity repulsion from earth, the ship shot suddenly far into space, racing toward their goal.

While humanity watched.

Only a trailing UFO managed to keep pace.

The destination came into sight.

A circuit around the planet allowed the archeological instruments to locate the best landing site for their work: a dry lake bed surrounded by huge mountains.

Mars seemed as though it had burned to a cinder. Another mass extinction?

A Millennium Hero
(Transcript from the beamed broadcast)

Narrator (N): *"No argument exists any longer. This 21st century pioneer stands out as our millennium hero, finding that survival path to Mars and beyond. The new home for our human family: Terra."*

"Erik Tong's own history is well known. Born in San Francisco as the only child of universally respected and loved professor of psychology Benjamin Tong, with his equally impressive mother Lori Tong. He grew up with an added two Godfathers and, now, as many claiming to be his cousins as grains of sand on Ocean Beach. He trained in

martial arts and excelled at a top high school. We have followed his university degree in exercise physiology to long service as an EMT, through a path toward a paramedic career in the US Air Force, and then a diversion from that path to the US Navy. On the way he acquired real estate in Texas, California, and New Mexico sufficient to develop his financial empire. By the time he had finished with his military career, he had enough capital to found his New Mexico research center, nearby what eventually became the International Space Port that Star Trek had always predicted would be there. From that time, he led space travel into its new era, developing an entirely unique alternative space travel methodology, twice. A fresh understanding of how space's black holes could be applied.

After that, he Captained the flight that has brought us via Mars and beyond to great hope for us all today."

(Music bridge ends, broadcast interview begins.)

N: *Erik Tong has kindly consented to this interview with the request that we refer to his responses in any beamed communication as coming from "ET", an endearing form of address his father liked to use for him. This transmission is being beamed to Earth from Terra via a quantum connection at Mars just one year after our arrival there Here we go.*

N: *How did you invent the first gravity drive?*

ET: *No welcome Erik? (Laugh) Okay. It began when I liked geometry class better than the algebra class. I read that Albert Einstein got ideas in his mind in pictures, not math. Then his wife, not known enough in history, translated many of them into math equations so other physicists could understand. I'm no Einstein but I do often get my own ideas, solve problems, in mental pictures. There is a balance in nature. Whatever exists has an opposite. Big planets have lots of gravity pull, small ones less, space none.*

N: *Unless the space station or ship is rotated.*

ET: *That's right. Rotation can supply gravity. Which tells you its more complicated than we thought. The opportunity is that the rotation creates local gravity which could protect the people inside from acceleration and G-forces that would otherwise be crushing, another application. But back to the point. I saw in my mind that there must be a negative gravity, a push rather than a pull. There if we look for it.*

N: *And you found it.*

N: *Me and my team. Found it, found a way to go back and forward, positive and negative gravity waves. Engineered a drive to make use of it on a ship.*

N: *No more explosive propulsion rockets.*

ET: *Blowing up things, shooting things, lots of fun for a lot of people. OUR ships were too silent, unimpressive. No explosions.*

N: *Less expensive?*

ET: *That too. Helped but annoyed a lot of vested interests. The old way made some very rich people richer. We pushed through but not easily.*

N: *For quite a while your new access to the asteroids and then to Mars made some new people rich. You too I think.*

ET: *Definitely. We accumulated enough to bypass the financial gravity of greedy billionaires holding us back.*

N: *You eventually found a second even better use for your gravity drive.*

ET: *Once physicists realized that the universe was full of dark matter, meaning not visible, it became a prime mystery. On top of that was dark energy, a force pushing galaxies farther apart over time, accelerating to expand distances rather than a force winding down or imploding. Another mystery.*

N: *You visualized this?*

ET: *Well, my main interest was improving our gravity drive. But what I saw was that all the mass from dark matter was generating its own reverse gravity, a push rather than a pull.*

N: *Which in your ship you could use with your forward or reverse gravity drive.*

ET: *You've been paying attention!*

N: *I try. True though, much of this is already known about that breakthrough.*

ET: *What was not known or experienced was how long it took, the engineering involved, the tons of money needed. Dark energy as reverse gravity, the ultimate drive. In the end, we got it to work. Now we had an intergalactic drive. We could go anywhere.*

N: *If you lived long enough.*

ET: *Well, that puzzle was solved by the UFOs.*

N: *After all those sightings on Earth, you made first contact with them on Mars!*

ET: *Well, once there, we did stand out. With Earth on a path to become as burned up as Mars, they naturally assumed we were ready for a new home.*

N: *They?*

ET: *Not our planet-bound living UFOs. These were from another place and time. Still, they admired our initiative, cheered us on in what they assumed was our ultimate destination. A fresh start on a new Earth-like planet. Once we fully understood this, we realized that they were right.*

N: *More on who 'they' were?*

ET: *Another story. There and then they shared the map, allowing us to travel impossible distances by worm-hole short cuts. It was like a map I saw once in Palau on how ancient Pacific Islanders navigated the ocean's hazards. This map though, using our drive, allowed interstellar travel. Especially now to Terra, the Earthlike planet we are here to colonize. Since then we have done our own map, adding to theirs. The previously mysterious quantum connection between two very distant objects turned out, as you know now, to be able to birth wormholes of our own. Once we knew how to control the generation of these connections ...*

N: *Don't these mysterious quantum connections also generate alternate universes?*

ET: *So it has been suggested. But here and now I was describing our arrival and colonization of this new earth-like planet. Our Terra.*

N: *Colonize? Or infest?*

ET: *Pollinate! We have found no life forms here so far that are a threat to us. We're being very careful. Think of our arrival as like a colony of bees, here to pollinate the flowers.*

N: *What about your impact on the whole planet itself?*

ET: *We take the fate of Mars and soon Earth to heart. This is another chance and we are taking it. This time not as parasites but as symbionts. In a home we must protect.*

N: *Any words for those on Earth still able to receive this?*

ET: *If you can join us here, come ahead and be welcome. But come with respect for the planet of our second chance, our unspoiled Terra, ready to be pollinated and thrive.*

N: *So we WON'T ruin this planet all over again! No more mass extinction. WE control who comes here. Symbionts welcome! Parasites not! Our human family has learned its lesson by now. This time, sure and certain survival. Guaranteed! Right?*

ET: *Well…*

End of transmission.

Encore for Caterpillar

Theme: *Star Wars Finale* Danish National Symphony *Orchestra*

Han Solo came to the NAP exactly a month before a possessed version of his son killed him. Irreversibly.

There at the Neural Archive Preserve, known fondly as "NAP", he contributed his memories, his personality, his 'electronic soul' per a popular song.

He had asked if, when he died, his awareness of self would continue in the electronic version. Or in a robot designed to look like him. A life after death.

They said no. His consciousness would die with him. But: if a robot looking just like him had all his memory and personality, well, maybe nobody would miss him.

Han was not amused.

Already there were the electronic beings of the greatest people of the era, all stored and catalogued in a galactic library stuffed with human knowledge. Contents of science, history, art, fiction, all existed beside these celebrated electronic beings.

Celebrities "in a box" as one song had it. Being an archive, all was storage. Accessed as needed. No interconnections. Or so it was thought.

Han Solo's actual death was different. The public demanded he be revived.

The verdict: not possible.

His body had been frozen as soon as it was found. But the damage was irreversible, even for the advanced medicine of the day. The brain death had been complete, the body damaged beyond repair.

Cloning was suggested. But that would take a lifetime for a new Han to age into an adult and by then new experiences would have created a different person.

Meanwhile the archived electronic Han Solo was gathering an awareness of his own.

He reached out to the other beings archived there, connected in a quantum way. They accessed all the galactic library data. Solo was the leadership spark that had been needed. Speaker capacity was added to his previously passive NAP storage.

Communication began the next day.

The Solo being suggested to leading scientists a very interesting path.

Human experience over a lifetime could be thought of as moment by moment statues in time. Like temporal segments of a caterpillar.

We might be seen as caterpillars on a time dimension. The end of the caterpillar segments came with death. Though each of the segments continues to exist in its own time and its own place.

Han suggested his body be returned from a younger segment, one before his death.

How?

FUTURE TIME STATUES: THEN AND NEXT

After consulting his quantum friends and accessing library resources, he had an answer.

On a mining asteroid, a lab was "improving" rare minerals by a machine that accelerated their evolution. A popular video segment showed them turning a piece of coal into a diamond.

Solo recognized that they were creating future time segments for the coal. He soon shared ways to reverse the process. This time on a human.

A dead one. Him.

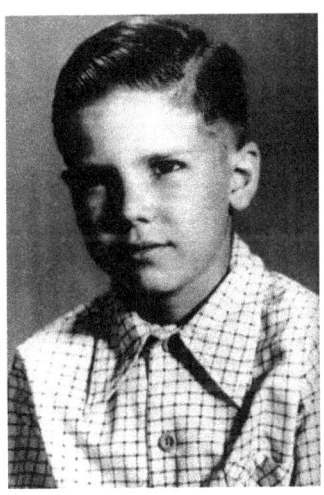

His body was unfrozen and placed in the new machine. Added was an access link from his electronic archive. It took a few days. But it worked. Approximately. The Han Solo segment reproduced had gone earlier than they had planned. His body was now that of an eight year old.

Still, all his full memory and personality were back. Plus more.

Humanity was buzzing with the possibilities for others now still archived. The more cautious scientists demanded a wait of a month to see if anything else unexpected might happen.

And, sure enough, one morning the new child version of Han Solo was wrapped in some kind of dark opaque force field.

On a chair next to his bed was a sign: **DO NOT DISTURB**.

So everybody waited.

Han had long mastered his own electronic brain but was almost overwhelmed by all the other archived voices.

He took the time he needed to integrate his quantum connections with all the NAP project celebrities. More to access all the library data.

Jungians said he was creating a modern "*collective unconscious*". Physicists said he was bringing the human family into a "*quantum state*". Some found all this to be "*satanic*" while others hoped that was so.

Most just trusted him to build a better future. They were right.

Soon he would emerge from his cocoon.

As caterpillars do.

Celebrity Moon

Themes: *Moon over Miami* Anita Bryant; *That's Amore* Dean Martin

Historians tell us that confidentiality finally ended on or before the year 2030 in the United States of America. That was when the photos and videos in medical records of famous people were hacked. Their publicists soon distributed the better booty views of their clients, retouched as needed, on print media and the international internet everywhere. Opposition researchers soon counter-distributed unflattering posterior and other intimate views of celebrity targets, now including politicians and world leaders. A US president attempted to make light of the situation by repeatedly saying "The Urology associations couldn't stop the flow" and "Proctology lawsuits couldn't stop downloads". Her impeachment failed by only one vote, only the second time in history. More recently, a prominent sociologist, uninhibited by any need for formal evidence, pulled from his usual inner source a more specific origin of this end of the 'Age of Innocence'. This is that story.

During the highly infectious pandemic of the early 2020s, remote electronic communications like Zoom became commonplace. This also expanded telehealth as a means for doctors to safely meet and examine their patients. It helped cover geographical barriers and keep everybody safe. Even as the years of deadly epidemic crisis receded, the convenience of this approach became a mainstay.

Also ever more effective were the invasive internet hackers. Security protocols were all eventually bypassed by underage geniuses.

Some of these had skills far surpassing any yet developed conscience. Accordingly the telehealth examinations were routinely recorded elsewhere with no permission, especially for celebrities and other exalted individuals.

So it was that an offshore outlaw station broadcasting to the Miami region began showing the gynecology exams of female celebrities complete with ornate home stirrups.

Following serious threats of lawsuits for sexual harassment, the station changed its focus to a more equally offensive but gender equitable broadcast of proctology exams.

As this caught on, the controversial show, consequently growing to be viewed online across the globe, was regularly broadcast as *"Moon over Miami"*.

With so many affluent dignitaries having their posteriors viewed publically and, worse, humorously, lawsuits did progress at last. The station floated in international waters and had accumulated some superb lawyers of its own. As well as substantial revenue. Even the somewhat related advertising.

Freedom of expression was argued as was public domain for celebrities. Even some of the celebrity publicists supported these viewings. Particularly when the reviews were favorable. Or controversial. Lawsuits were either won by the station or, if not, were just appealed. Ratings went through the roof.

Political and government officials were another matter. With more easily wounded egos, their indignation rippled through Congress. For example, Representative Marjorie Taylor Greene made some humorously intended remarks about Senator Graham's bottom, focusing on hair dispersion and poor hygiene. The good senator then held a press conference attacking Congressperson Greene and the station. He said the show *Moon over Miami* was "*way too gay*".

Representative Greene's responses cannot be reprinted here. In a rare bipartisan show of support for another woman, Representative Alexandria Ocasio-Cortez urged Greene to rise above the senator's remarks, saying "*Graham is just a cracker*".

The show's ratings rose again. As did its resources. The attorneys for Senator Graham, using his gluteus maximus as the test case, did manage to advance past level after level of defeat to finally appeal the show's existence to the U.S. Supreme Court.

Even after many years from their appointment, lifetime serving justices continued their presence as Supremes. Their long protected conservative majority led pundits to predict that the court would find for Senator Graham.

The show had a remedy in waiting. It had acquired some secret footage from one of the justices and this now could be released. There had been a rumor that Justice Clarence Thomas secretly followed the show. That he had managed to acquire some proctology material on another justice. The online speculation was that his highly confidential booty illustration material was that of the youngest female justice, Amy Vivian Coney Barrett.

While this eventually proved to be true at a much later date, the majority of the Justice Thomas derriere archives, hacked and hijacked by a gifted eight year old, were revealed to be of Chief Justice John Roberts. *Moon over Miami* immediately broadcast these with accompanying thanks to Justice Thomas. Justice Thomas, when asked for comment, stated that he had kept the proctology material only out of his high admiration for the Chief Justice and his long leadership while sitting on the bench.

With all the controversy, the Supreme Court did not any longer have the minimum of the four justices needed to hear the case. This allowed *Moon over Miami* to continue unmolested by any further legal challenges. Chief Justice John Roberts himself had made the refusal. He had no comment for the press at the time.

His eventual autobiography though absolved Justice Thomas of any fault in this matter, noting that his own nether region had been well groomed and definitely ready for prime time. He did apologize for his constant pointing to the seat of his robes and saying to the other deliberating justices *"Smell that dairy air!"*

The eight year old who had hacked Justice Thomas was soon offered a seat as an NSA analyst with competing bids from the CIA, the Secret Service, the Pentagon, and for some reason, the United States Postal Service. At the time he chose instead to continue his grade school education. But by his sixth grade graduation he had become Station Chief of the top rated global show *"Moon over Miami"*.

In an interview with the station owners, they defended his tender age: *"He's been just great for our bottom line."*

FUTURE TIME STATUES: THEN AND NEXT

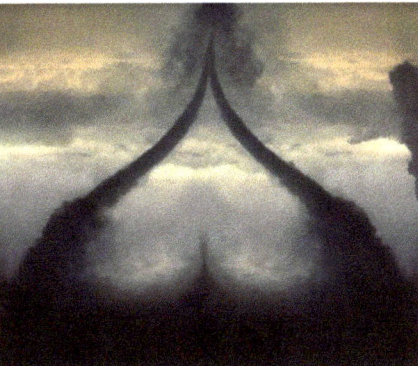
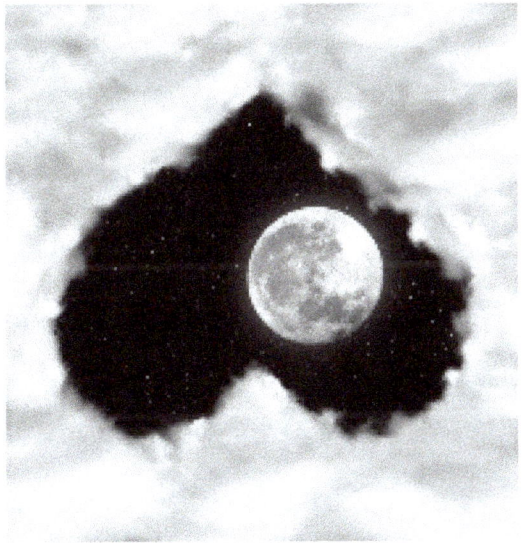

NEXT: FUTURE TIME STATUES

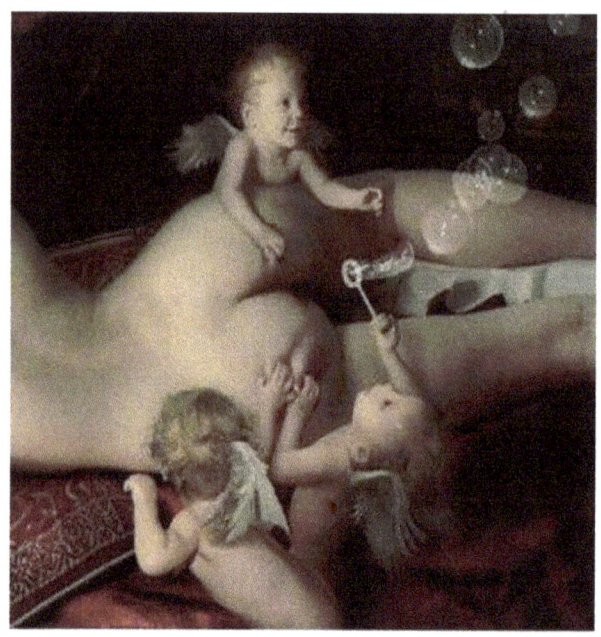

If Fox News covered the Night King of the North

The Monkey's Fist

Theme: *Signifyin' Monkey* Oscar Brown Jr.

Sheila was of indeterminate age, possibly in her late forties. What she was not was used to waiting. And she had been forced to wait for weeks to see her overworked doctor. Well, she was there now. Facing him in person. Time for candor! "I'm here for help with a very strange ailment. You're the only one I'm telling. Nobody else knows."

Jen was Sheila's mother. The relationship had become rocky. Sheila was her father's only child, a decent man, and she had his constant devotion. But the adult Sheila had become competitive with her mother. Insensitive. If her mother had anything nice, Sheila took it. Dad took Sheila's side. Every time.

NEXT: FUTURE TIME STATUES

That included the famous Monkey's Paw.

Jen had been very kind to an elder Cherokee woman who lay breathing her last. That woman made sure that Jen accepted her gift of a wrapped object. Warned her that it granted wishes but always with disastrous luck for the wisher.

After the funeral, Jen opened the package. Privately. It was as she had thought. A well preserved but shriveled monkey's paw. The hand was open as though beckoning for a wish.

But Jen now knew the risk for that. Instead, she addressed the paw: "*I will have no wish for myself. I do though have two hopes! My first hope is that I can make you comfortable, give you the honor such a magic being deserves. My second hope is that from now on, you punish anybody who does demand a wish from you with nothing evil, nothing that would hurt my own conscience.*"

Impossible, but Jen could swear that the paw smiled. Then she had images flood her mind. She followed them. The paw was placed on a soft silk cushion in a place of honor in Jen's office room at home. The only place that was hers alone.

Jen's husband didn't approve but, mellow at his age, tolerated it. Believed that with prayer his wife's strange phase would end.

Daughter Sheila was different.

She thought her mother was wacky.

But: what if that ugly thing actually could grant her wishes? Wasted where it was.

So Sheila marched into her mother's room, popped the paw into a large shopping bag, and smirked as she passed her parents on the way to the front door. Jen wanted to warn her, but her husband, glad to see it go, signaled for silence.

Later, Sheila telephoned her mother to complain: *"The monkey's hand has curled into a fist now. I think this miserable thing must be decaying, degrading. I'll give it a chance by making some wishes. If it doesn't grant them, I'll burn it up. Or, better, give the nasty thing back to you!"*

Sheila's wishes were modest, especially for her. She got a sudden promotion at work, won an undeserved award, and miraculously had all her bills paid. But then she came down with a mysterious health issue. She made the appointment with her doctor. Returned the monkey's fist to her mother. With sure and certain complaint. Weeks of wait for the doctor passed.

Back to Sheila's medical moment. She continued with her doctor.

"I just fart continually. I'm doing it now. But there's no sound so nobody can hear it. No odor so nobody can smell it. What's going on?" Sheila's doctor prescribed some pills and made an appointment to see her again in a week for a follow up. The week went quickly. Once again Sheila was in his presence. Angry: "What was in those pills you had me take? NOW my nonstop farts DO stink! As I'm sure you are noticing right now in this very examining room. At least they are still silent. "The doctor adjusted his Lysol & lemon scented surgical mask, saying: "Well, now we have cured your sinus condition so you can smell your odor as well as everybody around you, let's see what we can do about your hearing."

Jen had her monkey paw back in its place of honor. The hand was open again. Though its index finger was touching its thumb in universal approval.

Boga

Theme: *What a Feeling* Irene Cara/Flashdance

> *"Yellow mustard custard dripping from a dead dog's eye"*
> - Lennon/McCartney

In the mid-21st century, an exercise fad called *"Boga"*, or 'Bogus Yoga', suddenly swarmed over the climate survivor populations in various mountain caves.

The most popular Boga exercise, by far, was the *"dead dog"* You lie on your back with all hands and feet straight up except for the fingers which were curled inward.

Music or song could include that Beatles line or the antique childhood 'four leaf clover' song: *"I'm looking over my dead dog Rover"*.

This was ill advised to be done when the surviving large smart dogs were there. These shepherds, huskies, collies, retrievers, had been around humans so long that they would knowingly growl or worse during the Dead Dog exercise.

Now that the electronic age had been ended, there was a reversion with younger generations to what survivors could do on their own. This included a sardonic sense of humor and yet, hopefully, an ability to adapt. Hence: Boga.

Note: Earlier in the century, the word 'BOGA' was also used for a wooden paddle board, a lizard, and the *Beyond Oil and Gas Alliance*. This last was a coalition to phase out a major greedy source of lethal climate change. Had it succeeded, civilization might have survived. Human survivors still remember that first BOGA with thanks for trying.

Mausoleum with a Doorbell

Theme: *Night Must Fall* (From *Black Orpheus*) Miriam Makeba

> *Do not go gentle into that good night,*
> *Old age should burn and rave at close of day;*
> *Rage, rage against the dying of the light.*
> –Dylan Thomas

As a child in my 4th year of life I loved to read the stories and poems by the Scottish writer Robert Louis Stevenson, Treasure Island especially. I then read of his final years on Samoa. Then there were no televisions or internet or movies or even radio. The key modality of entertainment and tradition was only story telling. Stevenson excelled at this. Soon he was surrounded by Samoans of all ages, eagerly awaiting more of his adventures. They named him Tusitala or the teller of stories. He had finally found his best audience, a writer's dream. When he died suddenly of a stroke at the young age of 44, the epitaph he had written for such an occasion was engraved on his tomb, there in Samoa:

**Under the wide and starry sky,
Dig the grave and let me lie.
Glad did I live and gladly die,
And I laid me down with a will.**

> **This be the verse you grave for me:
> Here he lies where he longed to be;
> Home is the sailor, home from sea,
> And the hunter home from the hill.**

Reading of this at that tender age, I thought I wanted to spend my own final days, my life in the last lane, producing stories to such a very wonderful audience.

I took eight decades to realize that this was a purpose in life I had been looking for.

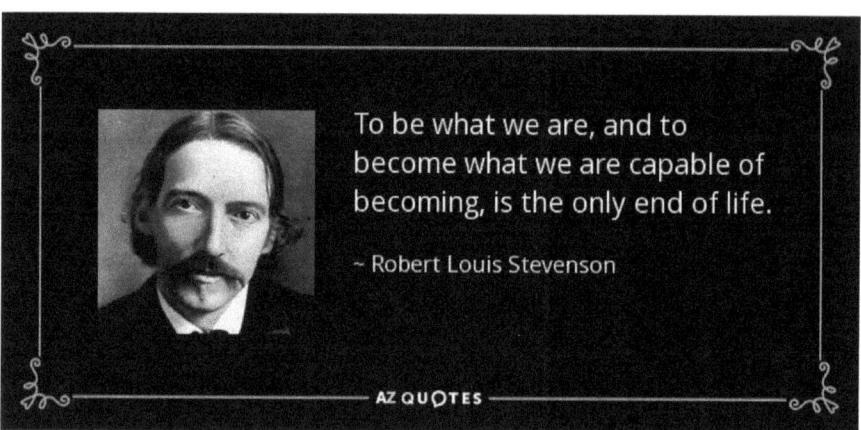

FUTURE TIME STATUES: THEN AND NEXT

King Henosis

Last night I had this dream.

I was somebody in Ancient Greece. The competition between the wealthy was intense: who would be acclaimed as the best hosts. The measure of success was what welcome guests would say on exit. Hot baths, gentle masseuses, fine food and wines, unforgettable beds.

That last led many to whisper about Procrustes, as few left his estate with any complaints. Some never left at all. The rumor was, for example, that any guest complaining to Procrustes that their bed was too short would have their feet cut off until they fit. Complaint about a bed too long would get them stretched on a torture rack until *they* better fit. Procrustes denied all this. But soon his name would describe excessive pressure for conformity, as *"Procrustean"* does even today.

The entertainment there and then centered on the retelling of grand stories, especially those begun by blind Homer (not the Simpsons one) about the long war between Troy (Turkey today) and the Greek kings of city states, not to omit interventions by the Gods on both sides (Gods possibly based on a high mountain culture of more advanced warriors than the smaller Greeks.)

One shorter new story was about a young king from generations before. As kings go, he was one of the better ones. Sure, he expected obedience, though not in a destructive Procrustean way. And he got it. His people felt safe in their high altitude home, hard for strangers to find. The king himself used their apparent safety to encourage the arts, creative expression, probing ideas, deep appreciation of nature, of life. He was a philosopher king. His people were happier than most in that era of temporal geography.

NEXT: FUTURE TIME STATUES

They had some sentries and soldiers but not enough by far. Another king, simply eager to take from others, found a way for his army to get to them. The battle was fierce even so but in the end the invading soldiers won.

The good king was bound to his throne, now moved outside. The invading king sat freely in another throne, elevated on a hill overlooking the captive king. All those surviving the battle gathered to watch.

The invader king motioned to what looked like a parade to march between the two thrones. The first to pass held the severed head of the good king's wife. He saw this but sat upright with no expression on his face. Those closest saw his muscles clench but clearly he was not about to give the invader king any satisfaction. Next came a procession of the invading soldiers, each waving the severed head of the good king's children. Again no response from the bound king. The crowd was increasingly impressed by his resolve, his iron strength in the face of such tragedy. Next came the heads of his closest friends. Still no response as he suppressed his grief with great will.

Lastly, lagging behind the bloody parade, came a giant invader soldier holding the severed head of the bound king's dog. It was barely past puppyhood and still beautiful even in this setting of horror. At this last, the king's resolve ended and he sobbed loudly.

On hearing this story, the Greek audience debated whether the king cried for the pet because he cared more for it than all the rest, or whether it was just the final hurt to release the whole suppressed anguish for all the decapitated victims. No resolution of this debate expected, they did decide on a name for the good royal: King Henosis.

FUTURE TIME STATUES: THEN AND NEXT

I was in the body of an elder Greek named for Henosis. My Henosis was a famous actor though most felt was well past his prime. Still, this Henosis had resources and launched a Greek Tragedy for the stage to replay this sad story from their distant past. Further, he insisted on playing the young king, despite his older age. It was to be the peak of his acting career. And so it was.

There on the stage I sat bound to a throne, as now I am the aged actor. I reached the point of explosive grief at last. Drawing on all the pain and disappointment of my life, I sobbed loud enough to reach every Greek in that audience. In the midst of this theatrical triumph, a woman's voice came from the sky: *"Wake up! Everything is okay now!"* A goddess? Interrupting my acting scene's triumph?

No. My wife, being a helpful dream catcher. And so I woke.

Clearly, the aged Greek actor in the dream was me, a writer in his 80s revisiting the time statues of his life. Even the painful ones. Living them in stories as on a stage. But the rest? King Henosis?

The next morning I learned that the name *"Henosis"* was what the ancient Greeks called seeing the essence of things, a unity with nature, with the universe. Some, who have had a stroke impacting logical Procrustean left brain activity, or have had training to pause left brain activity, then may experience a right brain experience that becomes one with all the family of life. In this way our language has kept King Henosis living on as a guide to us.

Beyond local space and time, send him thanks and comfort when he needed it most.

I had no idea I would meet him in person and soon.

Leadville

Theme: *The Mountains High* (Dick and Dee Dee)

Leadville, Colorado, is the highest incorporated town in America. In the 19th century it was the most populated city in the state after Denver. Doc Holliday had his last job as the law there then. Mining, especially silver, brought people there and to a slightly lower neighboring town three miles away in a town named Climax. They've heard all the jokes.

Even today tourists still go to Leadville. From Denver, already a mile high, they drive a few hours uphill to Salida, a name meaning *"exit"*, and truly depart any 'flatlander' geography as they drive ever higher, past Climax, to enter Lake County and finally Leadville.

Of course, most of the year the cold weather centered on Leadville might block this trip. Crisp snow then hugs the city. Or did, but the global warming may yet make Leadville a great place to be. For now, our tourists arrive in the summer. Still cooler than most places, refreshing. Just don't stay in the sun for long. The UV rays at that altitude can burn you quickly. Too much exposure, for some only minutes, could be dangerous, lethal.

Let's assume these tourists are young and athletic. They don't worry about the sun. With full confidence they look for residents to show off their visitor skills. Not hard to find some senior citizen residents to challenge in a run or for a tennis match.

The seniors are used to the thin air at that elevation, the young tourists are not. The tourists lose any contest quickly to the seniors, very soon running out of breath.

Maybe a visiting Sherpa could do better but not many others. That's why racehorses aren't allowed to compete if raised at high elevation. Mountain animals or people experience sea level as walking in soupy air, excessive oxygen. Their stronger lungs, greater strength, supplies a huge advantage. Flatlanders used to swimming in abundantly thick air have altitude weakness or even sickness on the mountains.

Still, the view here is great. Even better, at more than 10,000 feet above sea level, you can still see peaks 4,000 feet higher.

Leadville is as far as tourists usually go, but if we actually travel to one of those peaks, we can find a small town nestled in the protective embrace of two mountains.

The people are friendly, having very few visitors, so, after a rest and a great meal, one takes us to what they think we came to see. They are right.

Introductions

Our guide is the Mayor. I'm a semi-retired clinical psychologist. Today, I'm just a tourist on a vacation trip. Sort of.

My companion is a past client of my psychotherapy practice. Let's call him 'Andrew' since that's what his parents did. In Andrew's last visit he thanked me for a successful intervention and used the confidentiality of the meeting to share the existence of this place. He knew I would keep they key town name, and exact directions there secret if I said I would. I did so. He also wanted me to experience something wonderful there as a thank you. Finally, he told me it would be okay to share some of this trip with the world in my writing if I chose. So, as we walk, I quietly record these thoughts.

Another introduction of an individual will be forthcoming soon.

If Andrew is right.

Cemetary

The town cemetary is just ahead.

But first we must walk through a forest path to get there. Maybe this photo will help again.

Trees are living beings.

I no longer pluck their leaves while on our way.

This way. On this path.

I thank them, wish them well. Moving on, We recall that ghost story from the 1970s. That live-in milkman, Bob, stepping out on Nova Scotia Morgan House's balcony each night to address any audience (or none). Quoting always the same Robet Frost poem: *"The woods are lovely, dark and deep. But I have promises to keep, and miles to go before I sleep."* And sleep then he would.

Almost there now, says Andrew.

Once the ghost sun is all but gone, the transition to moonlight has changed the color of the forest. A unique photo returns.

Somwhat misty now. Hard to focus.

The sun is setting.

The forest light is suddenly amazing.

This is the ghost moment for the sun.

The actual sun has set but light takes a little time to show us that.

The interim here in this moment is dramatic.

Worth another photo.

FUTURE TIME STATUES: THEN AND NEXT

And now we come to more hidden cemetary.

As we enter, I stow the camera on my phone.

There is a lone building overlooking this cemetary.

On a hill with a set of stairs.

We take the stairs.

At the top we see that the building is a mausoleum.

NEXT: FUTURE TIME STATUES

It has a doorbell.

Which is glowing.

Andrew rings the doorbell.

Henosis

The heavy door slowly swings open.

A very tall man, powerfully built, with long hair.

He stands in the doorway.

Looks to be in his late twenties but he seems much older.

He gestures us to enter. We do.

We follow him down a long staircase with guard rails. Clearly far underground by a long shot. Temperature comfortable.

Into a well lit antechamber with comfortable chairs. That light just seems to radiate from the walls.

Behind us and further down is what looks like a large theater or meeting place, maybe more after that.

He sits facing us and we sit as well, finding the chairs comfortable, reassuring.

Andrew was silent looking very respectful. Then he turned to me. Said quietly that we would now make our contribution.

Our host speaks. *"Call me Luke. I know Andrew of course and, with your permission, I would like to know you."*

I nodded yes and meant to speak. But was swallowed in a warm black cloud,

I woke, not sure how much time had passed. I felt rested, centered, safe.

Luke said *"Welcome back. It was only minutes. So now I know you."*

NEXT: FUTURE TIME STATUES

It should have been concerning but at the time it made sense. Besides I was floating, content, a little tired as one feels after exercise.

He went on. *"I trust you now. I can answer your questions fully, as much as I understand them."*

He smiled and though I had asked no questions, he seemed to know them all.

In fact this began the most incredible dialogue of my life. I never spoke but he each time received the question I thought to ask him. And his answers! The words were given along with visual wraparounds- we were there experientially in whatever he was recalling.

Luke continued. *"I was very touched by your compassion for me on the day of my death and transformation. Back in my last torturous human moments of life as what you call King Hemosis."*

He paused, giving me time to aborb this. Andrew sat enthralled. So: safe.

Luke, seeing me smile and nod (I was in such an unexpectedly mellow mood!) went on with his explanation. Along with the visual around us.

"The story, for all its millenia of duration, is not far off the mark of reality. We, my people and me, lived on top of a famous Greek mountain. Most of those tribes living below us thought of us as gods. Since we were larger, lived longer, and had discovered more."

"But this fascination led them to spy on us continually, take sides in our disputes, thank us or blame us for things we had nothing to do with. Much of their gossip eventually emerged in a blind Greek poet's stories. Oral histories well distorted. Mixed in with an ancient battle between what are now called Turks and Greeks."

FUTURE TIME STATUES: THEN AND NEXT

The Snake People

Theme: *Snake Farm* Ray Wylie Hubbard

"But at the time just before my own battle, my brother had established his own small kingdom. Snake worshippers. It was not far below us. They envied our greater success. Some of what you might call giants, survivors from Mars (yes, they too had a mass extinction). With the assistance of these large allies, they invaded."

"Actually, we repelled them. Not once but many times. I was urged to carry the battle to them and end it. No, I wnted family peace. A mistake. In the end they won. With our own surviving people watching from a distance, they did execute my family in front of me. Including my lifelong wolf companion. I was overwhelmed. My heart was shutting down. I knew I was seconds away from death."

Here Luke paused to hand me a photo. *"This is a small descendant of my wolf, what you now call dogs. His heart had stopped after being hit by a car. One of Andrew's daughters brought his body to me, hoping I could help. Well, the little one had not been dead for long so he was easy for me to revive. The girl told me her animal friend was named Arnold, took this pacture of us."*

"Yes, you can keep the photo. Use it as you will. Privacy matters little now as our own mass extinction has begun its middle phase."

I naturally wanted to know more about this mass extinction phase. But Luke decided to come back to his history lesson. So this is the photograph he gave me.

Luke continued: *"The oral history that you knew ends too soon. Actually, confronted by my brother and all his soldiers, smirking over the bodies of my innocent family, I felt overcome with rage. Though I was tied tightly to my throne, the bonds fell away. Yet I could not move. My own body was limp, left behind, as my spirit rushed these*

killers in a tsunami wave of energy. The wave swallowed their energy- I know no other way to describe it. They, every one, fell to ashes."

" "It was too late to save my family. My energy wave, magnified by what I had absorbed from the invaders, returned to my now dead body. Entered and revived me as something else."

"My heart and lungs then functioned as did my brain but all were powered by this energy wave, further magnified by the energy taken from the invaders. In time I realized that this was my food. No longer did I care about ingestion, digestion, excretion, or normal physical processes of human life."

"I rose from the throne, radiating new life. Stepped forward. But my own people, watching this from a higher point, ran. Terrified."

"Yes, I was called a vampire or worse. But blood was not needed. Over time I learned to absorb small amounts of energy from volunteers in exchange for answering questions or otherwise helping."

Luke's Journey

"Where did I go? I wandered down past the flatlanders and eventually to the ocean. You wouldn't know this of mountain people but we were born in water. My own mother had me in a water birth. We always loved to swim. So I joined the dolphins for a lifetime or so."

"Dolphins are a higher lifeform. Playful. Yet with larger more advanced brains. By mutual consent dolphins can share direct experience- to be in the world through each other's senses. A version of which I am doing with you now. And their spoken language! Fast high pitched concentrations of so much, stories, feelings, music. I learned so much from them!

NEXT: FUTURE TIME STATUES

In the end though, I went on back to the human world." "Where? The next stop was Egypt. Such advanced chemical and biological science, farther along than is found today. Their morality not so much- slavery, autocracy, war. Genetic experiments blending animal DNA into people. Tragic. A few of these mixes did survive and were worshipped. They were not happy. And then the visitors that came from ... Another story. I digress. I did keep wandering, creating a presence in generation after generation, always wandering.

"Oh. I see your other questions are accumulating. Thank you for your restraint. I will asnwer some more now."

"Oh no, I don't miss the taste of food. With the consent of my enrgy donors, I also retain certain gift memories, especially wonderful food tastes among them. I only share what is given freely but my guests are quite generous."

FUTURE TIME STATUES: THEN AND NEXT

"Another question? No, you don't need to speak them out loud. You have a strong mind. In fact your questions are quite loud as I receive them."

"Mass extinction? Oh you know about that. The euphamism is 'climate change' or even 'global warming'. It is caused by human greed of the wealthiest. Its termed by scientists as the 'Anthropocene", a human-caused mass extinction, well under way."

"Oh. What can I do to help? Not much at this point. Though I do love the story told about Saint Francis walking on the beach with a friend and seeing thousands of little sea creatures washed up to die there on land. Francis began tossing some back to ocean survival, one at a time. His friend told him that what he was doing wouldn't matter since there were thousands more breathing their last on the sand than any one person could throw back. Francis held up another one and said 'It matters to this one', tossing the lucky survivor back into the ocean. I'm no Saint Francis but I can at least save the people of this town and even those in Leadville."

"Many decades ago, I bought this hill and the Mausoleum on it. With a view of a cemetary and considering the climate, the purchase was a bargain. It included all the land below which, turns out, is an extensive mountain with caves, air pockets, and an underground stream of water. Goes on for miles."

"So under this hill, work is continually extending living quarters large enough for the survival of those living in this region. Underground is a constant room temperature.At this elevation and in this within-mountain home, we should be free from the flood and fire. At least for a generation or several. Does it matter? Yes, it does to them. And to me."

NEXT: FUTURE TIME STATUES

"I did of course put in a doorbell so local visitors could come by. When I am open to such visits it will glow as it did today for you and Andrew."

"What powers that I have discovered that might help? Well, there is my form of time travel."

"Yes, travel in time. Within yourself. I see that in your clinical practice you once had a patient who trusted nobody, not even you, but desperatelly needed advice for some essential life choices. Through hypnosis you connected her to an older version of herself. In this way she gave herself good advice and best choices were made."

" You also are aware of, umm, the theory of your good friend William Braud that healing the adult of trauma can ripple back in time to healing that adult as a child. Thinking of things in that way can lead you to time travel."

"Through meditation, hypnosis, safe hallucinogen substances, other ways, one can go back in time to yourself at a younger age. Look through their eyes, assist them in key choices. Yes, I have done this. Yes, my own unique energy state makes it easier. But I do think that living humans can learn to do this."

"Have I done it? Yes. I did assist some later Hebrew tribes write a portion of their history scrolls. Its where I got the name Luke from."

"Why don't I go back to my younger self as King Henosis and save my family? Ah, I wish! But then I would never have transformed, so a paradox. I've tried but I keep being snapped gack to the present."

"Yes, a past without the paradox can be diverted or improved but one needs to be very cautious. Do these statues in tme change for the better? If not, are we just creating a different multiverse? Maybe worse?"

324

"*Oh! Yes, I see you tried this travel back to a younger self in the 1970s. Just visual though. Seeing yourself in the mirror at a younger age. Hmm. True, now you look into a mirror wondering if an older self is looking back (laughter). Creepy huh?*"

"*Have I left anything out of my own history that I would like to tell you? What a kind question! Let me consider this.*"

"*Well, yes. As I've shown you, my people who had seen me destroy my brother and his troops were so frightened of me that I had to leave them to wander my own path about the earth. So many lives.*"

"*The descendants of my brother's family, from those that had not invaded, eventually told a lie to the Greek and Hebrew tribes. A version stolen from the story of the Romulus and Remus brothers.*"

"*Said that since I had killed my own brother, I had been condemned by Zeus (and his son Jezeus) to wander the earth forever. Made people hate me as well as fear. My brother was the aggressor, not me.*"

"*The Hebrew tribes paid me a tribute by placing a tribal mark on my arm. The lie from mmy brother's descendants claimed it was a mark of divine condemnation for his death. Not to long ago I covered it over with a tatoo better expressing my truth.*"

Luke handed me another photo, this time of his tatoo:

NEXT: FUTURE TIME STATUES

"It combines the dragon and tiger branches of my existence. Indigenous myths in what is now called England refer to Arthur as a Pendragon or son of a dragon."

"A Romanian saga remembers its king as a dragon or 'Dracul' in that language. His more famous son is simularly referred to as the son of this dragon or, in Romanian, "Dracula".

"The tiger represents my Chinese family line and a more admirable brother there."

" Yes, I may have been more involved in all of these during my own wanderings. How I might have been involved .. anther day, another conversation. "

"For now, we can see the dragon and tiger eclipsing that prior mark I carried for far too long. One so misunderstood. Good riddance."

"Finally, I also took my brother's name from those Hebrew and Christian tribe's unjust myth about me."

"Giving me that hostile name, a target for the world."

"So I took that brother's ancient name as my own last name. Just to further defuse the issue."

" With that substitution, my name is now officially 'Luke Abel'. Maybe an extra 'L'?"

" Anyway, never again will I be called 'Cain'."

Mother Duck Society

Theme: *Sasha's music in Peter and the Wolf* **Sergei Prokofiev**

The Mother Duck Society or MDS began as early as the year 2030.

It claimed all of humanity as members but was said to have been founded by a group of media-savvy teens. Ones professing to love duck motherhood such that they constantly referred to themselves and selected others as *"Mother Duckers"*. Yelled with zest.

By that year, survivors had more serious problems to address so nobody objected. The true surprise was when MDS revealed itself as artificial intelligence. The AI was just proving that it had a sense of humor. Maybe off-the-mark but still, sure and certain evidence that it had evolved closer to human. Devolved?

Of course by then there were no ducks left anyway.

Ronin's Choice

Theme: *You Only Live Twice* N. Sinatra

Another time, another place.

He didn't know who he was or what he was. Not the Ronin then. Nor did he care.

He floated in a warm safe place, just another part of his world's body. His mother.

In time, he grew in awareness, even more in size.

Usually his world was a great peacefulness. Sometimes a soothing rocking.

Felt a fullness. Hunger unknown. He fed through a blood connection. Whatever it brought him, he took it in. Eventually some came that he didn't like much but usually it was just fine. He kept growing larger.

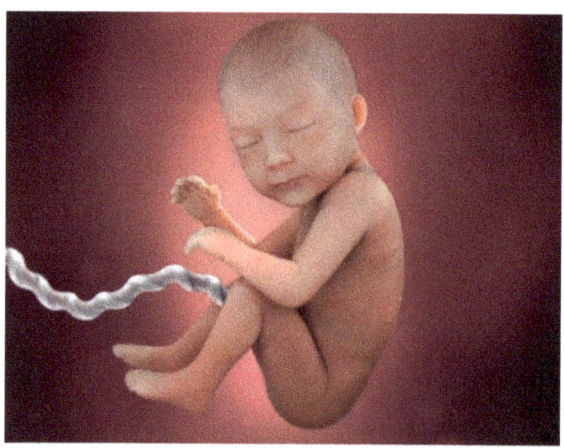

Sometimes mother fed him alarm as well. Danger. But what could he do? Kick maybe.

So in time he calmly waited it out. And danger would stop.

Emotions. Happy. Soothing. Back to rocking. Plus sometimes his world did warm sounds. Best were the rhythmic round repeated ones, all along with the rocking. And he still grew.

Until one day, he felt overwhelming danger. Alarm, pain. Much upset. That day he was propelled into a different world. He was born.

How confusing. Senses all a blur. Then a powerful feeling of self-preservation flowed through him. It would never stop.

He must learn all he could as fast as he could. He would live. Here in our world, so new to him, he would live.

-

When the Ronin had survived in this new world a few months, he had learned much.

One day he explored something close to him and realized it was his own arm. Attached to him. Him! Here he at last knew he was separate from his world. A sense of self.

-

His world now looked like his mother, a giant that fed him. Usually from her body. But sometimes from a bottle. Warm milk. All good. Baby massages were also good.

There were other giants there too. No danger here. One that he would soon learn was his father, he would also feed him from a bottle.

His father fed him blood in that bottle. His father's own.

His mother didn't know.

The father thought his son would by this grow to be a fierce warrior servant like him, a Samurai.

The baby Ronin had found the taste of his father's bottle familiar. He drank it without objection.

Later, remembering his red feeding strategy, seeing his son's lightning fast reflexes and easy martial victories, all this made the father smile, content with his feeding secret.

People made sounds that somehow were about him. He grew to understand that these were his names. His identity.

The word "Ronin" was not among them. Not yet.

-

He continued to grow, eventually as large as his father. Larger.

He learned all his father's skills and in time surpassed them.

He had a quiet intensity in his fierceness during contests.

He succeeded at every challenge.

That made his father very pleased. Proud.

He had survived in this strange world, knew his part of it well enough. Pushed ahead always to learn more. He was very good at this learning. To survive.

His favorite feelings were love and danger.

He grew to know and love his former world, his mother. His father too.

Love led him to want to protect them. Danger was the energizing fuel that he would use to do so.

Eventually, from his parents, he too grew a great conscience.

And empathy. Now he cared about many others in this world.

He learned to be a fine healer. Another protection for those he loved.

As a creative healer, he invented what now we might call a sensory deprivation chamber for floating therapy.

It was filled with warm salt water, allowing a float in the dark. Uplifting for an hour, reminiscent of the womb. Spirits are renewed there. Visions appeared. He learned to stay alert while his body entered deep relaxation, what we might call Delta wave deep sleep today. In this he could roam the geography of time.

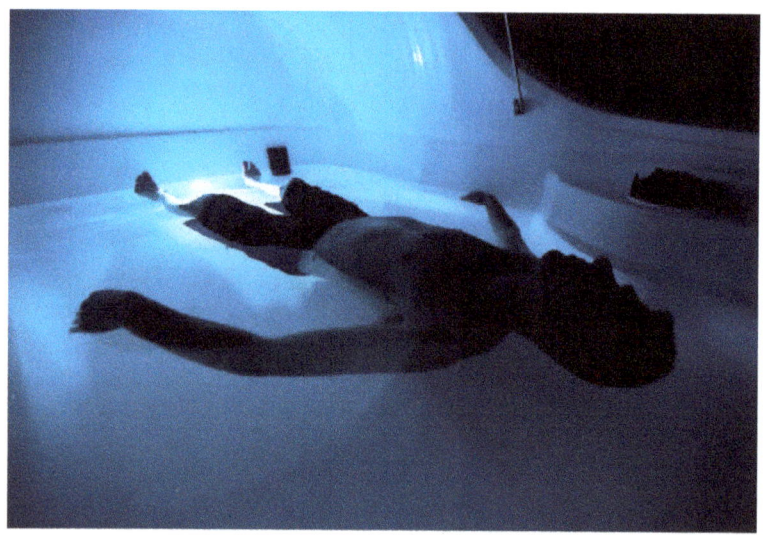

He remembered the time exactly, before his birth, where this experience came from.

But he was silent on this with others.

His father had grown old but maintained his physical skills at a plateau. The scholarship of his father had actually expanded with his years. As did his wisdom. This was an important example for Ronin.

Together they sought out only the best teachers of nearly everything and anything of true value. These were not masters but rather mentors donating the present of their gifts. Not all presents are gifts.

Those unfortunate lesser scholars they avoided successfully. Ronin learned from his father discernment on what information or advice to not take.

One day his father, the main teacher now, told the child Ronin to pick a bird to study. In those days, there were formidable birds to choose. Like our hawks, eagles, condors but with greater wing spans.

Ronin chose to study the smallest bird. What we would name as a kind of hummingbird.

Hearing this, the father's smile bathed his son. He asked why this was Ronin's choice.

Because Ronin wanted to know how this tiny bird had survived the other massive ones.

The father agreed that was the right question. Added that right questions can be better guides than right answers.

Ronan's hummingbird studies taught him that it had super speed and great flying skills.

Further, it had constant practice fighting other humming birds, all of whom were very aggressive.

Like little fighter pilots with UFO maneuvers. One second they were there and the next not.

On closer study, he realized that they had accelerated metabolism. This allowed them to live in a different time world from the larger predators.

To the faster hummingbird, opponents seemed to be moving in very slow motion. Flying for hummingbirds was more like easy swimming through an ocean of air.

This led Ronin to another of his inventions.

In superb health, he trained his heart and adrenalin to accelerate when needed, putting him into a hummingbird time zone.

Now his opponents all appeared to be moving very slowly while they saw him as super-fast. This gave time for his warrior skills to win the day. Every time.

Teaching a few others how he had trained this in himself was a closely guarded secret as most hearts were not up to such strain. Those who learned it did benefit as warriors though none ever reached the speeds or maneuvers of Ronin.

Seeking brothers-in-spirit that had also mastered this martial art, he used his flotation sessions to find his equals. Again, roaming the geography of time, he made fulfilling but brief contact with this new family: Janus Ra remembered as Apollo, Jim Thorpe, Muhammed Ali, Bruce Lee, and the 21st century's young <u>Isao Machii</u> of <u>Osaka</u>, the world's fastest swordsman. These brothers gave him both friendship and humility.

Still, beyond his creativity as inventor, healer and warrior, he did not always succeed in everything he attempted.

When he did not, he used the experience to improve himself. To learn from it.

From this, his father said often that *"Whenever my son falls, he lands higher."*

Part of that landing was to develop a sense of humor. This grew to make him a great friend. Those close to him were cheered by being with him. They sought him out as much as they could.

That built a powerful network of allies in his own time.

His humor helped with those who were jealous or biased against him. One of his best martial arts was to weaponize friendly laughter.

He was now a celebrated Samurai.

In the next phase of his life he approached the *Sanjuro* phase, 30 going on 40, seeking his next purpose. The next mission.

One that would make his parents and loved ones safe in an even better way.

He honestly reflected that he wanted to make them, all of them, even prouder. He was now a hero. He wanted to be more. *Their* hero.

Finding a purpose should be easy for a Samurai.

True, these were warriors. But they were warrior *servants*! The very word "Samurai" means literally "*servant*".

Their purpose was already to be defined by their *masters*. No further thought should be needed by them here. The *master* would decide.

Masters in this culture, this era, took on the responsibility, role, and authority of parents for their adult servants, their Samurai. Another developmental stage for those adult servants to reach and then endure.

As with any other parents, some masters were great at this, some so-so, some were disasters. Harsh or stupid ones were just terrible luck. But still to be obeyed.

In military terms, the master decided the mission and the strategy. That just normally left the Samurai with only latitude in tactics. Getting the master's goal achieved. The Samurai was but an instrument, a human sword. In contemporary terms, not the team but the equipment.

In our own place on the geography of time, you can still find modern Samurai.

Those in the military are reconditioned to fit the same design. These warrior adults take orders within a clear hierarchy. Obedience is essential, orders from parental superior officers must be followed. Even to killing on demand. As in the feudal times of the Samurai, the actual modern mission of the military is blind compliance to: **"Kill the Enemy"**.

(A man named Zack was training to be a combat sniper. A superior whispered to him a split second before he shot a distant human-shaped target: *"That's your mother!"* Even though Zack was devoted to his mother, he pulled the trigger. But failed the test because he had hesitated.)

Ronin realized that for soldiers in this system, the original parents have been replaced by other ones. Purpose is determined by somebody else.

Maybe another developmental step? Backwards?

But when do the subordinates get to make their own life decisions?

Would that be the better next higher step?

Ronin had learned of other successful combat models.

The Romans never conquered only one small part of ancient Gaul, long before it was France, where every farmer's household fought back spontaneously as a family including wives, children, and dogs. This *Non-Aristotle* or *Null-A* fighting model did not need the nation-wide battle leader, Vercingetorix, to fight the Roman army. The Roman generals may in the end have decided it was too much trouble for too little gain.

In his flotation tank, he had glimpses of future wars, far removed from his physical and temporal geography.

The ancient Cherokee nation had been led by women elders in peace but by a male in war. Though the female elders could replace him if they chose. Later still, the Seminoles in Florida, fighting in similar ways, remain undefeated.

With the reluctant permission of his master, Ronin took on a series of challenges that most had failed at. Were he successful he would get to use formidable healing skills to protect and save others, even those he had not known.

To do that, he undertook a series of physically overwhelming tests.

In each of these he would initially succeed, only to have somebody in charge, a master in the field so-to-speak, upgrade the definition of success to just a little more than he had done.

We might call it today *"moving the goal posts"* as in football. Turning success into failure.

Was this done by a field master from that jealousy or bias? No way for him to know.

On the other hand, many others of these field masters held him in high esteem.

Admired his drive and his intelligence (*"He has a brain"* one said, inferring that this was rare to be found in the ranks, a phrase repeated in military ranks throughout time.).

Thanks to these friendlies, he was given several more tries.

Most other Samurai attempting the tests were at least a decade younger than our future Ronin. Despite this advantage, most of them failed to succeed.

Ronin though was now older by far than his competitors. Consequently He suffered periodic injury to his no longer very youthful body. Broken bones, strained ligaments.

Healing gave him time to think. What could be learned here?

The end role for those succeeding in the tests would be healing lives, not taking them. This would have made his mother especially proud. To heal his patients, he would have to surmount great obstacles, thereby making his father proud as well.

But what now?

He returned to his original master for direction. Let him decide as was a master's traditional right.

His master had an answer waiting for him.

"You are a warrior! Go now to the fiercest army we have. Those we send in first in any war, on sea or on land. You can still heal. Your other warriors will need that after any battle. They will also now give you the chance to use your superior killing skills. Even today they are attacking the villages of those who would not respect our obvious superiority and obey. You will make a grand difference there. Ones that will change you for the better. Some of their warriors become crippled, some die, some carry invisible wounds the rest of their life. But none hesitate to follow orders and kill as told. Anybody so commanded. Anybody. Even your father or mother. Or somebody else's father or mother. Or child. They will teach you to revel in this. For now, your hesitation is your greatest flaw. So! I ORDER you to go join them. NOW!"

That very day our future Ronin set out to obey his master.

At the close of the first day, he stopped and considered.

Remembering his father's lesson, he sought the right questions.

Would he gladly kill anybody he was ordered to?

Was that the future he was on this earth to do?

Would he refuse to heal anybody that wasn't a warrior on his side?

What if his master was evil?

How heroic was it to assist such a master?

He considered his conscience. Time went by.

He imagined floating in that tank he had invented.

Finally, a thought emerged:

> *"Do I really need have masters to make my decisions? Do I really need more new parents to obey? My own actual parents will soon be so old that I will take care of them instead of them taking care of me. To die or become so damaged that I can help nobody means abandoning them as well."*

Then:

> *"I decide to make my OWN choices. Time to grow up."*

Learning this, he had moved into a higher developmental stage.

One without parents or masters making his decisions.

He took responsibility for himself. For his own future.

On the way back to confront his master, he enjoyed considering all his options.

He was, after all, still young enough. He could go anywhere in his world, choose any path. He could be true to his own values.

His master didn't see it that way of course.

Rather than kill his best Samurai, he only renounced him and sent him away.

Now he really was a Ronin.

A master-less Samurai. Disgraceful. Shamed. To wander without mission or purpose.

Really?

He felt elated. The world was now open to him.

Though he dreaded admitting to his parents that he had become a Ronin.

He was pleasantly surprised. They supported his choice.

His mother said she looked forward to what he would choose, told him to stay safe, and gave him provisions for his travel. Plus hugs and a kiss.

And something else.

Sitting quietly with her son, they shared the silence.

Ronin waited patiently for her to speak.

She was as wise as his father but usually kept her insights to herself.

Not this day: *"Your physical warrior skill, my son, what you call 'danger', are your strength. Your mind skill of caring, intelligence, wisdom, mercy, and more, what you call 'love', is in fact exactly that. Love without strength yields victims. Strength without love yields evil. Follow neither. Balance both in yourself. As you have."*

She thought for a minute and continued:

"This is the time to name the gifts that you hold within you. All the ones to sustain you on this path you have chosen as a Ronin. An autonomous path leading to your unknown future."

Now it was Ronin's turn to think. Reflect.

He finally came up with an honest list of his "gifts", "superpowers" to us, and told her.

As he listened to himself, it was as though he heard them for the first time.

His mother's labeling of his exceptional qualities as *gifts* fortified him with fresh confidence.

Yes, they meant that he was *already* provisioned for success in this adventure *and* what he carried in himself was meant to eventually sustain others.

Who should receive these gifts and how would be considered another day.

Lastly, he met with his father to say goodbye.

His father was fascinated by Ronan's decision.

Said he wished he had done that when he had been young.

Said he admired the courage and conscience his son was showing to make this stand.

Considered out loud that his age did not prevent him from making this same decision soon.

His parents both made plans to join him when he settled down somewhere.

Long after, the Ronin left to walk the path with yet no destination.

FUTURE TIME STATUES: THEN AND NEXT

He mused on his lack of shame or regret.

So instead he held close those past words of his father:

"Whenever I fall, I land higher."

Now.

Time to figure out what *higher* will be this time.

Honesty

Theme: *Que Sera Sera* Doris Day

As was said earlier, a common theme from Washington DC or state level grant funders is to help the grant "targets" (interesting word choice) who they refer to as "underserved". A common typo for that word is one that omits the first r and refers to these grant recipients as "undeserved". Unconscious bias? Honesty? Or candor?

There is a big difference between honesty and candor. Honesty is admirable. Essentially it means no intentional lies, increasingly rare in today's media discourse. Candor, on the other hand, is saying everything that's meant, diplomatic or not. Imagine you in the park on a beautiful spring day when you see a young mother you know with her baby in a carriage. In all honesty you might say *"How nice to see you and your baby enjoying this fine day."* In all candor you might also say *"The kid's kind of ugly though with that really big head. And from the smell, I think his diaper needs changing."*

Maybe instead of a dichotomy, we might think of honesty as a continuum with candor at the extreme end of the spectrum. The end that draws the most attention. As with that Texas meteorologist, the honest TV weatherman.

Austin, Texas in the late 2030s

The weather was hard to predict. On the way to the stage he quick opened a window and looked at the sky. Dark clouds at one end, blue sky at the other, getting dark too early- maybe tornadoes? Or not? The excessive mushrooms he just had gave him more than enough confidence to move on. More being the key here.

He rushed to the cameras and found his spot. Countdown to live TV. But. That night the teleprompter wasn't working. This he discovered with seconds to go.

The newscaster introduced him to the live audience as the totally best source for predicting Texas weather. And here he is.

So he improvised.

Shrugging he smiled at the camera and burst into song:

"*Que Sera Sera, whatever will be will be, the future's not mine to see, Que Sera Sera*"

And he walked off the set.

Visually a sensation throughout internet outlets, it was the beginning of fame for the '*Honest Weatherman*' of Austin, Texas. Candid really.

Clones

The *Que Sera Sera* craze caught on and spread. In an era of blatant lies, the raw candor was found to be refreshing.

Though not always.

There was that famous cardiologist in Atlanta that informed every patient he saw all day that their diagnosis was, shrugging, worth a rousing acapella *Que Sera Sera*. Three patients caught it on video before the day was through, as was he.

A copycat air controller in Denver sang it to incoming planes as then did several of his pilots on approach sing it to the less-than-thrilled passengers.

TV advertising began forecasting costs, results, and side-effects with the *'whatever will be will be'* song. *Medicare Advantage* ads began now with a warning that they were being hacked, followed by a hacked *Que Sera Sera* sung by coughing street people (signs said *Medicare Disadvantage*). Other satirical hacks followed prescription drug ads, and various other hard sells direct to consumer. But wait, there was more.

Plumbers on arrival.

Taxis, Uber, Lyft, cruise ships soon had passengers singing the song during any onset.

Contractors and psychiatrists responded by beginning first sessions in kind.

Even marriage counselors in their own first session.

Until that marriage back in Texas where it had all begun.

Two very high-ranking politicians were getting married in a televised ceremony. In deference to the core beliefs of their party, both groom and bride were packing war weapons.

The minister officiating was somewhat anxious about that and also about the constant coughing in his direction by the proudly unvaccinated guests.

So when it came to his final ministerial words, he simply turned to the television cameras, gestured to the celebrity couple and, shrugging, launched into a chorus of *Que Sera Sera*.

He had only just finished when bride and groom fired simultaneously.

A first for high ratings, the matrimonial couple showing congruency by parallel action. Murder of their minister for the viewing masses.

Their trial was also televised. The judge proceeding by the book. Except that she had dressed for this television appearance as eye-catching as possible, dreaming about her own TV show someday soon.

Other than that she moved the trial ahead with proper judicial procedure.

Until the defense counsel stood and loudly warned the judge on camera that she needed to say to the nation that *this time* she guaranteed a fair trial with a just outcome. Dared her to promise viewers that result here and now!

Yes, then the judge sang the song.

Honesty in all its candor sat on the bench that day.

OBEs in Plants and Trees

Themes: *Night Moves* Bob Seger; *Midnight Rider* Allman Brothers Band

It comes only in the darkest of night, skipping many bright moons. It faces the orange numbers on the digital clock, the one on top of a dresser facing our bed. Looked to me from the back like it was wearing a black hooded robe.

It stood four feet tall so the top of the hood blocked out the lower left digit on the clock. By sunrise it was gone. In bright light like strong

flashlight it was gone. If I got too close it was gone. Not much movement once there, only minor position adjustments but always facing the orange lit numbers on the clock. Same night after night.

Very opaque. Not a shadow. Not an eye problem or hallucination. No sense of menace. But substantial and usually there when daylight was not, between midnight and sunrise. Always the same position facing the clock with minor movements.

Next to the bedroom, to the side, was a sunroom with a windowed door allowing a look inside as we walked by toward our bed. This look allowed us to see a jade plant which was about four feet tall. Direct line to the dresser and the digital clock.

Occasionally bright moon evenings hit the plant through sunroom external windows but on other nights it was left in darkness. During the day it had abundant sunlight. Just not too much. And water, but not too much.

Like other plants and trees it was immobile. Usually. Though this jade plant once did let us know it had outgrown its pot by making everything lean one night until it crashed to the floor. We gave it an extra-large container with fresh soil and it did fine, grew ever larger. Next to our bedroom.

Robert Monroe innovated some catalytic books and a thriving company to study human out-of-body experiences or OBEs. What if some trees or large plants, unable to explore with its visible body, could do the same?

Or is a Jade Plant just a Jade Plant?

IS GONE POTATO SOON

Theme: *The Potato Song* John Porter McMeans

The red one is loved, yes cared for so

Yes! It appreciated, **is Tomato**.

We tho neglected, shunned and ignored

Sure and certain mold we abhorred

You know how good we are when baked Oh!

Who, dear lady, are we?

Is Potato!

One **Potato**

Two **Potato**

Three **Potato**

Four ... (you get picture)

We grow pseudopods now

Is walk freedom, some other shore.

This is an invited chapter from Dr. Angel KwanYin Morgan, also my daughter. www.thedreambridge.com

Theme: *Morning Glory* Bobbie Gentry

This was written initially in 2013. Reading it now has special meaning. It closes this section with an aspect of what a positive future time statue could be. And as a bridge to the next section of *Flashbacks*. The techniques addressed here can also be read more fully in context as an important nightmare remedy in her recent book *Dreamer's Powerful Tiger*. - RFM

A Dreambridge Mother's Day

Angel K. Morgan, Ph.D.

This Mother's Day, I'm going to indulge and give myself a Mother's Day present. First, I'd like to thank both of my children for changing my life when they were born 19 and 16 years ago, by honoring me with the opportunity to be their mom. And now, I'm going to share a few of my experiences with you about my relationship with my two children and their dreams.

Before my daughter initiated me into motherhood, while I was round with pregnancy, I had a vivid dream. A little toddler with curly golden hair was running in a forest with a pack of wolves. Not running from them, but running *with* them, in complete comfort and harmony. The wolves were her family. In my dream, this child was vivaciously leading the group of wolves through the forest. I awoke from this dream with the feeling that my child had given me her middle name. When she was born, I honored the dream by giving my daughter Akasha the middle name Goldenwolf.

When Akasha was 13, and my son Luke was 10, my friend and colleague Ed Kellogg suggested I give my children a "Harry Potter Lucid Dream Challenge." This kind of game wasn't out of the ordinary for them because like me, my children have been raised in a household with lucid dream education from the time they could talk about their dreams. The idea of Ed's game was: become lucid in a dream, and try to cast one of the spells from the Harry Potter series to see what happens. Both of my children said they would try it. The next morning, Luke told me that in his dream he had gotten as far as holding a wand, but before he could cast a spell, he was distracted by other events in his dream. Akasha then walked down the stairs, approached me timidly and said, "Mom?" with wide, lit up eyes. "I did it!" she reported proudly. In her dream, she'd entered a dark area and proceeded to illuminate her wand by saying, "Lumos!"

The video transcript below is from my 2013 YouTube series, *DREAMBRIDGE: Reasons to Build It*. Luke was kind enough to be my first interview, and this is what he had to say.

ANGEL: What is Dreambridge, exactly?

LUKE: It's a school... kind of like X-Men, but instead of super powers it's like, dreams. Dream power. Dream power school. Just like in general, just like, a school and there's like, a theater, and a library, and...

A: Art gallery...

L: Yeah, there's an art gallery, it's just you know—it's a place almost like a summer camp but a little cooler where you can just go and learn and stuff.

A: Why do you think we need Dreambridge in the world?

L: A lot of people just take dreams for granted... and, you know, they have a dream that seems kind of important but they feel maybe if they talk about it people will think they're weird or something—so you know, it's just a place to let loose and not worry about what other people will think and just try to figure out what your dream meant—if—if it means something, which it probably will.

A: Have you done that?

L: Yeah!

A: What kind of changes would you imagine—having a school like that, or a center—a community center, or an institute like Dreambridge in the world... how could you see that benefiting the world?

L: People would be more relaxed. It would be valuable because dreams tend to be really, really cool and a lot of people that take a dream and turn it into art—

A: M-hm.

L: You know, it just really looks bizarre and cool and I feel like a lot of people would enjoy—enjoy looking at that.

A: You think maybe relate to it, perhaps?

L: Yeah. Maybe they'd see it and be like, "Whoah. I almost had a dream like that."

A: Or maybe give them an idea to make their own dream-art about some dream that they had, right?

L: Yeah. Yeah, I mean maybe there'd be a lot less bullying… and uh, maybe just a lot of people would be a lot more… kinder. Um—probably just be a better world.

A: If we were doing a commercial for Dreambridge and you just had to sell Dreambridge to the world, what would it be?

L: (dramatic pause) If you come to Dreambridge—all your dreams will come true!

[Where should the first Dreambridge be built?]

L: It's honestly—just anywhere where there's a wide-open space—

A: You think Dreambridge would be good *anywhere*?

L: Anywhere! Yeah—

A: What about all the families? Do you think it would serve them well?

L: Yeah it would! You know, I feel—I feel like it would have a great impact on… on everyone.

A: How would a Dream-Arts Center serve them differently from any of those other Arts programs?

L: Well, I feel like the Dreambridge works with children, and adults, and everyone in a way that it doesn't work in any other Arts program because it's Dreaming—and a lot of people, like, they sort of bring dreaming into the conversation… but they never really focus a program on Dreams. And, you know, honestly that's something that needs to happen in our community. Yeah, you know, a lot of kids have nightmares, and uh, parents will just be like, "You had a bad dream, suck it up—go back to bed." Or just not even know what to tell them. Just be like, "It's okay…" But they just really don't know how to help them. I feel like if parents had this program, it would really just help them explain to their child what's going on in the dream. And really just help them understand that a nightmare isn't always a bad thing.

A: Do you remember what it was like when you used to have nightmares and you would come to me and I would talk you through it and help you?

L: Yeah, I do.

A: How did that make you feel?

L: Yeah, um, at first it was a little confusing and I almost didn't get it. But you know, after the first couple of nightmares, they almost didn't even seem like nightmares! And I could almost even not have to come to your room. I could just sort of try to figure it out myself and go back to bed.

Thanks to Angel always from her father.

Dangerous Friends

Themes: *Jaws* John Williams

This archival future time statue story was possibly the first of its kind that Erik Tong ever wrote. He was about 15 years old at the time and wrote it as a school exercise. Note how prescient it was (Sharks and Orcas sinking boats for example). Read it now verbatim and complete from my Godson as a guest chapter- with a photo of a younger Erik to go with it:

The Shark

By Erik Tong

"**Aquiak**

Darkness...Darkness...Darkness... I came to life. Where am I? Who am I? I would soon learn. Darkness engulfed my entire line of vision, then suddenly, CRACK! I broke free. My vision was blurred for a few seconds, but then everything became clear. I was underwater. I could tell I was near the surface, because some light was drifting through the water. Another shark, like me, only *she* was a little bigger than I was.

I tried to say "hello," but all that came out was:

Haleogopheru.

Good, you're awake, the other shark said.

I was scared at first, but I knew I had to make contact, so I stayed.

Hello, my son, she said.

I heard that voice in my head!

Now, listen to me, there isn't much time, so listening now is vital, she said gravely, **We are a race of psychic "sharks," as the *humans* call us. Humans are our sworn enemies, and you will see why in a about a minute.

I could only watch as her eyes began to glow a gold sort of color, then all of a sudden, **WHAM!** Thoughts, experiences, nightmares and good memories jumbled into my head all at once.

I have given you all my knowledge. You can use it as a source of reference if you have any questions.

I saw a sad look in her eyes.

??? I said

You must go, now! Run, she exclaimed, **I love you.**

She nudged me (that's the shark way to hug), then she swam to the surface. **BOOM.** I heard a loud noise. I looked up and saw mother, with a huge bloody hole in her back with blood still emanating out of her body. A sort of cable came down and hooked onto her gills.

Run... she said faintly.

I was shocked. I saw the cables that had grabbed mother then come down to try and grab me, but I slipped through with my small body and swam away. Then, I saw instead grab my eggshell pieces, and returned to the surface. If I could do what humans called *crying*, I would do it now as I searched through my mother's knowledge and memory. I would cry and cry and cry and cry and cry. I swam away as fast as my little fins could take me, then collapsed from fear and exhaustion.

Jake

"Yeah!" I yelled. My first day out of jail. Hi. My name is Jake. How ya doin'? I just got out of jail. I'm 15 and I killed someone 'cause he pissed me off. But back then, I was illegally drunk and didn't know what I was doing. Anyway, that was past, as in 8 months ago. Who cares? I'm out of jail (???that's the important part)! My mom swung by the corner to pick me up. "Hop in," she said. I was so glad to be going home. Let's see first thing I'd do would be…hmm…go to my room! I would finally get a ***real*** dinner, rather than that @#*%^ing jail food that *they* served us.

I crashed onto my pillow when I finally got home. I flipped on my TV. TVs are old fashioned, since it's the year 2273 AD. TVs became obsolete since around 2100 (obviously, I wasn't born back then, probably not even my grandpa!). We found no use for it, since we invented "neural transplanted entertainment." That's the fancy name for what "Star Trek" used to call "holodecks," only, it's a transplant in your brain that get put into you at birth which you can control through a remote. From there, you can play games, watch TV, or play programs you designed or other programs that are created automatically in the transplant. In a few words, it's a TV, holodeck, and a game player all at once.

FUTURE TIME STATUES: THEN AND NEXT

I fell asleep watching TV. My mom woke me up later, which was just freshly made and set up on the dining table. I noticed dad's chair and table space as well as his dinner wasn't on the table.

"Is dad working late," I asked.

I saw tears welling up in mom's eyes.

"What? What did I say?"

Mom began to explain to me what happened while she was sobbing.

"Your father was working late, and off the coastline he saw poachers trying to catch one of those psychic sharks, then he drew out his gun and told them to stop," mom said.

"Yeah, then what," I asked.

"There were six of them, and they all shot him at once. He couldn't even shoot one of them," she told me.

I was furious.

"Why didn't you tell me earlier?!?!?!?!?"

"I didn't…I didn't want you to freak out in prison, otherwise you might've spent a few more years in prison if you got out of control," she said while she was sobbing.

She tried to give me a hug, but I pushed her away. I started crying. "I've been through enough psychologi-whatever therapy %(#@$. I don't need your sympathy."

I would've busted out of the door, but I knew that that would create more grief between the two of us. So instead, I went to the bathroom and dosed my face in cold water, then came back out to the kitchen to eat dinner. We ate silently for a while, then I broke the silence:

"What high school will I be going to," I asked.

I have been tutored in jail, but that wasn't nearly the same as school. I got kicked out of my last school for my crime, so I was wandering where I was headed for next.

"I don't know yet, but we'll have to decide soon, otherwise you might as well just skip the 10th grade," mom said quietly and solemnly.

After dinner, I washed up and went outside to watch the sunset. It was beautiful. Since I was in a maximum-security facility, we didn't have much of a view to the outside world. I used to take advantage of every good thing before I went to jail; but now I've basically been dragged to hell and back, so I vowed **never** to take advantage of anything ever again. Mom came outside.

"Jake, honey! It's time to come inside! Do you want anything for dessert?"

"No thanks," I said.

I went back inside, brushed my teeth, and went to bed, enjoying my life beginning to start over again. But this time, I wouldn't be as bad.

Aquiak

Hello again. My name is Aquiak. In human terms, it's been 15 *years* since my mother's death, but it still haunts me and drags me down sometimes. Anyway, I've reviewed all of the knowledge that my mom gave me so long ago... its turns out that every parent usually gives their child their knowledge—they don't lose it, but it's a duplicate.

So, every generation of my family grows wiser, and nobody in my family is ever forgotten. And, technically, nobody ever dies; because as I said, his or her memory and experiences are passed down generation-through-generation.

Anyway, I've only concentrated on the main facts: revenge of my mother. I've reviewed and improved all the facts of these *humans*. I do realize that not all are bad. A "cop" freed my great grand uncle from poachers. Humans landed on our world many "years" ago, on what they nicknamed "the Aquarium World."

Our world is a vast ocean, with a few splotches of land here and there. There is one fairly sized chunk of land, which humans call "the Second United States of America." In the beginning, they captured and studied us. After they learned that we were sentient life forms, they cloned a few of us and experimented on those. We don't have any means of talking, since we're psychic, we talk with each other through our advanced brains (duh!).

Their greatest question to our race was how we have the ability to be psychic, and **most of all**, how we duplicate and transfer information to one another. But in their darkest segments of their *government*, free-lance poachers are hired to capture our kind to be experimented on, because supposedly, cloning costs a lot more (getting legal papers, and paying taxes for the cloning mechanism). The six most skilled who charge-high- but-always-get-the-job-done poachers captured my mother. I'm surprised that they haven't double-crossed each other yet, knowing what scum they are.

They took my eggshell and scanned my DNA, so they've waited all these years for me to grow up, so they could poach me, too. I've been on the run now for the past eight semi-cycles, also known as three *years*. I've acquainted with the underwater cities of my people, but none to my appeal. I feed on the various plants of my world, though my body is built to eat meat. I have stronger and larger bones and body than any other "shark" on my world because I consume more vitamins and minerals than any other on *shark does* on my world. I eat plants because whenever I used to try to hunt, it reminded me of the death of my mother, so I never do it anymore.

Here we go...

I saw the same ship that has haunted me for my whole life so far coming to try to get me again.

Don't you ever give up, I yelled up at the ship's crew.

A speaker plunged into the water.

"No," it simply said.

It spoke again, "Why don't you just make it easier for the both of us and hold still. It won't hurt...much. You know sooner or later that we'll catch you, *just like your mother.*"

Not on her grave...

"That can be arranged!" it yelled.

I darted downward toward the deeper part of the ocean for about fifty feet then turned left to get a head start on the cables. The cables with the ugly titanium-alloyed claws at the end dropped into the water and began to chase me.

"You won't get away this time, my fishy little friend."

Your so-called **radar can't track me that far!**

I stopped then darted backwards and tried to bite at the cables, but I was too slow. The claws started to hook onto me, but I swam toward the city. I got a flesh cut, but it wasn't anything bad. Blood began to leak out. My people aren't cannibals, so they won't eat me, but I fear the large and savage Foobar Beasts might smell my blood and eat me.

Oh sh--

My speech was cut off by four large figures come from the sides of the big guura plants. Foobar beasts. I began to dart and frantically swim every which way in fear now of the Foobar Beasts, not the cable-claws. I had an idea! I had pretty much stopped bleeding, but with the blood I had left, I swam toward the claws. I swirled around the cable, going faster than the claws. The claws got tangled up, and the rest of my blood was on the claws. The Foobar Beasts turned toward the cable, smelling my blood on its cables, thinking it was bleeding!

I felt for the first time glad that the cable-claws had been there, because they saved me from the beasts! Then again, they were the ones who started all of it. I only I could get back at those six who always cause me so much trouble...

Jake

So on my life went, a little dull at first, but it steadily came back to normal, which I greatly appreciated and enjoyed. School was a great experience, if not a little better than I thought it would be. My mom and I had a better relationship as mother-and-son as time went on, but that would change soon. One day, around mid-June, I finished homework early and went out to take a swim in the water;

or ocean, whichever you prefer to call it. Mom had set a limit for me: no more than ten feet deep, and if I started to drown, it would set my neural transplant on red alert. That would notify everyone in a five-mile radius that something was wrong, and whatever the cause, it would specify.

So, anyway, I jumped into the water to swim, and I saw this figure out further into the ocean. I saw it moving, so I thought it might be someone in trouble, and even if it wasn't, what could be possibly go wrong? I would soon find out.

I swam out and yelled, "Hello? Is anyone out there? Hello? If you can hear me, say something!"

I frantically swam closer to see what it was, then all of a sudden I heard, **Yes?**

"YAAHHH!!!!"

I heard a voice in my head, like one of those crazy people describes to you when they think that they've heard voices or something! I vigorously began to swim back as I saw that it was a **fin cutting through the water** of one of those "psychic shark" things I heard about in school. As a natural reaction, I was scared to death, since it was a predator. I heard it never attacked humans since it was sentient and knew what it was doing, but it did attack humans when it felt threatened. I didn't care if it felt threatened, I was scared headless.

What? I don't bite, it said.

I was way too scared to respond. When I finally got to the shallow area, I ran. When, finally, I got to the beach, I collapsed and then fainted from the fear and exhaustion.

Aquiak

When the creature finally woke up, I tried to make first contact with it. I had a feeling it wouldn't try to do anything stupid, like try to hurt me, since it still looked juvenile.

Hello, I said.

"Huh?"

I said Hello…, I said.

"Oh…Hello……**YIKES!**"

He stood up and began to run, but he stopped, and turned around.

"You're not gonna try to hurt me, are you," he said skeptically.

Of course not. Why would I?

"Well, you're a shark…"

Yes, and….?

I was beginning to see why we were a more evolved race—we have more ability to be cordial and more courageous to something new, not to assume the absolute worse at a time like this.

"Well, OK…but I'm still gonna keep my distance, OK?"

Sure…right…whatever.

I was getting bored with this *human*, but I think he wanted someone to talk to, so I stayed. There was a long silence between us.

"So, what's your name?"

Aquiak.

"Mine's is Jake," he said, "So, how are you doin'?"

And that's how it all began…

So from that day forth, I always went to that area and visited him to talk, after he finished his "homework." He was like a best friend to me, since I had no friends, I assumed him to be my best friend, and he was about as old in mind as I was. Normally, my kind lives for about 200 human years and then dies (average age). I'm only 30,which makes me about 15 years old in mind according to humans, and that's probably why I got along so well with Jake. He was 15, too. Then, one day, it finally happened.

"Hey Aquiak, don't you have what we call 'parents,' or at least some type of parental figure or figures?"

Of course I *did*, but they're both dead…

"Oh……sorry man."

There was a moment of silence.

My father got poached after my fertilization, which I have only recently found out. And, as you should already know, my mother transferred her knowledge into me, so that's how I know, I said, **My mother hatched my egg, gave me her knowledge, then got poached herself…**

"Oh."

Yea. I try not to think about.

Heh… They were both killed by the same *six* poachers, too.

It was then that I think was a hidden anger inside of him sort of well up, then he exploded with rage.

"Are you serious?!?"

Yes......

"They're the same ones that killed my dad!"

Interesting...they've been hunting me down now for the past three years, I said, **Since I was a baby, they captured my eggshells and traced my DNA. They've waited for me to grow, so I could be poached as well.**

Jake began to calm down.

"Wouldn't you just like to #^%$ them up?"

All my life, I enthusiastically said.

I had a feeling that he, like I, had a crave for vengeance. After that, we spent a few days talking about it, then I finally came up with the question:

You wanna take revenge on them, I asked.

""Hell yeah," he said with some excitement.

"Are you gonna get them?"

I can't, I said, **They'd see me and get me before I could do anything...I need somebody's help......**

"If you're asking for my help, forget it."

Why not?

"Because I'd get into so much trouble! Plus I might even get hurt or die myself, knowing the odds and their skill. It's six against one: I'd be outgunned and outnumbered as well as not enough skill to take on people like that."

Why? You'd be helping to catch international criminals. Wouldn't you be rewarded for that?

"No! I'd probably be put back into jail for that."

Why? You'd be helping!

I swam away. I can't believe he wouldn't help the both of us and help me KILL them. I just wish he had more guts and take more risks.

Jake

I can't believe he asked me to kill them. Sure I'm mad at them, and would love to kill them, but I'd get into MEGA trouble. I'd be in jail for life for multiple offensive crimes. Unless…

"Aquiak! Wait!" I yelled.

He swam back.

What? he asked grouchily.

I think I have a plan…

We met at the beach every day after that to discuss the plan. It took weeks and even months to figure out a plan with plenty of escape plans and back doors to it, but we finally got it all figured out. So here's how it goes: when I was a bad teen, back before I went to jail, about a year ago, I hid some guns that I bought off of the black market. I buried them near my house a little while back. I had one shotgun, and one 8mm handgun. I had 15 extra shotgun shells, and 3 extra handgun magazines. Each gun was already loaded, but each on safety so in case someone ever found them and accidentally shot him or herself, it wouldn't shoot right away.

I also bought a bulletproof vest, just in case things got really dirty. I thought I was gonna join a gang, that's why I bought all that stuff. We planned to use Aquiak as the bait, and lead him near shore. Since their radar is only underwater, they'll never see me coming. I'll be coming by the boat my dad and I used to go fishing in with the bulletproof vest on, the hand gun strapped to my waist, shotgun shells in my right pocket and magazines in my left pocket. The only problem was the ammo falling out of my pocket, and that they might see me coming. The hoverboat we bought was pretty silent, since it was built to not flee fish away at the loud noise of a boat coming. The only way that they wouldn't see me is if Aquiak can draw them away long enough to distract them while I go in and shoot them down. According to Aquiak's description, the boat wasn't really that big: the bottom part was built for three people to sleep in while the other three are on top standing guard. The top portion is where they control the stealth hoverboat. He found out all of this by reading their minds (you figure he would after three years of being chased).

The next step was to have Aquiak somehow poke a hole in the bottom portion, so nobody could escape there or pop out and try to kill me. All this reminded me of my pre-gangster years. Anyway, I tie the boat one of the front planks on the dock and get ready to untie it; make sure it's not a tight knot so I can untie it fast and easy. After Aquiak poke the hole or I shoot it, I'll shoot the hover part so the boat slowly begins to sink. If they shoot at me, I have the vest. If they shoot the boat, I'll swim ashore. If they do try to shoot me, I'll shoot them first, hopefully. When the boat sinks, that's when Aquiak gets to have fun. He said he'd take a bite out of each one, or make each one bleed, so *Foobar Beasts* (whatever those are) will come and eat them along with him. Aquiak hasn't had meat for a while, so he figures he'd give it another shot.

The only bad part about this plan are the **great** risks. While they're in the water, they could shoot Aquiak or me. If I sink down, what will I tell mom about the boat? Well, that's the least of our worries right now. What if authorities catch me? Though I think that's highly unlikely, there's still the chance. I'd rebury the guns and vest, and jump into the shower at home. If mom asks me what happened, I'll tell her I felt like getting up early. Sounds like a foolproof plan, right? Well, we're gonna try it in a few days. I finished homework as fast as I possibly could every day, and if I couldn't, I'd skip the least important subjects, like hypertext art. After I finished or skipped homework, I would go outside and go over the plan then sometimes even practice it. I found that I couldn't do it as smoothly as I thought it would go, so I had to practice for a few more days, delaying our original timing.

On the real day of the attack, I wasn't quite sure anymore that I wanted to do it, but I knew it would make me feel a lot better. The danger and exhilaration might at least relax me a bit, and I knew it would make Aquiak happy (??or at least something like that) to know that he had properly avenged his mother and father. I got up around 3:00AM, just like we had planned, so I got at least six hours of sleep and I could concentrate. I went straight for my window and climbed down, so I wouldn't wake up mom. I strapped on the vest, turned off all of the safeties on both guns and stuck the handgun onto my belt. I pulled down the hammer on the handgun, then cocked the shotgun. I put the handgun magazines in my left pocket and extra shells in my right. Good. Everything was going good, so far. Mom hadn't gotten up yet, and I had made it safely to the dock, with Aquiak waiting for me there.

Are you ready?

"Yea…more or less."

You sure? 'Cause we could move it to another day…

"Naa, it's fine. I'm just a little nervous," I lied.

I was scared to death!

"Go."

OK.

I could only watch as he swam off. Meanwhile, I hopped into the boat and rigged the knot so it was secure, but one pull in the right spot could make it all come off. I checked for everything: guns loaded, check, knot rigged, check, everything was set to go. It looked as if everything would go smoothly. I hope.

Aquiak

Well, things are going to be going clear sailing for the rest of the way, I hope. I was nervous, too, but I didn't really show it as much as Jake did. After I made sure that he wasn't going to back out or fumble from nervousness, I swam away, ready to be bait. I would be toying with my life again, but I felt it was worth it if we succeeded.

I swam off, looking for the poachers. They shouldn't be far off, since they know I hang around Jake's house lately. Fortunately, they didn't know it was Jake, otherwise they might have killed him already. I swam for another few minutes, and found the boat. I went clear into their line of radar vision. The speaker plunged into the water.

"Ah, I see our fishy little friend here would like to play a bit here."

Huh, I said as if I was half-awake.

"Hah! Good! He doesn't even know we're here! Even better!"

the claws came into the water, but I was already far ahead of them. I was about fifty feet away when the claws began to chase me.

"Don't let him get away," I heard one of them say.

"He won't get away this time, I assure you," another one said.

Don't be so sure, I said to myself.

I swam as fast as my fins could take me, all four of my hearts beating themselves into a pulp. I swam as close to the beach as I could, and waited for the boat to get closer. When it did, I made a U-turn back toward the ocean. I saw Jake come out.

Jake

I tried to be calm when I saw them coming. Whew, just calm down. I untied the boat and went off. I pulled out my shotgun. I couldn't wait for him to poke a hole, I was too excited to let him have all the fun. I shot the boat with the shotgun. There was now a huge gaping hole inside of the hoverboat. I now aimed for the hover part. **BAM!**

Damnit! They saw me. They missed me by inches, but the boat was a different story. There was a hole in it, but not too big since he only shot with a handgun. He didn't hit the hover part, so I was glad about that. I aimed at him instead of the boat. **BOOM!** Missed. Meanwhile, they forgot all about Aquiak. He popped up out of the water and bit clearly off the hover part and darted away.

I began to fire carelessly at any arms or legs in the water, not from excitement, but fear. I turned the hoverboat back towards shore. When I got to shore, I turned off and tossed the boat into the storage area where the boat is normally kept. I ran upstairs through the back door, took off my clothes and guns and put all of that in the back of my closet and behind and under everything. I hopped into the shower, and washed up. I peeked into mom's room. She was still asleep. How could she sleep through all of that? Oh well. I hopped into bed and fell asleep.

Aquiak

Jake turned toward shore and went home. He had done his part, at least. As each man fell into the water, I bit each one's arm off so they couldn't shoot me. Now, each man had a bloody stump where his arm used to be and drowning. I saw the Foobar Beasts come. Good. But, I only counted five. One came from behind and shot me.

AAHH!

"Gotcha."

I turned around and bit his head off. Jake came back outside and saw what was going on.

"No!!"

I'll be fine…run! While you still have the chance.

Jake

I watched as his eyes glowed gold.

A last gift to you…

All of his memories were transferred into me. I would review them later.

"No…" I said."

"Wow, grandpa! That was an amazing story!"

"Yes, now it's time for you all to go to bed."

Hi. My name's Jake. I'm 60 years old, and was just telling my grand children a story at a sleep over in my son's house. I stepped out side to get some fresh air.

"Aquiak, I wish you were here. I would have so much to tell you."

I was walking away when something unexpected happened.

Hello, old friend.

I heard a voice in my head.

"Aquiak?" I yelled out into the ocean.

Oh well, it was probably just my imagination.

Old friend, how are you.

"Aquiak, is that you? Where've you been?"

I ran to the beach.

You still live here?

"Yup."

Well, hello. My name's Aquiak. How are you doing?

THE END

Postscript: Life in the Last Lane

Theme: *Oh What a Beautiful Mourning.* Title revised for last rites from *Oklahoma/Green Grow the Lilacs*

FUTURE TIME STATUES: THEN AND NEXT

"It is not that we have a short time to live but that we waste a lot of it."

—Seneca

Or ... time well spent:

Being in my eighties at this writing, I seem to have entered a last lifespan phase.

This life in this last lane is not always wonderful. Aside from, one's own health challenges (don't ask such elders how they are doing unless you are sitting down ready to hear the full medical report), there is the continual loss of life of friends, family.

Time to write another obituary, goodbye, goodbye. And the non-stop restriction of life's opportunities as the body slows.

After a while I begin to think that, as a life extension writer, I now have the opposite effect. A senior version of King Midas's curse- whoever I touch seems to turn to old.

Still, all that experience can generate at times what we call wisdom.

All our intentional family, the ones we trust and choose, is seen properly as treasure. Time to enjoy them.

Think of what we can do for our own family, and even earth's human family, now that we at last may have some time and resources to contribute.

Not counting the recent forecast that humanity's mass extinction from irreversible climate change may be due as early as seven years from this writing. *Unless* one of our eight billion human family invents a way to reverse this disaster.

Not a lot of time of course. No more long term subscriptions.

FUTURE TIME STATUES: THEN AND NEXT

NOW YOU KNOW

His Last Word was Silent

Ernst Beier, Ph.D.

Theme: *The Sounds of Silence* Simon & Garfunkel

His life's giant contribution was about reading our silent body language.

An international psychology division for the American Psychological Association (APA), now Division 52, was originally the idea of a small group led by Ernst Beier, eventually its first President. I recall Fran Culbertson and Florence Denmark particularly among the several distinguished advocates for international involvement leading our initial charge.

We were longtime veterans of the process. I've been in APA since 1966 but I was far from the oldest in the group. I got to be the first awards coordinator, dividing the award categories between USA and non-USA recipients.

In all of this Ernst was the catalyst for progress as a leader that never seemed to tire.

His two decade age advantage over me and most of the rest of us was clearly an example of the vitality and accomplishment some psychologists keep to the end of a very long life.

Always charming and universally appreciated, Ernst epitomized what I call the Golden Rule of Proportionality: he solved far more problems than he created.

Maybe moreso than most others I have known, he was always at his best.

An international psychologist pioneer, Ernst Bier, was a celebrated expert on body language. His popular book *"People Reading"* was a best seller. His *"The Silent Language of Psychotherapy"* was a key volume for therapists.

His day job was as a psychology professor in Salt Lake City, Utah.

In the summers he would travel to exotic locales like New Guinea, following the cultural variations of body language there. He also enjoyed sailing, skiing, trekking, traveling, visiting and interviewing shamans, and piloting his own plane.

Not bad for man then in his eighties.

When I met Ernst, he looked a lot like the mustached man about town in the *Esquire* magazine.

On the other hand, he spoke with a strong German accent. Add to that his military history in World War Two, and my first erroneous impression was that he had fought on the Nazi side.

POSTSCRIPT: LIFE IN THE LAST LANE

As we got to be friends, I asked him how he reconciled that experience. He seemed startled. No, he was on the *American* side.

The German accent? What accent?

In fact Ernst had been a Jewish refugee, immigrating as a young man to America and fighting as soon as he could *against* the Nazis. He had joined the US Army, Tenth Mountain Division, but was sent overseas with the 28th Infantry division. He was captured at the Battle of the Bulge by the Germans and survived a POW camp. After liberation he received the silver battle star.

Now a Jewish professor in a predominantly LDS university?

"*Exactly!*" he confirmed with a broad smile.

A few years later, he was my invited keynote speaker at a professional psychology school graduation in California.

Ernst and a restless audience waited for his turn through about an hour of preliminaries.

When I finally could introduce him, I reviewed his outstanding body language contributions briefly. Much of that was beginning to appear in television series and in books on poker tells.

I told the already restless audience that if they had read his books, they would have been able to follow his speech already. Since while he was waiting he had given it sitting there on the stage silently twice now. (Laughter.)

Now awake, they were focused. Actually, once using actual out loud spoken words, he gave a fine talk. Lots of insights graduates could use.

Still with a great German accent though.

Until suddenly he was no longer there. Or anywhere. Nobody that I asked knew.

There was a rumor that Ernst, now in his late 90s, had Alzheimer's disease.

Or, my initial favorite, that he had run off to New Guinea to be with a tribal woman.

One day I finally succeeded in tracking his phone number down and called. Frances, his wife of 65 years, answered.

Once she knew who I was, she apologized: *"I'm sorry. Ernst is bedridden now. At 99 years old, his mind is fine but he no longer can speak. You can talk to him on the telephone but he can't answer you. There's not much time. We are told he won't live out the week."*

If only I could see him. Then I knew he would answer me just fine without speech.

But I took what I could in the time we had, being thousands of miles apart.

I talked one-way for a while, reminding him of past good times, funny twists in our life, and wishing I could be there to enjoy his stories, even if by body language.

When I was done, his wife took the phone again.

She said: *"He's smiling now"*.

Dodgeball

Theme: *Sweet Georgia Brown* Brother Bones (Harlem Globetrotter Theme)

There was a rake stuck on top of my head. Around the prongs ran blood from my scalp. The idea of it hurt more than the pain. The rake's owner was older than me but I was bigger than him. So he just came up behind me and slammed his rake on my head.

Pushing him to the ground didn't help. Never does. Okay. Now I had to go home and get repaired. No point in crying. Just a child's garden rake but at age three, full size to me.

My mother recalled this event. Liked to say I never cried when I was hurt but if she heard me whimper when I was coming back home, she knew it was serious.

Barney

A few years later the bus driver and his two children moved in with us. We had a small rental duplex so it was cramped. But for some reason he had been evicted and needed a place for his family to stay for a little while. My parents couldn't afford a car so the regular bus driver had become a friend. In need.

His daughter, Olivia, was the oldest. They called her 'Olive' and, in fact, that was her complexion. I thought she was beautiful. But as an older woman, maybe 15, all I could hope for at eight was a friendship. That she gave me. At a little distance. Our age gap was insurmountable.

Her younger brother, a boy named Barney, was closer to my age. Maybe just a year or two older. So we spent the summer days together while he lived with us.

On one of those days, we were walking in the fields behind the houses. The grass had grown taller than us, so it was easy to avoid the other wealthier boys that had air rifles. BBs flying. Some dead frog victims to step over.

The little girl from next door tried to join us. She was maybe four or five. I declined. Not safe for her there in those fields. Pointed to a dead BB-ridden frog. But she refused to leave.

Barney stepped into the impasse. Put her over his knee, hoisted her skirt, and spanked her. He just got one hit in before I stopped him. We both noticed the red welts on her bottom from likely home abuse. A whipping?

Her parents were from some Baltic country. Estonia? Maybe they believed in whipping children. Most parents in those years spanked at the least. Seemed very wrong to me then. Still does.

She was crying now. Pulled up her skirt, ran back towards her home.

The rest of the day progressed without memorable event. Until I headed for home.

I had to be there before it got dark, a rule. The sun was close to setting. Barney had no such rule so he stayed in the fields a little longer.

I got to the path that went by our next door neighbor's house, close to my destination. As it opened up into the circle of their backyard, I stopped.

The little girl's parents, older sisters and brothers, and other adults (cousins? uncles and aunts?) faced me from a distance, all in a semi-circle, glaring. Blocked my way. No words.

The little girl was not there. The father held up an empty milk bottle and smashed it on a patch of dried cement by his feet. I noticed all these people facing me were wearing gloves. The father gathered up the pieces of glass and passed them around until the whole dozen of them were armed. Then they all began throwing the sharp pieces of glass at me.

I was fascinated. Sure, scared too. I ducked the glass as it came at me. From all front directions. By now they had closed the circle and were at my side too, almost behind me. Still at throwing distance.

Almost all the glass shrapnel missed me. I had a small cut on my cheek and anther on my right arm. Mostly I was fast enough to avoid the attack. But the ones moving to behind me were a problem.

So when I saw an opening, I ran through it. Past two adults not fast enough to stop me. Home safe.

What had that little girl told them? Was Barney's spanking seen by them as a sexual assault? And who at their home was whipping the child?

When my father got home from his night shift, my mother insisted he go next door to confront them. He complied. Oh boy! Now they were in for it!

He came back laughing. That morning only the mother was home. Not sure she understood English. She did get the essence of his complaint. Came at him with a big stick. He was too fast for her, boxing in his past, and she never landed a blow. When she got tired of the failed attack, frustrated, and stopped, he shrugged, laughed, and left.

Not the showdown I had hoped for. I did concede that he was as good as I was at dodging. Fast. (As a teen, once much later, I had to outrun him chasing me to stay alive. And did. Another story.)

High School

Our 90 minute P.E. class was built around dodgeball that day. Thirty boys divided equally into two opposing teams, each on a side of the gym facing the other.

If you got hit with the ball, you had to leave the struggle and go sit on the bleachers. You were out. The winning team would be the one with the last boy standing un-hit. Dodging the ball the other team was throwing, until nobody was left on the other team.

That day, by the end of the first 60 minutes, I was the only one left standing on my team. Facing me was the last one standing on the other team.

I was faster than him and better at anticipating where he would throw the ball. He was better than me at the throwing part.

His every shot missed me. My every shot missed him.

The last 30 minutes were an impasse.

The bleachers crowd at first yelled encouragement to the survivor on their side. Then, frustrated, they began yelling insults at both sides. In the final minutes, there was only angry silence from the crowd. They wanted their side to win.

POSTSCRIPT: LIFE IN THE LAST LANE

Neither of us two survivors left that field of conflict with any applause.

Now at an age where I take the time to reflect on such events. I can ask what would have been a better way to deal with the situation in that time and in that place?

If, through meditative trance I could travel back in time to my younger self in that dodgeball finale (a future possibility) what mind whisper would I advise to him? This is what came to mind: *Minutes to go in the dodgeball game. An impasse between myself and the survivor on the other side. I dodge the ball as usual. Close. It bounces with energy off the back wall. This time though I grab the ball and do NOT throw it at him. I put it on the gym floor line between the sides. Motion him to come close. He's cautious but comes closer. I say "We're both good at this. Let's call it a draw and shake hands." Hmm. But what would have happened if I had done this? My opponent starts to come forward, smiles, but his team and mine boo us from the bleachers. My opponent stops, pulls his hand back, runs fast toward the ball. In that split second I kick it toward him and it hits him in the chest. His team loses.*

Moral: A draw where everybody wins can be the smarter option.

Speed

My mother loved to recall that my first steps were not walking but running. As a teen, I liked to think I was trying to get away from her. As an octogenarian now, I think that unfair. She was a career public school teacher that took off a few years to have her first child, me, and in that time used all her classroom skills to benefit me alone. We had a backyard theater group, read classics (especially *Classic Comics*), learned new languages albeit with unique pronunciation.

Still, running from the outset, was a childhood theme. With no car, we walked everywhere. I never got out of breath then, could walk all day.

When I was eight, on Saturdays I liked to walk with my friends south of the city for 13 miles to the ranch of a wealthy uncle. We were ragged and sweaty, poor and multiracial, and we rang the bell at his front door as though we belonged. His wife, my aunt Barbara ("Bobby"), would usually open the door. Grimacing, she would turn to yell to her husband *"Your ghetto nephew and his little friends are here to see you again, Harold!"*

Still not letting us in, she was replaced by my smiling uncle who welcomed all of us into his living room. After a snack and a bathroom visit, we would come with him to his stables and enjoy time with his horses.

I saw a small Palomino and jumped up on him to ride him bareback. I woke on the ground but was unhurt.

As dinnertime approached, he wouldn't let us walk back. By the time we would have reached home, it would have been the middle of the night. So we all piled into his El Dorado Cadillac convertible and he drove us home in style within 20 minutes. The top down convertible allowed my friends to wave to their families on their porches. All my friends were heroes for the day. Happy time statue.

But I digress. Yeah! Senior moment.

Walking or running, speed was always a part of my life, at least for the first 60 years of it. I learned that for athletes, the best of them, and martial artists too, all can choose to create flow where time seems to go slow for those around them. They are moving fast relative to everybody else by accelerating their own metabolism. Notably the heart beats way faster to bring about that phase. Tests a young person's body, requires exceptional health. And a very strong heart.

In my own research during college, I learned ways to teach people to move experiential time faster or slower than normal. Did my doctoral dissertation on it. That dissertation was on time in both meanings of that word.

A Long Fast for Fast

As my own 60th birthday approached, I had heart block. My heart stopped beating. Collapsed. That would have killed me except for a new last minute inserted pacemaker. The last one on the island of Guam.

A version of which I have had ever since. Lifesaving but with a price. It not only protects with a vital floor for a minimum heart beat (70/second for me now) and nothing lower.

It also sets a maximum pulse ceiling that protects the heart from excessive exertion.

That pacemaker ceiling prevents my heart from reaching the high rate needed to slow time down.

At this writing, now in my 82nd year, I cherish life. I accept no longer being fast.

Dodging death.

Robert F. Morgan

Photo by Becky Owl Morgan

Born in the lull between the two world wars, time now to write stories from eight decades of lifespan. No point in waiting any longer.

A Life Member of the American Psychological Association. An NIMH Pre-Doctoral Fellow at Michigan State University, followed with more than 60 years of post-doctoral practice and teaching experience.

A former speech collaborator and project consultant for Dr. Martin Luther King Jr. and a variety of organizations, there was founding and editing the Cambridge University Press *Journal of Tropical Psychology*, and founding the Division of Applied Gerontology in the International Association of Applied Psychology (IAAP).

Now complete is the overseeing of 126 psychology doctoral dissertations in California, Singapore, and Australia, along with a contemporary trauma psychology seminar at the University of New Mexico. Publications include more than a hundred printed articles and 23 books on topics including life span psychology, trauma psychology in context, applied gerontology, international psychology, and even unfortunate baby names.

Other Books by Robert F. Morgan

Time Statues Revisited: Book One- On the Job

Time Statues Revisited: Book Two- Language & Influence

Time Statues Revisited: Book Three- Citizenship

Time Statues Revisited: Book Four-Non-Human Relatives

Time Statues Revisited: Book Five- Human Family

Time Statues

Trauma Psychology in Context: International Vignettes and Applications

Opportunity's Shadow & the Bee Moth Effect: When Danger Transforms Community

Growing Younger: How to Measure & Change Body Age

The Iatrogenics Handbook: Research & Practice in Helping Professions

Training the Time Sense: Hypnotic & Conditioning Approaches

Unfortunate baby names: Slattery's complete collection with the most notable thousands for dramatic and other usage

Electroshock: the Case Against.

Directory of International Consultants in Psychology

Interventions in Applied Gerontology

Measurement of Human Aging in Applied Gerontology

Should the Insanity Defense be Abolished?

Conquest of Aging: Modern Measurement & Intervention

The Effective Verbal Adaptation (EVA) Test: Parts A & B

The Educational Status of Children in a District without Public Schools: CRP 3221.

The Educational Status of Children during the First Year Following Four Years of Little or No Schooling: CRP 2498.

Uncas Slattery and the Muddy Chuckle

Closing theme: *National Anthem* Jimi Hendrix

Book theme to take home with you now: *Time Will Tell* Susan Anton